THE
ROI
OF HUMAN
CAPITAL
SECOND EDITION

Measuring the Economic Value
of Employee Performance

Jac Fitz-enz

AMACOM

American Management Association
New York • Atlanta • Brussels • Chicago • Mexico City • San Francisco
Shanghai • Tokyo • Toronto • Washington, D.C.

Special discounts on bulk quantities of AMACOM books are available to corporations, professional associations, and other organizations. For details, contact Special Sales Department, AMACOM, a division of American Management Association, 1601 Broadway, New York, NY 10019.
Tel: 212-903-8316. Fax: 212-903-8083.
E-mail: specialsls@amanet.org
Website: www.amacombooks.org/go/specialsales
To view all AMACOM titles go to: www.amacombooks.org

This publication is designed to provide accurate and authoritative information in regard to the subject matter covered. It is sold with the understanding that the publisher is not engaged in rendering legal, accounting, or other professional service. If legal advice or other expert assistance is required, the services of a competent professional person should be sought.

Library of Congress Cataloging-in-Publication Data

The ROI of human capital : measuring the economic value of employee performance / Jac Fitz-enz.—2nd ed.
     p.   cm.
  Includes index.
  ISBN-13: 978-0-8144-1332-6 (hardcover)
  ISBN-10: 0-8144-1332-3 (hardcover)
  1. Human capital.   2. Productivity accounting.   3. Labor economics.
HD4904.7.R33 2009
658.15'226—dc22

                                                              2008050809

Printing number

10   9   8   7   6   5   4   3   2

To
Laura,
My love
My strength
My inspiration

Contents

CHAPTER 5

End-to-End Human Capital Value Reports   144

CHAPTER 6

Human Capital Analytics: The Leading Edge
of Measurement   165

CHAPTER 9

Outsourcing: A New Operating Model? 252

CHAPTER 10

How to Change the Game 272

CHAPTER 11

Eleven Principles, Seven Skills, and Five Metrics 291

Preface to the
Second Edition

In reviewing the first edition I found that many of the predictions made in 1999 came true. This is because the fundamentals around human performance still apply . . . and always will. The environment may change but people don't. Specifically, my early prediction about the labor shortage came true, only now with greater urgency.[1] I described the rise of outsourcing along with contingent workers as the first step in restructuring organizations. My declaration about the need to focus on leading indicators has come to be accepted. My points about the quality of work life have become mainstream topics. Other projections within the first edition also proved accurate. This edition continues to be on the leading edge with the introduction of Predictive Management, a new paradigm for managing the future today. You will see the concept in various places and the model in Chapter 10.

Business Changes

Businesses are finding that they have to change the way they do business. The model that emerged after World War II has run its course. Dot-coms came and went with much fury and left behind an e-world that has profoundly affected the way everyone does business. When you change the communication system, you shift power bases and you expose weaknesses. The flaws of the past that could be papered over are now more obvious. New forms are rising as a result of communication analytics and computer technology. Change is the order of the new century.

In terms of management trends, outsourcing has made quantum leaps. From the advent of the first full human resources process outsourcing contract in 1999 to today, the concept has exploded. According to Everest Research there are four thousand companies currently offering those services worldwide. Human development has shifted from a reliance on classroom training to a blended approach that incorporates various media and job experiences.

Globalization has come to the fore. The growth in China, India, and the Arabian Gulf countries has called forth a new power that is affecting everyone everywhere at all levels. Even managing a local small business is different today. Ever hear of pollution, global warming, health insurance, immigration, or education deficiencies? How about mega-brands like Toyota, Wal-Mart, Starbucks, Amazon, or Google?

Of course, recruitment is the main game now. In 1998 the labor shortage was a factor but it was isolated largely on technical skills related to dot-com ventures. Today, professional and managerial shortfalls in many disciplines are emerging and will not be alleviated by temporary market downturns. Multigenerational workforces had barely surfaced. Now they are the norm. Baby boomers were in charge, now they are looking for an exit strategy they can afford.

The Good News

Despite a continuing reluctance of some human resources people to address quantitative analysis, there have been major advances in the past decade. When I was writing the first edition of this book, I would have estimated that only about 5 percent of human resources departments were doing anything significant in this area. Most of those were still mired in basic measures of HR efficiency—that is, cost of hire, time to fill jobs, compensation and benefits expense, and effects such as turnover rates.

Now my estimate is that at least 30 to 35 percent of human resources departments are doing some kind of quantitative measurement. Unfortunately, only about 10 percent have moved upscale to measure effects on the enterprise. Thanks to the work of people like Jack and Patti Phillips, John Boudreau and Pete Ramsted, Mark Huselid, Brian Becker and Dick Beatty, Dave Ulrich and Wayne Brockbank, Jesse Harriott and Jeff Quinn, Ken Scarlett, Debbie Mc-Grath, Erik Berggren, Doug Hubbard, Kent Barnett, and Jeffrey Burke, among others, the state of the art has improved dramatically. In Argentina Luis Maria Cravino and in Brazil Rugenia Pomi are leading the way. Software packages are coming to market from companies such as Authoria, KnowledgeAdvisors, Oracle, Scarlett Surveys SuccessFactors, and others that make quantitative analysis easier and more meaningful. We are moving from merely measuring to finding and explaining meaning.

Looking Ahead

This edition updates its predecessor in several ways. In the past two years, I have collected more than three hundred cases, models, and survey results, many of which are merged here to replace and update those of the first edition, to give currency to the narrative.

The basic metrics in the book are now widely used and quoted around the world. In addition, I have developed leading indicators and intangible metrics that were not proven as well in 2000. Intangibles have attracted a great deal of interest since Baruch Lev's 2001 book, *Intangibles*. Concurrently, benchmarking has peaked. The more advanced human resources professionals are looking for something new and leading indicators and intangibles are satisfying that need. There is a new chapter (Chapter 7: Predictive Analytics: Leading Indicators and Intangibles) to cover this development.

Chapter 1 reflects the changes since 2000. Chapters 2, 3, and 4 are refreshed with new material, but the structure is unchanged. In addition to new text and new graphics, the number of case studies has been increased.

Chapter 5 displays an updated reporting model. The latest balanced scorecard approach is added along with an updated human capital profit-and-loss model. These link HR's reporting language more closely to the accounting system.

The structures of Chapters 6 and 7 are reworked in the light of recent developments. Chapter 6 expands and offers more details and depth to human capital valuation. It revisits the value of indexing. Benchmarking is repositioned as a tactical rather than a strategic activity, which it was when I introduced it in 1985 with special attention paid to context as a means of understanding benchmark data.

Chapter 7 focuses on the future. It expands on predictive analytics. Leading indicators and intangibles are covered. Trending and indexing examples are shown.

Chapter 8 is the original Chapter 7 and is largely redone. Outsourcing is removed and placed in its own chapter. Restructuring, contingent management, mergers and acquisitions, and benchmarking are all reworked. Employee engagement is added.

Chapter 9 is given exclusively to outsourcing. Since 2000, outsourcing has exploded with both good and bad results. It is changing the structure of organizations.

Chapter 10 is an entirely new subject. Based on a major research program that yielded a new management model, this chapter describes how to change the game and gain competitive advantage through predictive management.

Finally, in Chapter 11, the guiding principles are updated into eleven principles for success, seven skills of valuation, and five metrics of life.

Acknowledgments

A project as complex and extensive as publishing a book involves many people with many talents. The content people who supported and contributed ideas are acknowledged in the Preface to this edition. I want to also cite the people at AMACOM who helped get this tome out the door.

My gratitude goes out to Executive Editor Christina Parisi and her assistant, Janet Pagano; Publicity Director Irene Majuk; Managing Editor Andy Ambraziejus; especially Erika Spelman, who kept the project moving between me, the copyeditor, the proofreader, and the indexer; copyeditor Mary Miller who picked up all my typos and grammatical errors; proofreader Robin O'Dell; and Production Manager Lydia Lewis, who coordinated with the designer to get the design completed, negotiated schedules with the compositor and printer, and made sure everything got where it needed to go on time.

Thanks everyone. This is your book also.

References

1. Jac Fitz-enz, "Getting and Keeping Good Employees," *Personnel Journal,* August 1990, pp. 25–28.

Preface to the First Edition

The Missing Piece

The classic books of management have ignored, avoided, or thrown platitudes at the question of human value in the business environment. When and if the authors did give passing attention to valuing the human contribution, their comments were either gratuitous or simplistic. Nineteenth-century capital theory claimed that wealth was leveraged from investments in tangible assets such as plants and equipment. It held that workers were entitled to compensation only for their labor, since the incremental values of the business came from investment in capital equipment. This type of thinking lit the fire under people like Karl Marx and Samuel Gompers. From the early work of Fayol[1] and Barnard,[2] which supported this thinking, to the more enlightened insights of Drucker, Peters, Handy, and others, no one has successfully taken on the challenge of detailing how to demonstrate the relative value of the human element in the profit equation. Invariably, writers attempting to do so have opted out at the last minute with weak-kneed excuses for not closing the loop with specific examples. The only exception has been some of the human resources accounting work, and that has not been accepted as a practical management tool.

The term *human capital* originated with Theodore Schultz, an economist interested in the plight of the world's underdeveloped countries. He argued correctly that traditional economic concepts did not deal with this problem. His claim was that improving the welfare of poor people did not depend on land, equipment, or energy, but rather on knowledge. He called this qualitative aspect of economics "human capital." Schultz, who won the Nobel Prize in 1979, offered this description:

> Consider all human abilities to be either innate or acquired. Every person is born with a particular set of genes, which determines his innate ability. Attributes of acquired population quality, which are valuable and can be augmented by appropriate investment, will be treated as human capital.[3]

In business terms, we might describe human capital as a combination of factors such as the following:

- *The traits one brings to the job*—intelligence, energy, a generally positive attitude, reliability, commitment

- *One's ability to learn*—aptitude, imagination, creativity, and what is often called "street smarts," savvy (or how to get things done)

- *One's motivation to share information and knowledge*—team spirit and goal orientation

The great irony is that the only economic component that can add value in and by itself is the one that is the most difficult to evaluate. This is the human component, which is clearly the most vexatious of assets to manage. The almost infinite variability and unpredictability of human beings make them enormously more complex to evaluate than one of the electromechanical components that comes with pre-determined operating specifications. Nevertheless, people are the only element with the inherent power to generate value. All other variables—cash and its cousin credit, materials, plant and equipment, and energy—offer nothing but inert potentials. By their nature, they add nothing, and they cannot add anything until some human being, be it the lowest-level laborer, the most ingenious professional, or the loftiest executive, leverages that potential by putting it into play. The good news is that measuring the value added of human capital is possible. In fact, it has been going on in a dozen countries since the early 1990s. Why this is known by only a relatively few managers will be addressed later.

Viewed from either an economic or a philosophic perspective, the thing that matters most is not how productive people are in organizations. That is a by-product of something more fundamental. The most important issue is how fulfilled people are in their work. No amount of compensation can restore the soul of a person who has spent his or her life in mindless toil. In fact, even a modicum of economic comfort cannot overcome the bitterness of that experience. Curiously, fulfilling work is truly its own reward for the individual and the enterprise. In the final analysis, there is clear and abundant evidence that an organization that makes work as fulfilling as possible will develop and retain the most productive workers and enjoy the most loyal customers.

One of the key drivers of fulfillment is knowledge. Knowing how well we have done leads directly to job satisfaction. The only thing that is more satisfying than seeing data that show our accomplishments is having our supervisor see the results of our labor and compliment us on a job well done.

Facing the Talent Shortage

For the foreseeable future, organizations in most developed countries will be faced with a talent shortfall. In the United States, the demographics are such that it will be impossible to sustain strong economic growth due to the paucity of talent. Since 1965, the end of the baby boom era, the birthrate has declined by about one-third. This decline has resulted in a workforce population that is decreasing. Concurrently, the national economy as measured by the gross domestic product has nearly doubled over the same period. Obviously, the economy and the working population are on diverging growth curves. Although the current robust economy will surely slow to some degree, the availability of indigenous talent is not going to reverse its course overnight. From 1996 to 2006, the percentage of workers ages 25 to 34 will shrink 9 percent, and those 35 to 44 will slip 3 percent.

Such data are available to anyone who chooses to look for them. Drucker accuses organizations of focusing data collection on the inside of the enterprise.[4] These data treat only costs. Yet results are outside, and management has largely ignored demographic and customer trend data. He claims that the most important factor for planning and for strategy is whether the share of income that customers spend on an industry's products is increasing or decreasing. On the human side, it was pointed out in an article in 1990 that the most significant problem organizations would face in the last half of the decade would be a shortage of talent.[5] The economic and population data were available to management and were ignored. If we want the economy to continue its upward pace, something has to be done to compensate for the declining number of qualified workers at all levels.

There are several ways to accomplish that—some potentially more effective than others. The first reaction is to bring in millions of immigrants to fill jobs. This is not going to happen. Congress is under pressure to control immigration by various self-interest groups such as labor unions. Immigrants will help, but they will be a very small part of the solution. Even if the gates were opened, the data show that between 1980 and 1990, 41 percent of new immigrants age 25 and older did not have a college equivalency education, compared with 23 percent of native-born Americans of the same age-group.[6] This is not going to fill a knowledge economy's talent shortage in the near term.

Outsourcing work to other countries is an increasingly popular method of coping with the shortage. Manufacturing has been doing this successfully for the past thirty years. However, managing professional workers engaged in qualitative, judgmental designs thousands of miles across oceans and continents is a more complex matter and not so trouble free.

Another simplistic answer stems from outmoded beliefs about people. Some managers believe in their hearts that rank-and-file workers are not a whole lot smarter than Skinner's pigeons who learned to peck levers to obtain food pellets. Those managers believe that providing tangible incentives, the human equivalent of food pellets, is the answer. However, it doesn't matter how tasty the incentives might be; a pigeon who doesn't know which lever to peck is not going to get a pellet. This is a way of saying that if we don't have people with the inherent talent, training, or work experience, along with the right tools and information to do the job, we are not going to get the results we need. All we will have is frustrated pigeons. To maintain a competitive position in the marketplace of the twenty-first century, management will have to find methods for increasing the power of the human information lever. The availability of valid and reliable performance data is at the heart of the issue.

The most cost-effective, long-term solution to the talent shortfall lies in helping each person become more productive. This charges management with the task of figuring out how to invest in human productive potential. During the Industrial Age, the primary production tools moved material. In the postindustrial age, the production tools move information, which in turn tells us how and when to move the appropriate materials and services. Electronic technology is just beginning to be employed to generate useful data and move them quickly. The loop of productivity begins to close when human beings learn what data are needed, where, when, in what form, and by whom. The loop is completed and productivity enhanced when people learn what the data mean. Training in data analysis and interpretation turns data into information and eventually intelligence. That is the only feasible path to solving the talent shortage. Schultz was right, decades ago.

Acknowledgments

The models and methods described are the result of the collective insights and efforts of many people over a long time. At the beginning, in the 1970s, Bob Coon tested the earliest methods with me in the human resources department of a Silicon Valley computer company. Over the years, Bob worked with me again at the Saratoga Institute, when we went public with our first crude survey of human resources benchmarks in 1985. The staff at the institute, through their daily work of supporting clients with valid, reliable data on human capital, added immeasurably to the content of this book. The work of Eric Stanger, David Flores, and Charlotte

Cox was especially valuable. Clients too numerous to mention have tested our ideas over the past fifteen years.

Finally, I thank the thousands of indifferent and contentious people whose apathy and sometimes hostility spurred me to prove that it could be done.

A special word of thanks to my acquisitions editor, Adrienne Hickey. She never let me produce anything less than the best I had to offer.

References

1. Henri Fayol (1841–1925), *Administration Industrielle et Générale* (General and Industrial Management), trans. Constance Storrs, with a foreword by L. Urwick (London: Pitman, 1949).

2. Chester Irving Barnard (1886–1961), *The Functions of the Executive* (Cambridge, MA: Harvard University Press, 1938, 1962).

3. Theodore W. Schultz, *Investing in People: The Economics of Population Quality* (Berkeley, CA: University of California, 1981), p. 21.

4. Peter Drucker, "The Next Information Revolution," *Forbes ASAP*, August 24, 1998, pp. 47–58.

5. Jac Fitz-enz, "Getting and Keeping Good Employees," *Personnel Journal*, August 1990, pp. 25–28.

6. Hudson Institute, "Workforce 2020," 1999.

CHAPTER ONE

Human Leverage

"We can have facts without thinking but we cannot have thinking without facts."

—JOHN DEWEY

The Shift

No longer is management of the human resources department a human resources issue. When personnel and training came into being during the 1930s, it was in response to the growing strength of organized labor. The main contribution of personnel and industrial relations was to deal with that incursion. After World War II, as corporations expanded, there was a need for someone to handle the administrative issues around employees. Personnel got the job. By the late 1960s, it was becoming clear that there were more complex challenges, so personnel changed its name to human resources. Today, the game is human capital management. Conceptually, this is recognition that people are the bedrock of the organization as we stumble into the Intelligence Age. The fundamental question has become, how do we improve the return on our investment in human capital?

We find ourselves in a world where yesterday is a distant memory and tomorrow is an uncertain dream. The only reality is now. Yet, by taking the long view of any issue, we better understand not only where we have come from and where we are now but perhaps where we might be headed. Consider how a technology such as telecommunications has evolved. It started as a box on the wall with a crank and a gizmo to talk into. Some people believed that it was a fad and that they didn't need one. Today, it is a gizmo stuck in your ear or a pad hung somewhere on your body and don't try to tell your teenagers that they don't need one.

So what does this have to do with managing organizations and especially with understanding how people—that is, human capital—need to be addressed within our organizations? Here is where it goes three-dimensional. The issue is not only the structure of organizations and the people within them. Now the external entity, the customer, has entered the organization in a new and as yet not clearly understood way. Whether we recognize the fact or not, the customer is as much a part of our companies as are our physical and human assets. The three types of capital—structural, human, and relational—are rapidly merging into just structural and human with what was the external relations (the customer) now imbedded in everything we do internally.

Let me try to explain it by paralleling it with the evolution of electronic technology. Computers became a reality with the production of ENIAC, which was the first truly workable, large-scale computer. By large, I mean room size. ENIAC was born in 1945 as a mass of vacuum tubes that truly took up the space of a room. Twenty years later, IBM came out with the System/360 that brought computing into the business world in a somewhat user-friendly way. Two decades later, minicomputers were common and the microcomputer appeared. The first portable computer weighed more than 20 pounds. Today, laptops weigh less than 5 pounds. BlackBerrys and similar devices weigh only 5 ounces and provide more computing power than ENIAC. So what? Stay with me, there is an end and a point to this journey.

As the computer and lately the telephone evolved and merged capabilities, the critical challenges also advanced from hardware to software to services. The product capability has grown to the point where the customer and the product are virtually inseparable. Today's telephone/computer is no longer in a room, on our desk, or in a purse or briefcase. It is attached to our ear. Already that gizmo is taking simple switching voice commands. Tomorrow it will do our computing verbally as we walk, drive, or sit on our patio. Arguments over any topic from who won the Stanley Cup in 1948 to where was da Vinci when he painted the *Mona Lisa* to what was Tonto's pet's name will be settled without lifting a finger.

Ten years ago, I told people at PeopleSoft that they needed to move toward services as the next natural evolutionary step. They told me to get lost. Lou Gerstner saw the future and had the power to shift IBM toward service. In 2007, over 60 percent of IBM revenues came from services.

The reason that the customer is now part of our organization is that we no longer sell a product or provide a service. We design, sell, and service a *customer experience*. We are stuck in the customer's ear, literally and figuratively. No matter what our product, because of the customer's emerging capabilities and the expectations that are coming with them, we are selling experiences.

Steve Berkowitz, former CEO of Ask.com and later senior vice president of Microsoft's online business group, hit it squarely in words that are paraphrased here:

We have to deliver the basics but that isn't going to get us to the top. Customers go where their emotions take them. We have to give the customer the richest experience they want NOW. In order to do that, I say we have to live 24/7 with the customer.

The New Human Capital Management Model

The human resources function is positioned by choice or fate to lever human capital. The simple delivery of a service or processing of a transaction is a nineteenth-century concept. For this new mandate to work, a new vision, attitude, and set of skills are necessary to carry out a comprehensive model. Chapters 2 through 4 systematically lay out such a model. It starts at the top with the goals of the enterprise rather than at the bottom with the question of what human resources should measure. This is the first point of differentiation. We are not here to focus on human resources. Human resources is charged with helping people make a greater contribution to the organization's raison d'être. So, our focus must be first on human capital and secondly on the human resources department. Once that distinction is clear, everything else falls into line. Then we can work down through operating processes to human resources service offerings. At the end, we have a structure on which to consider ensuing chapter applications and eventually build a performance measurement program.

Effects on Organizational Management

Organizations are undergoing wrenching change not only due to globalization, technology advancements, and labor demographics but also because of the force that makes truly global companies competitive—information exchange. Peter

Senge, author of *The Fifth Discipline*, puts a framework on this capability: "For the first time in history, humankind has the capacity to create far more information than anyone can absorb, to foster far greater interdependency than anyone can manage, and to accelerate change far faster than anyone's ability to keep pace."[1]

Although there are many forces affecting the management of human capital, there are two that stand out in my opinion. The combination of the recent on-demand business model and labor demographic trends is an omen. It tells those who are wise enough to grasp it that a seminal change has arrived. It is not coming. It is here, now.

Communication—Technology now puts the world of information at the fingertips of everyone with a computer and a phone line. It allows us to collect, modify, and transmit that information in a matter of seconds anywhere on the globe. Communication is power—and that power has made hierarchical structures obsolete. Management has to reinvent its organization into a power-sharing network. If nations cannot stop, Internet communications companies certainly cannot either.

Process—The on-demand business model is bringing supply chain management principles into all aspects of organizational management. Now, product development as well as marketing and administrative functions such as finance, information technology (IT), and human resources are part of the corporate value chain. As such, each is a target for external providers. This has opened the door to business process outsourcing (BPO), which has grown dramatically in the new century. When Exult became the first pure-play BPO provider for human resources and signed British Petroleum as its first customer in December 1999, the starter's gun sounded on a new era of human resources management. As a member of its advisory board, I had an insider's view of the evolution of BPO. Today, the early BPO contracts are up for renewal and a new version is being designed. In less than a decade, a second generation is already emerging.

Structure—When communications and processes change, structure must also change or be overwhelmed. Functional silos will gradually be dismantled and operations slowly integrated in support of the corporation's superordinate goals. As this picks up speed, the pressure will be on the resource providers such as finance, IT, human resources, and procurement to also break down their internal silos and act in a cohesive, single-process manner. For human resources, this means that planning, staffing, compensation, development, and retention will have to move strategically as one and tactically take each other into consideration in delivering their part of a single, value-adding process. Figure 1-1 is a depiction of the old functional model and the new strategic concept.

It is difficult to clearly show the interconnections of all the HR services. The point is that they are all interdependent and interactive. This is in keeping with the demands for a more fluid integrated process. As you read the following sections, consider how we can evolve the human resources function into an integrated, value-generating service. And before you get too enraptured with this or any other model, keep in mind Greenspan's Uncertainty Principle:

> **Every model, no matter how detailed or how well designed conceptually and empirically, is a vastly simplified representation of the world that we experience with all its intricacies on a day-to-day basis.**

The twentieth century's leading management theorist, Peter Drucker, claimed that the greatest challenge for orga-

Figure 1-1. Human resources structures.

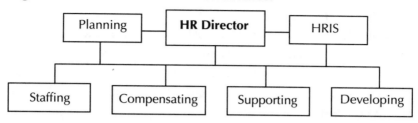

Twentieth-Century Human Resources Management Structure

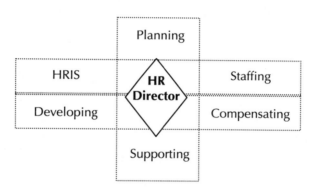

Twenty-First-Century Human Resources Management Structure

nizations today, and for the next decade at least, is to re-spond to the shift from an industrial to a knowledge economy. He reminded us that the purpose and function of every organization is the integration of specialized knowl-edge into a common task.[2] This shift toward knowledge as the differentiator affects all aspects of organizational man-agement, including operating efficiency, marketing, organi-zational structure, and human capital investment. Each of these directly or indirectly hinges on an understanding of the ability of people to cope with unforeseen, massive, and usually hurried change.

Nick Bontis of McMaster University in Hamilton, Canada, shows us that human capital, as the employer of information technology, is the critical antecedent in effectively managing the organizational knowledge that yields higher business results.[3] At the end of the day, it is blindingly obvious that without hard data on human capital's activity and productivity, there is virtually no chance of competing effectively.

Data for Management

A Conference Board survey in 2004 showed that only 19 percent of companies responding share people measurement reports below the senior executive level. This indicates that such data are not part of middle manager decision making. That has to change because human capital data is essential to daily management.

Well-thought-out, reliable, and rigorous metrics can:

- Provoke discussions with managers that lead to action plans

- Serve as educational tools helping to bring implicit ideas about the value of human capital to the surface

- Reduce the risk of marginal HR investments

- Support line management human capital decisions

A 2006 study by the Society for Human Resource Management (SHRM) asked members about the strategic contributions of their human resources departments to their organizations. Four hundred twenty-seven companies responded. The top five services selected were:

1. Employee relations   78 percent
2. Recruitment and selection   76 percent
3. Benefits management   69 percent
4. Performance management   61 percent
5. Compensation and rewards   57 percent

Far down on the list were leadership development, employee engagement, retention, and succession planning. More important, the list should have been focused on business effects, not on HR's activities and services. Once again human resources shows that it is a cost center not a value generator. They should have reported examples of gains in quality, innovation, productivity, or service. From this survey, it is clear that HR people don't understand what it takes to earn the strategic partner title they claim to want. Holding hands, hiring, and administering are useful, but not strategic. We need to lift their eyes from their desks and toward the business.

The new on-demand imperative is both a prod and a tool to carry us into a better world. To cope with this development, we need to:

- Be flexible in our response to changing demands

- Grow or shrink based on the variability of demand

- Be prepared to function anywhere at any time under any condition

- Continually minimize unit costs

- Make operations transparent both internally and externally

Inside this model is the demand to build integrated operations. Siloed organizations are slow and expensive. From command and control structures we shift to networks where communication moves easily, thereby accelerating production and shortening time to market. Synchronicity smoothes the flow of information and materials across the organization.

Making the Change

Efforts to change to a new model are inhibited by constraints as well as supported by enablers. The positive and negative forces battle each other and in the end contribute to the emergence of a new order. Constraints challenge old thinking and make old structures obsolete. Enablers include both tools and technologies but also the passive vacuums left by the demise of the old.

- *Constraints.* Uncertainty is an inhibitor. It makes us hesitant, fearful, and regressive. The uncertain global market and increasing regulations inhibit bold ideas.
- *Enablers.* Communication technology, decision science tools, and outsourcing all help us design and install better systems.

In time, enablers overpower constraints, because progress is inevitable in a free society. It is predictable that the structure of organizations will change significantly in the next decade. The market demands it and the tools are available to drive it.

Data Conundrum

The irony underlying the need for data on human capital is that the capability that information technology puts at the disposal of organizations can be a barrier to understanding events and responding effectively. The vast majority of data resident on organizational databases is not gathered and organized in a manner that helps executives manage their human capital problems or exploit their opportunities. Because employee costs today can be anywhere from 20 percent to 70 percent of corporate expense, measuring the return on investment (ROI) in human capital is essential. Management needs a system of metrics that describes and predicts the cost and productivity curves of its workforce. Beyond that, and more important, are qualitative measures. Quantitative measures tend toward cost, capacity, and time. Qualitative measures focus on value and human reactions. The quantitative tells us what happened, whereas the qualitative gives us some idea of why it happened. For the wise, it yields clues as to what is most likely to happen in the future. Together, they offer insights into results and drivers, or causes. For example, if we see costs or delivery times increasing, we might find that quality problems are at the source. Product defects cause work to be recycled, thus slowing down delivery time. In turn, this causes customers to be dissatisfied and perhaps to look for other suppliers. Lost customers drive marketing costs up, which increases product cost, and so on.

> Because employee costs today can be anywhere from 20 percent to 70 percent of corporate expense, measuring the ROI in human capital is essential.

Two Aspects of Human Capital

When we speak of measuring the value of people, we have to acknowledge the two aspects of that issue: the economic and the spiritual. We can accept the intrinsic spiritual value of people and focus on the economic side. In essence, all measures of value contribution are really measures of human value as economic units and as spiritual beings. Only people generate value through the application of their intrinsic humanity, motivation, learned skills, and tool manipulation.

In addition, we must deal with the myth that only standard financial information is accurate. Because we have practiced double-entry bookkeeping for five hundred years, we have come to believe that the numbers on financial statements are truths. This is not the case. They are just facts. There is only one number on a balance sheet that is verifiable as a truth. That is the first asset: cash. All other numbers are a combination of hopes, agreements, and expectations. In effect, we have constructed a system that changes whenever the Financial Accounting Standards Board (FASB) decides to change it. We admit willingly that the system works to some extent in telling us what happened last period—so far as the agreed-upon practices show it. But the data are only as accurate as the inputs, which every businessperson knows are manipulated.

Standard accounting fails to solve today's mandate at two levels. First, accounting looks inside the organization. Its primary role is to conserve the assets of the enterprise. Second, it is focused on the past. If we want an internal, backward look, accounting does the job. Conversely, today we need to focus on the issues that will create future wealth, the actions that will extract value from the marketplace. We need to focus on the future, for we cannot be successful backing into the future with our eyes locked on the past. The advent of new forms of accounting—namely, economic value added and the balanced scorecard approach—is a promising step in the right direction. Recent developments on leading indicators and the measurement of intangibles described in Chapter 7 open vast new opportunities.

Next, we must confront those who say that invested capital greatly determines the productivity of people. In an absolute sense, that is correct. If you give me a gazillion-dollar supercomputer, I can solve large mathematical equations faster than I can by using my laptop. But the question is: Can I do it as fast as a mathematics professor using the same equipment? No way! This is the human leverage.

A related argument says that brand equity has much to do with the success of a given salesperson. It's true that if I am selling Coca-Cola versus Joe's Cola, I will probably sell more Coke than Joe's with less effort. But if you are a better salesperson than I am, you will sell more Coke than I will. It is fair to claim that factors other than human knowledge, skill, and effort affect the outcome of a given situation. Nevertheless, it is also true that human knowledge, skill, and effort make the marginal difference in just about every situation. As the would-be facilitators of human effectiveness, we must step up to the challenge.

What Human Resources Can Learn from Finance

Consider how finance has evolved in recent years. At most firms, finance professionals have moved up from being seen as merely accountants or so-called bean counters to suppliers of genuinely strategic analytics to the C-Suite. How did that happen?

Accountants became more valued as the service economy evolved because the deployment of financial capital grew to be more important relative to physical capital. The function evolved because the accounting profession developed common standards—generally accepted accounting principles (GAAP)—that were accepted across entire industries. These enabled senior finance professionals to develop higher-value analytics that were specific to their own firms.

Today, HR is in exactly the same position. First, people

are now clearly the most important issue for companies. Second, since 1985 there has been a common set of metric definitions in the marketplace. That was the year we published the first benchmark reports at Saratoga Institute. These definitions are now in common usage. The missing piece is they have not officially been adopted. That is the charge for the Society for Human Resource Management. As the national professional association, it is SHRM's duty to step forward and make the defining statement. The definitions are no longer the exclusive property of Saratoga Institute, so SHRM would not be endorsing one company to the exclusion of others.

From there, HR ratifies through application the concept of *generally accepted human resources practices*. The goal would be to have the routine infrastructure in place to do for human capital investment what finance colleagues have done for financial capital. Then, the profession will be in a position to move beyond the HR equivalent of bean counting and offer senior management a real inventory of human capital assets and methods for how this talent capital can best be deployed across the enterprise.

If HR professionals embrace the many faces of change driving organizational decisions today, effectively manage human capital, and drive for measurable results, they can make higher value contributions to their organizations than ever before—and elevate the status of the HR profession in the process.

HRP

I am taking another run at this notion by forming HRP (Human Requirements Planning)—a base for research, standardization, and advanced applications. With the support of a number of major organizations such as Accenture,

American Management Association, Blue Shield, Ceridian, Fidelity, KnowledgeAdvisors, Lehman Brothers, Monster, Oracle, Scarlett Surveys, SuccessFactors, Target, and the Conference Board we have designed a future-focused management model and operating system that we call HCM:21®, Predictive Management.

The model lays out a human capital management system that will carry us into the future. It is described in Chapter 10. The point of it is to serve as a base for collaborative research on human capital management, analysis, measurement, and reporting.

Building on the principles of this model, the research methodology focuses on the study of human capital management and is based in new age metrics. Just as finance builds on accounting, we use HRP as a stepping-stone to open up an entirely new field of human capital predictability. Emerging from those static concepts of the twentieth century we apply advances in decision science and statistical analysis to build a human capital business intelligence field. This moves us from benchmarks and coincidence toward true correlations, causality, and predictability.

Measurement here is concerned about describing why something happened as well as what is most likely to happen in the foreseeable future. Most of the metrics are strategic—that is, they describe high-level integrations of activities and/or results. Rather than study costs of a discrete issue such as cost of hire or cost of a training program, HRP is concerned with complex effects. Today, we are measuring leadership, culture, readiness, knowledge management, engagement, and corporate culture not just as stand-alone metrics but as drivers and predictors of organizational outcomes. The marketplace of the twenty-first century is moving, expanding, and changing so rapidly that management must have tools that help it look ahead rather than backward. Accounting provides concrete measures of the past. HRP produces leading indicators and measures of intangibles. Most important, it makes connections that drive predictability. The basis of success today is information about tomorrow, available today.

People and Information

The knowledge, skills, and attitudes of the workforce separate the winning companies from the also-rans. It is a complex combination of factors. Still, people are not the only force behind the inherent power of human capital. If the key to wealth creation were only head count, then the dullest, lowest-level person would be as valuable as the brightest, highest-level person. In actuality, it is the information that the person possesses and his or her ability and willingness to share it that establish value potential.

Data and people are inexorably linked as never before. Either one without the other is suboptimal. Rather than bigger buildings or more equipment, employees need timely, relevant, and, most important, organized data. Management's imperative is to put useful data at the fingertips of its human capital on a timely basis and to train them in how to use such data. The ability and experience of a person allow him or her to:

- Convert data into meaningful information

- Turn information into intelligence related to a business issue

- Share that intelligence with others

The motivation to share data is the unrecognized barrier to information systems and value extraction. Once more, having data per se is no more useful than having any other resource unless we know how, why, and when to share it. Experience has proved repeatedly that without the knowledge of what to distribute and the motivation to do it unselfishly, information is just another expensive, underutilized asset. The inevitable conclusion must be that long-term profitability is dependent on the creation of an information-sharing culture. It is the perquisite to any attempt to manage intellectual capital.

Modern success stories exemplify the value of information in changing the game and leading an industry. Wal-Mart was built largely on its inventory and sales information system. Knowing what was moving at what rate in each store kept it from being out of stock, which is a cardinal sin of retailing. It also helped drive down costs, which gave it a competitive advantage in the marketplace.

Amazon gathers data from each sale to each customer. Anyone who is a regular customer receives notices frequently on books that reflect buying patterns. If you buy a cookbook you will receive notices of new or specialty books on topics related to food preparation and presentation. If you buy golf books, you receive notes about golf instruction, equipment, resorts, and historic matches.

Information is the driver of almost all economic activity today. Human capital information is essential to any organization that desires to be a leader.

Data-to-Value Cycle

At the heart of the data-to-value cycle is people. It is a cycle rather than a continuum, because data from one phase can cycle back to influence the previous phase or phases. To understand how to assess the value of human capital, we have to look at it in application. Value adding always starts with the enterprise's goals. Operationally, those goals flow down through the business units to the starting point of human capital management—the activities of the human resources department. At this point, the process of connecting human capital data to demonstrate value begins.

> Human knowledge or skill is of no organizational value until it is applied to a business situation. Value adding always starts with the enterprise's goals.

Value can be traced from the inception of data collection through processes to economic results. The cycle starts in the processes having to do with the planning, acquisition, support, development, engagement, and retention of human capital. The values are the economic effects resulting from investment in human capital. Human capital is organized in the human resources department and transferred into operating units. There it is invested, along with other resources. As improvements are realized, value ensues. Value comes through a reduction in expenses as well as through revenue generation, which ultimately lead to profitability and other enterprise goals. The cycle is seen in Figure 1-2.

Schematically, it works like this: Phase One of the cycle is the point of obtaining, supporting, and retaining human capital. Internal efficiencies within the human resources department lead to expense reduction. Improvements in cycle times, incentive compensation plans, greater employee engagement, or development programs also can affect revenue generation. In Phase Two, human capital is applied to tasks and processes within the various business units. It is then a matter of determining whether the gains are attributable in part to human actions. Phase Three focuses on the competitive advantages those improvements generated, which lead to economic goals. When this is viewed as a continuous recycling process, we can find many points at which to assess

Figure 1-2. Data-to-value cycle.

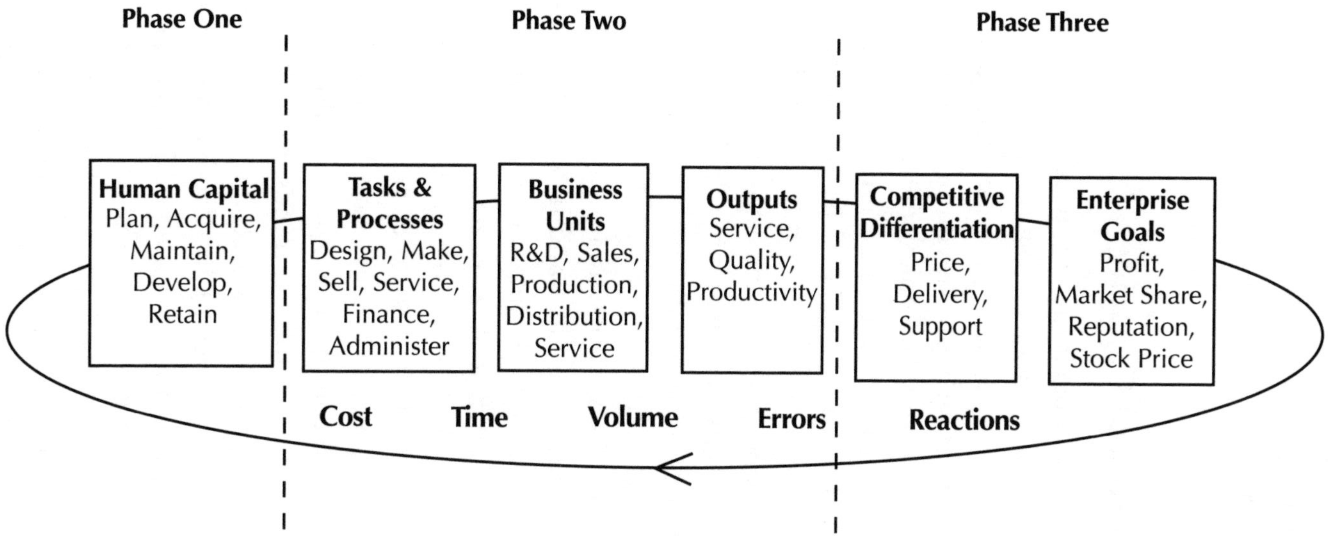

Phase One

Human Capital
Plan, Acquire,
Maintain,
Develop,
Retain

Phase Two

Tasks &
Processes
Design, Make,
Sell, Service,
Finance,
Administer

Business
Units
R&D, Sales,
Production,
Distribution,
Service

Outputs
Service,
Quality,
Productivity

Phase Three

Competitive
Differentiation
Price,
Delivery,
Support

Enterprise
Goals
Profit,
Market Share,
Reputation,
Stock Price

Cost   Time   Volume   Errors   Reactions

the impact of internal improvements on a corporation's profitability.

Organizational Capacity

Organizational capacity, as it is used in this area, is the ability of a company to extract value from the organization's physical and intellectual assets, or relational and human capital. Intellectual capital is composed of intellectual property, the brand, and a complex intertwining of codified processes and culture. Relational capital is the knowledge and relationships with external entities from customers to regulators. Human capital is the combination of employee skills, motivation, engagement, and commitment. People are the catalyst that activates the intangible, inert forms of intellectual capital and the equally passive forms of tangible capital—material and equipment—to improve operational effectiveness. To optimize and measure the ROI in human capital, we have to understand how it interacts with other forms of capital, both intangible and tangible.

Executives often look at organizational capital from an internal ownership perspective. This is a protectionist view, which is not totally bad but is certainly limiting in terms of exploiting its potential. They want to know how to secure the intelligence contained within their documents and processes, as well as within the minds of their employees. It is relatively easy to slap a brand, trademark, copyright, or patent number on a piece of intellectual property. It is a bit more bewildering to find a method for putting one's brand on the human brain and heart. A judicial battleground is forming, with lawsuits flying in all directions, as we try to establish a body of legal precedents for intellectual assets. It has become a significant issue as some emerging countries do not value the sanctity of intellectual capital as much as do most Western countries.

The second organizational capital artifact is *process management*. Documenting how to do something makes it an asset. Superior inventory management helped Wal-Mart take the number one position in retailing. Fred Smith, the founder of Federal Express, created an industry by changing the process of small package delivery. Ray Kroc forever changed food service by automating the sale and serving of simple meals. Every major commercial advancement stemmed from some disruptive technology. Distribution systems, manufacturing methods, and administrative efficiencies represent potential value. Codifying and applying them is an attempt to build intellectual capacity.

One process capital issue that has been largely overlooked has to do with an organization's culture. This is arguably at least as important as process management. Culture dictates what is acceptable in terms of how a process can be run. Some would say that culture is a human capital issue, but it is primarily an organizational factor formed from the CEO's vision and the behavior of the C-level executives. Culture is the defining aspect of every organization. It is the organization's *signature.* Terrence Deal and Allan Kennedy launched the corporate culture concept in 1982.[4] They described how it covers the expectations, rituals, taboos, and underlying rewards and punishments of the corporate society. Fons Trompenaars and Charles Hampden-Turner extended the concept to global issues of corporate value systems and diversity around the world.[5] This has caught on to the point where a currently popular cultural goal is to become a "great place to work." Many companies are struggling to build environments wherein people want to work.

This brings us to the folks who are trying to corral another kind of capital or intelligence that is focused outside the organization, called *relational information*. Relations include interactions not only with customers but also with suppliers, partners, competitors, media, community, and government—indeed, all stakeholders or observers of the organization. A corporation's brand is a visible example of relational capital. Some brands such as Sony, Coca-Cola, Virgin, IBM, and Shell are worth incalculable billions.

Compelling arguments can be made regarding the economic value of knowledge about, and good relations with, any external force that impinges on the organizational corpus. Regis McKenna introduced the idea in 1986 when he argued that traditional product-focused marketing was an anachronism.[6] He claimed that building relationships was one of the three underpinnings of marketing, which are:

1. Understand the market.

2. Move with it.

3. Form relationships.

Whereas information may have a fleeting moment on the stage of consciousness, relationships have a permanence that can be very powerful. People might not remember what someone said yesterday, but they will remember what others did. Somewhere along the way, McKenna's third element got lost because it was not a traditional marketing activity and accounting didn't know how to put a value on it—and still doesn't. However, as one who spent several years in sales and then founded a company, I can state unequivocally that personal relationships are absolutely a competitive advantage. We will look at relational capital, especially customer relations as it merges with human capital.

Finally, we encounter the fourth position, which is dedicated to expanding the skills and knowledge of employees for the sake of the person as well as the company. There are two concerns here. The first is with trying to build *learning organizations*—a recent term for which there are a number of fuzzy definitions. In short, according to Peter Senge, who popularized the term, a learning organization is "a place where people are continually discovering how they create their reality."[7] This construct is undergoing a great deal of experimentation in its own right. A learning organization is not a simple idea. Senior executives, first-line supervisors, employees, trainers, accountants, and lawyers all take different views. The definitive model has yet to be proven.

The corollary human concern is the right of the individual to trade on the knowledge that he or she possesses. Humanists and lawyers argue over the rights of persons within whose brain cage and experience base lay the germ of human capital. Well-publicized cases of appropriation of knowledge through recruitment are surfacing periodically. Some are settled out of court while others battle to the wall. Eventually, one or more will work itself all the way through the legal system, and a body of human capital law will emerge.

Consultants and some academicians have joined the race to intellectual capital for what they see as an opportunity to sell their newfound erudition. Every major consulting firm has formed a human capital practice. The media are supporting this movement with clichés. Spouting platitudes like "people are the most important product," they encourage the building of new management panaceas, thereby inserting more ignorance into the race. By touting every new employee service fad for which there is scant evidence of effectiveness, they generate confusion and frustration. Figure 1-3 displays many of the management panaceas that have hit the market in the post–World War II era. The top is

Figure 1-3. Fifty years of management panaceas.

2010	? ? ? ?
	Engagement—*Intangibles*—Supply Chain—*Analytics*
2005	Knowledge Management—Execution—Talent Management
	Balanced Scorecard—Intellectual Capital—Outsourcing
2000	Reengineering—Delayering—Rightsizing—EVA
	Customer Service—Benchmarking—7 Habits—Downsize
1990	Empowerment—Continuous Improvement—Kaizen
	Corporate Culture—*Change Management*—MBWA—TQM
1980	*Intrapreneuring*—Relationship Marketing—Excellence
	Quality Circles—*Diversification*—One-Minute Managing
1970	Work Simplification—Hierarchy of Needs—Decision Tree
	Organization Renewal—Value Chain—Kepner-Tregoe
1960	Managerial Grid—Matrix—Hygienes and Motivators—Theory Z
	Theory X&Y—Plan/Organize/Direct/Control—Human Relations
1950	Management by Objectives—Management Science—*Decision Trees*

a question mark, because tomorrow someone will come up with the latest solution to all of management's problems.

Typically, each function—finance, marketing, production, and human resources—chooses just one of the lanes on the organizational capital track (structural, relational, or human). They drive off in every direction; each toward what he or she believes is the finish line. The irony is that each is partly correct, but only partly, and therein lies the rub. So long as they never need to meet, there will be no problem. However, organizational capital looks less like a racetrack and more like a maze. Having said that, there is still undoubtedly value in this frenzy, for it is by trial and error, the running in wrong directions and the collisions along the track that we will one day understand what organizational capacity involves. The race will be more painful and less successful until we accept that we must survey the track and understand the vehicles.

Surveying the Track

Figure 1-4 is an example of the intellectual capacity pathway. We need to turn the various lanes into one. When we grasp how to integrate them into our management thinking, we will be moving in the right direction at a faster speed. Strategy and tactics must fuse the four perspectives into a broad-based synergistic solution that can be economically valued. That integration represents the final step on the path to organizational capacity.

The ROI Race

The strategic business plan is like a race plan. The plan's goals are to reach the finish line first. Data systems are the vehicle. Information is the fuel. But the vehicle is not a self-propelled, perpetual-motion machine. It needs a driver, the human being. Measurement is the dashboard gauges. They tell us how fast we are going, the condition of the car, and how far we have gone. Only the driver knows if we are headed in the right direction. When management is the sole driver, the only one who has access to the travel plan and the odometer, we can go a long way in the wrong direction before we realize it. By having someone checking the map against the road signs while others watch the speed, fuel gauge, and temperature and pressure lights, we increase the probability that we will arrive at our destination on time, as well as enjoy the trip.

To have a successful trip to profitability, we need to know more than how to read both traditional and new dashboard gauges. We must design a human capital dashboard that gives us new data and then teach everyone how to read the gauges. The starting point is to know specifically what our goal is, as well as what our competitors are doing. This in-

Figure 1-4. Intellectual capacity pathway.

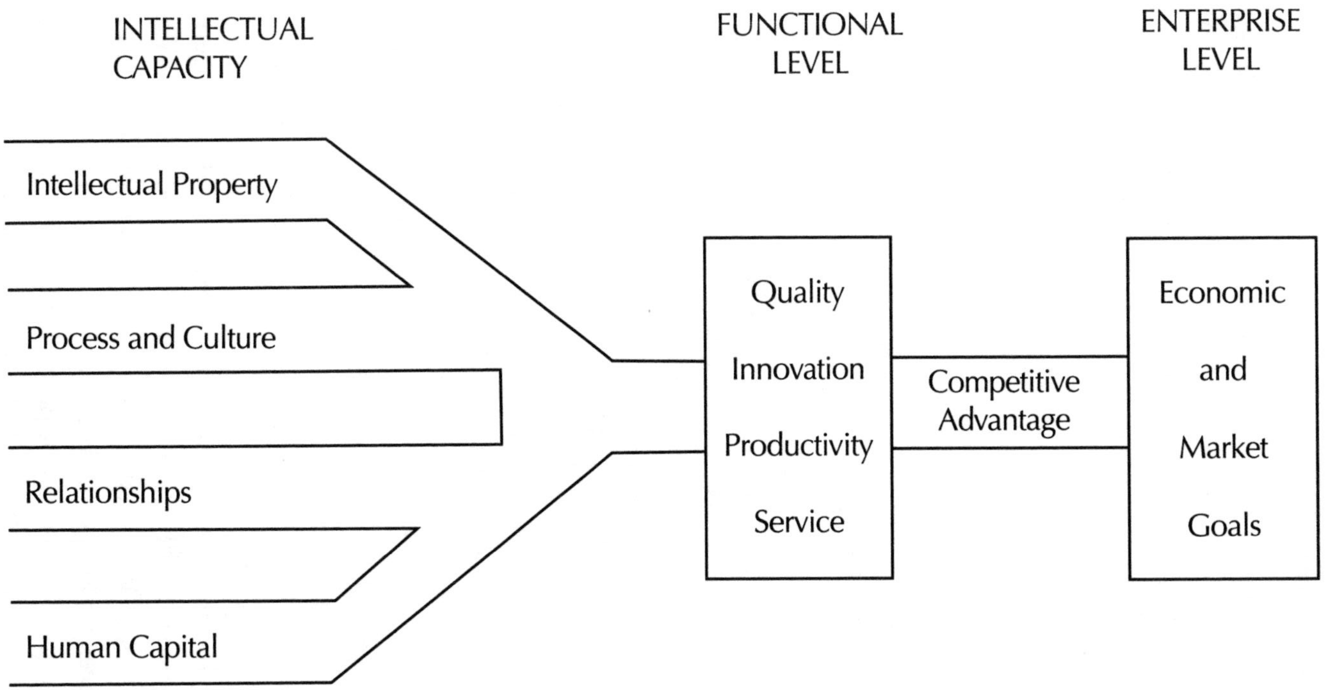

formation evolves into distance, direction, and time requirements. Next, we must specify the type of information that different people will need to manage the race. Finally, we have to learn how people, data systems, and information interact to impact profitability. It comes down to where, what, who, when, and how.

- Where do we want to be?

- What data do we need to capture and manage to get us to the finish line?

- Who should generate what data?

- When do we need it?

- How do we accomplish this most efficiently and effectively?

It is also useful to know how fast and in what direction the competition is moving. Currently, we call that *benchmarking*. The problem with benchmarking and best practice research is that the subject company is not comparable to ours. Second, even it if were, by the time we assimilate, copy, and install the practice, the competition will have moved on to something better. This keeps us always in the pack, but never leading.

False Starts

The most common reaction to the information challenge is to invest in technology. This is necessary, but by itself, it seldom yields a solution. Technology is a passive asset or, at best, an enabler of human intelligence. Computers and programs don't add value until knowledgeable human beings put their trained hands on the keyboard and begin to draw out the potential within the software programs. Technology plus training should make workers at all levels more productive. This is the first step. But there are two parallel steps that must accompany it. One is the issue of data production. All processes generate data as a by-product. Most data are not sorted, collected, and shared widely. Some executives realize that they have a vast pool of useful data beyond accounting, but they seldom make the investment to turn it into productivity-enhancing intelligence. I believe the reason is that they have been trained in financial data analysis, but not in the utility of human performance data. They know they can't run the enterprise without financial information, but they don't appreciate the value or necessity of applying human capital data. The one light at the end of the proverbial tunnel is the gradual adoption of the balanced scorecard.[8] Here, data beyond financials make up 75 percent of the information.

> Computers and programs don't add value until knowledgeable human beings put their trained hands on the keyboard and begin to draw out the potential within the software programs.

The first, last, and most important piece is information culture. Investing in information technology and training is necessary. But again, technology and data are passive. Even information possessed by workers is suboptimized unless it is shared. Putting up an intranet knowledge exchange does not automatically cause useful information to be shared. In the final analysis, it comes down to creating an information-sharing culture. Only then is it worthwhile to invest in information technology, train people in its use, and implement policies aimed at gathering useful by-product data. The fundamental question remains, what information do we need?

Points of Measurement

There are three levels at which the leverage of human capital investment can be measured. The principal focus must always start at the enterprise level. Here we are looking at the relationship between human capital and certain enterprise goals. These goals include strategic financial, customer, and human issues. The second level of measurement is the business unit. At this stage, we are watching for changes in intermediate-level quality, innovation, productivity, and service (QIPS) outcomes. Measurement is fundamentally about assessing degrees of change. All business objectives can be reduced to these QIPS categories. All changes can be measured through some combination of cost, time, volume, errors or defects, and human reactions. The third, but in a sense the primary, stage is human capital management per se. Now we can see the effects of the human resources department's work on planning, hiring, compensating, developing, engaging, and retaining the enterprise's human capital. When we break down the subject of human capital measurement like this, the mystery disappears.

I grant that it is not easy to measure the economic effectiveness of people in service work or professional-level activities. The problem has been that measurement initiatives often applied manufacturing methods. Except for clerical jobs, measures of efficiency or productivity are not appropriate in a nonmanufacturing situation. The input to white-collar work is data. The applicable skill is judgment. The output is information and, if we're lucky, insights and intelligence. There is no single metric for professional-level staff work. As I will demonstrate later, there are five basic paths to measuring the value of this type of output. The greatest value is found in the staff's impact on line function objectives and ultimately the corporate goals. The bottom line is that although it is not easy to evaluate staff work in quantitative terms, it can be and is being done.

I have spent thirty years explaining and demonstrating this by showing the linking methodology and publishing company, industry, national, and international benchmark data, but some people still won't let go of the myth and deal with the reality. Fortunately, every day more people with open minds, new values, and different perspectives are entering business, especially in staff functions. The following chapters show how to measure the ROI in human capital and process management, which leads to competitive advantage and economic value at the enterprise level.

Summary

Management's responsibility today is to combine people with information on a timely basis for several purposes. First, information on employee-based activities is necessary to partner with financial data. Second, financial data tell us what happened. Human capital data tell us why it happened that way. Third, if we are going to manage for the future rather than the past, we need leading as well as lagging indicators. They cannot be found in traditional profit-and-loss statements. Leading indicators are often intangible and therefore not susceptible to standard accounting principles. Yet they are the data that makes the accounting data happen.

Information is the key to performance management and improvement. Without it, we have only opinions with no supporting facts and no directional signals. Information does not move by itself. There has to be an information-sharing culture that promotes and rewards data analysis and sharing. Improvements in one area need to be published centrally, where people can access the information and save themselves from reinventing effective practices.

The three types of data—structural, relational, and human—must be integrated. Structural data tell us what we own. Relational data tell us what outsiders—customers, competitors, and other stakeholders—need or want from our enterprise. Human data show us how the only active assets—people—are doing in their commitment to drive the organization toward its goals. When we begin to understand how the three relate to one another, support and drive one another, we have started down the track to intellectual capacity. By introducing HRP to business, we are making a quantum leap from the static past to the volatile future—with greater hope and reason for success.

Not only is it possible to measure the effects of human performance, it is necessary for maintaining a leading position in the market. Because white-collar, information-focused judgment is fundamentally dissimilar from blue-collar, product-focused labor, a different measurement methodology is required. A spectrum of metrics have been developed that, in total, show the value added of professional-level work not only today but into the foreseeable future. The value is found in the effect it has on enhancing the outputs of its operating-unit customers. As staff groups utilize human capital more effectively, they increase their contribution to the goals of the enterprise.

References

1. Peter M. Senge, *The Fifth Discipline* (New York: Doubleday, 1990), p. 69.

2. Peter Drucker, *Managing in a Time of Great Change* (New York: Dutton, 1995), p. 76.

3. Nick Bontis, "Managing Organizational Knowledge by Diagnosing Intellectual Capital," *International Journal of Technology Management,* 118 (1999), pp. 433–462.

4. Terrence E. Deal and Allan A. Kennedy, *Corporate Cultures* (Reading, MA: Addison-Wesley, 1982).

5. Fons Trompenaars, *Riding the Waves of Culture* (Chicago: Irwin, 1994); Charles Hampden-Turner and Fons Trompenaars, *The Seven Cultures of Capitalism* (New York: Doubleday, 1993).

6. Regis McKenna, *The Regis Touch* (Reading, MA: Addison-Wesley, 1986).

7. Senge, *The Fifth Discipline*, p. 13.

8. Robert S. Kaplan and David P. Norton, *The Balanced Scorecard* (Cambridge, MA: Harvard Business Press, 1996).

CHAPTER TWO

2

How to Measure Human Capital's Contribution to Enterprise Goals

"In the business world, the rearview mirror is always clearer than the windshield."

—WARREN BUFFETT

At the corporate level, everything starts with the CEO's mandate and vision. Mandates change as market opportunities wax and wane. In the 1990s, cost reduction was the number one corporate issue. It led to massive layoffs and continual cost cutting. Then came the dot-com mania and innovation became the top priority. Following the reconstruction after the dot-com firestorm, cost management rose again like the phoenix out of the ashes. But now a 2007 Conference Board survey of 769 CEOs around the world claimed that excellence in execution and top-line growth were the top initiatives.[1]

This compares with the results of another survey published on CareerBuilder.com in 2007 that listed the top five topics that HR provides CEOs:

1. Training/leadership development

2. Succession planning

3. Company mission/values

4. Recruitment tracking and costs

5. Benefits costs[2]

There seems to be some correlation here as the chief executives seem to want to focus first on the future viability of the company and second on current costs. That is good news for human resources because it opens the door to strategic-level contributions.

Constancy and Alignment

Although initiatives come and go regularly, the CEO's vision is not so ephemeral. Unless there is a drastic change or until a new chief executive arrives, the vision is seldom changed. Vision leads to the organization's brand and culture. This triumvirate is the base on which all decisions can be, should be, and most often are founded. We have learned that brand and culture must correlate. The brand is a promise to the marketplace about what it can expect when dealing with the company. The brand can be an expression of quality (Tiffany), price (Costco), service (Ritz-Carlton), innovation (Apple), stability (General Electric), or other attributes. Culture connects with brand at the operating level. Employees are told directly and indirectly what is expected, acceptable, or taboo in this culture. It is the same in any organization from a family to a club, community, or church.

Problems arise when the brand promise is different from the cultural attributes. If the market is expecting rapid response and excellent service then employees must act accordingly. Trouble arises when the organization says one thing but encourages employees to act in a different manner. For example, a number of years ago, my bank advertised "your personal banker" who was supposed to know me and serve me better than a competitive bank. Yet, when I called the bank to talk to my personal banker, no one knew who that was or how to find out. Brand and culture did not meet. I'm certain you have experienced such disconnects when dealing with companies. The new firms selling computers, telephones, PDAs, software, and cell phones are notorious for this disconnect. This could be why there are such low consumer satisfaction ratings and frequent switching among providers.

These are classic cases of misalignment between marketing and operations. Misalignment has always been one of the fundamental problems of corporations. It is obvious that all organizational assets, business units, and employees should be directed to serving the enterprise's purpose. This purpose is expressed through a combination of financial, operational, and human goals. After the vision statement, top management shifts its attention to financial goals in pursuit of exceptional rates of return on shareholder investments. These are to be achieved through operational objectives laid into each business unit. Finally, the employees are assigned personal performance targets. In the perfect plan, there is direct alignment and connection from top goals to bottom targets. Of course, nothing is perfect and alignment is often skewed. Nevertheless, we will proceed as though it is possible to keep alignment, more or less, and design a system of measurement that illustrates the desired connections.

How to Become a Business Partner

For HR to assure that it is aligned with the business, it needs to know the intricacies of the business. It needs to know what is changing within the business. Human resources needs to know the fundamentals of the business, including the following:

- What drives revenues?
- Who are the major customers?
- What is our market share?
- How do our gross margins compare?
- Are earnings per share rising or falling?

Figure 2-1 shows the linkages among the enterprise level, business unit level, and human capital level. Notice I did not say the human resources level. The focal point is human capital, or the employees of the company. Human resources is an enabler that performs several functions vital to the optimum operation of the enterprise.

An HR executive survey in 2006 queried a number of human resources and business executives about how human resources can be more effective.[3] They coalesced the inputs into a set of five guidelines. Here we will take on one of those. The others will be discussed in following sections where they seem to fit well.

Five Ways to Become More Business Savvy

1. *Know your business.* Learn as much as you can about the technology, marketing, finance, and production

Figure 2-1. Organizational connections.

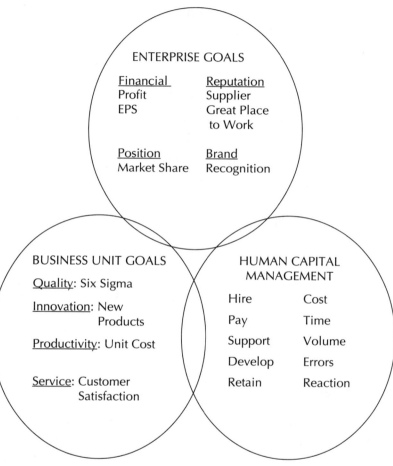

side of your organization. Work outside of HR on line projects.

2. *Learn to work with your CEO and board to build shareholder value.* Remember that we work for the shareholders. Develop data around the investments in human capital. Push up bad news as well as good.

3. *Absorb all that you possibly can.* Read outside of HR. Go to industry conferences. Learn to read financial statements. Be eager to broaden your general knowledge.

4. *Master workforce performance assessment.* Learn to apply data in forms that tell past, present, and future stories. Translate anecdotal data on skill development into effects on business outcomes.

5. *Become an outsourcing and offshoring expert.* Learn to manage vendors and set realistic cost-saving and service-delivery goals. Decide what level of service is most appropriate for your organization at this point in time.

In Chapter 3, we will see some examples of how HR works with business units to generate value. At this point, I will concentrate on corporate-level metrics that link financials with human capital.

The First Step

In the late 1990s, I led the development of a set of financial-operational-human ratios that expressed the link between people and financial results. We began by combining revenue, operating expense, profit, pay, and benefits with employee head count and full-time equivalents. We split pay by level from nonexempt through supervisor/manager and up to the executive level. Each combination yielded a different aspect of the relationship of people, their costs, and the economic results of the enterprise. In the course of the testing, we gathered insights into the forces that drove financial performance. It became clear that there were relationships among the many employee and operating variables. We could see that movement in pay programs, turnover rates, staffing strategies, employee relations services, and training investments influenced product quality, innovation, productivity, and customer service. Now, I call that **QIPS** for short. Although we could not statistically demonstrate causality, there were obviously some connections that were more than coincidental. From that work over the past decade plus, we have reached the point where we can suggest structures, practices, and systems that bring human performance and financial gains closer together. In the case of not-for-profits such as education, social services, government, and military the endgame is serving the organization's constituency and accomplishing or fulfilling its mission.

Human-Financial Interface

For many years, the general practice of matching human and financial variables at the corporate level was confined to that single gross measure derived from the income statements of corporations: revenue per employee. Its flaw is that it does not separate the effects of human effort from the leverage of other assets. For instance, we cannot see in revenue per employee the effects of automation, better inventory control, improved quality, training, effective marketing programs, monopolistic conditions, or anything else. All it yields is a general trend. Adherence to this single metric drove the myth that the impact of human resources and human capital efforts in general could not be measured at the enterprise level. The good news is that since the publication of the first edition of this book, and perhaps partly through its teachings, that myth has largely disappeared. The fact is that there are a number of metrics that can be applied to the relationship of investments in human capital to corporate financial results.

A Strategic View

A customer-oriented strategy for improving shareholder wealth would focus on three factors: costs, potential customer value, and customer needs. The activity-based costing methodology and its supporting software technologies have provided the ability to trace the unique costs of customers, channels, services, and products.

In contrast to calculating the profit from a past time period, calculations of projected financial returns use time/value-of-money principles that consider the timing of future cash inflows and outflows, as well as the cost of capital. A company's ability to satisfy its customers and retain their loyalty provides a sustainable competitive edge that allows higher average prices relative to competitors and drives the top-line growth that the Conference Board study listed as a key CEO initiative.

Evaluating customers requires calculating prospective metrics that when acted on intelligently, truly convert to bottom-line earnings and shareholder wealth. The employee-customer connection mentioned in Chapter 1 appears here.

- A company affects customer loyalty constantly through every interaction and interaction is a human, not a technical, issue.

- A company must continually analyze its customer profile in innovative ways to discover new profitable revenue-growth opportunities.

Becoming customer-centric requires a 360-degree view of data. I submit that includes human capital data, which is at least partly a function of human resources services. A customer-centric approach segments the customer base in multiple ways. Different customers need different treatment—that is, service. With an understanding of customer value and profitability drivers, a refined customer segmentation scheme and data on employee performance that directly affects customers, a company can use sophisticated analytic software to predict "what next?" for individual as well as groups of customers.

Typical marketing delivery systems are:

- Marketing automation software

- Interaction management software

- Marketing optimization software

- Channel analytics

We need to add human capital analytics to this list.

Refocusing

When we look at metrics, usually we are looking at a result, not a cause. So it is with corporate-level human capital metrics. It is the same as looking at gross sales or operating expense. These metrics are simply the end point of a large number of activities that occurred within the organization, many of which were affected by outside forces. For example, the gross sales metric does not tell us which activities within the sales and marketing function were the primary drivers of the result. It could have been due to a cadre of great salespeople, a brilliant advertising campaign, having the best product, price discounting, or a myriad of other factors. It also could have occurred despite having a marginal sales force, based on great customer loyalty, a competitive advantage in delivery capability, or a series of competitor mistakes. In order to find causes, we have to break down the corporate-level metric and look at it from various angles over time. This segmented, longitudinal view will eventually tell us what drove the end result, be it good or bad. So, as we view several combinations of revenue, costs, and employees, keep in mind that the causes will be found later in the organization's processes, along with the way in which we acquire and deploy human capital.

I used to think of organizations as manifesting a continuous series of events and reactions. Subsequently, it has become more apparent that organizations are in a constant state of actions and interactions, dependencies and interdependencies. It is very difficult to break them apart. What on the surface appears to be a discrete act or result is actually the visible aspect of many actions and reactions. Yet, because many people still view things from the traditional fragmented perspective, they launch improvement programs, such as quality projects, at a business unit process level without conscious consideration of its effects elsewhere in the enterprise. Value can be added only if the goals of the enterprise are foremost. Everything starts there. Figure 2-1 outlines the basic interactions and interdependencies among corporate goals, business unit objectives, and human capital management. In practice, we pull them apart to view them as separate variables although in reality they are one constantly interactive entity similar to an atom with neutrons and protons constantly circling.

Progress toward the enterprise's financial, market, and human goals is not linear. At any point in time, they are moving together and apart. This is what makes management of large enterprises so difficult and why they fall out of alignment so often. The business units derive their quality, innovation, productivity, and service objectives from the enterprise goals. The objectives are achieved or not achieved through the actions of people, or the human capital. All other assets are inert, passive, and not inherently value adding until applied by a human being. Hence, the flow of energy oscillates back and forth across all three elements thanks to human effort. Periodically, we stop it mentally to measure how we are doing. For this we need tactical-level metrics to measure improvements within the human resources–based functions and to monitor the human capital effects on business unit objectives. We need strategic-level metrics to show the effects of human capital on corporate goals.

Putting the Human Capital in Value Added

When choosing one measure over others for a performance-reporting system, keep in mind that what we select is a reflection of what we understand and value. What we select will be the issues on which our people will focus attention and energies. In addition, if we are going through some type of organizational change (and who isn't?), we can use metrics to focus the direction of the change. If the move is aimed at improving customer responsiveness and service, then we should measure that. Likewise, if it is targeting cost reduction or product quality, we can use those types of metrics to drive the change in that direction. Best of all, when we choose enterprise-level metrics, we are telling everyone that their change and improvement programs must service these metrics.

Gary Hamel and C. K. Prahalad claim that change programs often fail due to a lack of proper measures.[4] They describe one multinational company that watched its market share decline for years. Employees received messages urging them to do better or berating them for substandard performance. The missing element was competitive data. Without specific data, there was no focused sense of urgency around improvement. The fault lay on the doorstep of top management, who, when negative data were collected, explained them away. The impasse was resolved only after a new top management team was put in place. As they gathered pertinent data and acted on it, things began to change for the better. However, the denial and lost time cost thousands of employees their jobs.

Enterprise-Level Metrics: The Launch Point

Macrolevel data is the launching site of an ROI assessment system. The most common takeoff point is corporate sales or revenue.

Human Capital Revenue Factor (HCRF)

A first step in looking at the human capital aspect of financials is to revise the traditional revenue per employee metric. Sales per employee is the standard measure used by the federal government and most business media. This equation is inadequate and out of date. In the days when management first began to look at sales or revenue per employee, the corporate landscape was considerably simpler than it is now. In other than seasonal businesses, most employees were hired to work full-time. But in today's market, organizations employ human talent in several ways. In addition to the traditional full-time employee, many people work part-time. This changes the corporate denominator from employee to full-time equivalent (FTE). As a simple example, if ten people work half-time, the FTE is five people, although the number of "employees" is ten. The number ten represents what is commonly referred to as head count.

> Sales per employee is the standard measure used by the federal government and most business media. This equation is inadequate and out of date.

To further complicate matters, approximately 20 percent of the U.S. workforce today is what has come to be called *contingent*. These are often referred to as *rented* employees. According to government statistics, in the past ten years, contingent workers as a percent of the U.S. workforce have increased almost 10 percent. These people are not truly employees, because they are not usually on the payroll. Nevertheless, their labor has to be accounted for in order to have a valid representation of the labor invested to produce a given amount of revenue.

At the end of the day, we have converted revenue per employee into revenue per FTE (including full-time, part-time, and contingent labor hours). FTE is a surrogate for total labor hours invested. It is a basic measure of human productivity, in that it tells us how much time was spent to generate a given amount of revenue. Although this is a better starting point than revenue per employee, it is still too simple. We need more sophisticated metrics to understand the relationship of human capital to financial outcomes.

Human Economic Value Added (HEVA)

In the 1990s, the Stern Stewart organization popularized the term *economic value added*.[5] EVA, as it is called, is defined as *net operating profit after tax minus the cost of capital*. The objective of this measure is to determine whether the actions of management have added true economic value rather than simply generated the typical financial statements, which can mask actual outcomes. EVA is very useful, in that it shows how much true profit is left not only after paying all expenses, including taxes, but also after subtracting the cost of invested capital. As Stern Stewart has pointed out, this can be a revealing measure of managerial performance. EVA can be given a human capital perspective by dividing it by the FTE denominator described earlier:

HEVA = Net operating profit after tax—Cost of capital / FTEs

By converting EVA into HEVA, we can see how much EVA can be ascribed to the average amount of labor contracted for. I say *labor*, because the term *employee* is an anachronism in this case.

The following formulas are variations on a set of financial and human capital variables. For the sake of this example, I have produced a set of figures for a hypothetical company, SamCo, to illustrate the formulas. Figure 2-2 lays out the vital statistics of SamCo that are needed for this exercise.

Human Capital Cost Factor (HCCF)

Just as the income statement displays both revenue and expenses, we can show human capital expenses to go along with various revenue and value calculations. There are four principal costs of human capital, which are:

1. Pay and benefit costs for employees

2. Pay costs for contingents

3. Cost of absenteeism

4. Cost of turnover

Figure 2-2. SamCo financial data.

Revenue	$100,000,000
Expense	80,000,000
Payroll and benefits	24,000,000
Contingents cost	3,750,000
Absence cost	200,000
Turnover cost	3,600,000
Employees (FTEs)	500
Contingents (FTEs)	100

Other investments such as training are too idiosyncratic to put into a generic formula.

Each of the four cost variables needs some explanation. Keep in mind that contingent labor normally includes neither benefits expense nor the cost of absence or turnover. In some contracting situations, the agency pays benefits for its contract personnel, and this cost is passed on in the hourly labor rate charged to the contracting company. In the case of absence or turnover, contingent labor that does not report to work is most often replaced promptly by the contracting agency. Although there may be a couple of hours lost until the replacement arrives, overall the costs are too negligible and variable to track.

All measurement programs from business to politics to the social sciences have some error. Macro measures such as ours have a small inherent standard error. Nevertheless, they have been proved over almost thirty years to be at least as accurate as the other line items in corporate financial statements. When we use the same formula over an extended period, the effects of a minuscule error are fractional. Keep in mind this is not a life-threatening exercise. No one will die if our numbers are off by a percent or two. I can assure you that the inputs that go into making other corporate metrics are no more precise than what I am suggesting.

The term *pay*, as we use it, is simply the number that appears on an employee's W-2 form at the end of the year. It is all current cash compensation. Pay does not include long-term incentives until they are paid out. In the case of options that are exercised, we would include the cost to the company of the stock option.

Benefit costs are the monies paid by the company to provide employee benefits. Portions paid by the employee are not included, since they are not an expense to the company.

We use the U.S. Chamber of Commerce list of benefits as the standard.

Absenteeism is an expense to the company, in that the work ascribed to a given job is not getting done by the person paid to do it when he or she is absent. One can argue that someone else does the work when a person is absent. However, that cannot be proved, and the variations in how an organization copes with absenteeism are so great that we must take a consistent stand in order to have a reliable measure. A small cost of absenteeism is factored into our metric by taking out one-half the value generated per hour by all jobs. It works like this:

Revenue per FTE per hour is *X* (hypothetically $100)
Absenteeism is 2 percent
Subtract 1 percent or $1 per FTE hour

Although the cost is minuscule, we include it to keep the issue of managing absenteeism in view. There are vendors who make a good living out of absence and downtime data. Management needs to know when it is paying for time not worked.

Turnover is obviously costly. An argument has raged for many years about the true cost of turnover. Despite several credible studies, some executives like to argue over how to cost turnover. An individual organization can choose to measure turnover costs any way it likes. But to have a reporting system that transcends the idiosyncrasies of the individual, we have developed and tested a standard formula for calculating turnover.

It includes the cost of termination, replacement, vacancy, and learning curve productivity loss. These four variables generally cost a company the equivalent of at least six months of a nonexempt person's pay and benefits and a minimum of one year's worth for a professional or manager.

The combination of pay, benefits, contingents, absence, and turnover yields a total cost of human capital for the organization. Obviously, there are equipment and facility costs implied with the employment of labor, but these are not truly human capital costs. It is the responsibility of management to control these direct and indirect costs of human capital, just as it controls the cost of other resources. The HCCF is a convenient, tested metric for monitoring the base costs of an organization's human capital over time.

Applying the scenario and figures for SamCo, we find the following human capital cost:

HCCF = Pay + Benefits + Contingent labor + Absence + Turnover
HCCF = \$24,000,000 + \$3,750,000 + \$200,000 + \$3,600,000
HCCF = \$31,550,000

It is clear that labor cost is not \$24 million, but \$31,550,000, or 31.4 percent more than appears on the employee pay and benefits line in the financials. If we extend this a bit further, we calculate that true average FTE cost is not \$24 million for 500 FTEs, or \$48,000, but \$31,550,000 for 600 FTEs, or \$52,583 each. Both numbers include overtime, shift pay, and all forms of pay for time not worked. Now we have a more comprehensive and descriptive cost metric.

Human Capital Value Added (HCVA)

The issue of human capital productivity was seen in a simplistic form as revenue per employee. Then, we saw a more accurate form in revenue per FTE (HCRF). Next, we introduced cost with HCCF. Now, if we want to move to profitability per FTE, we have the following formula:

$$\text{HCVA} = \frac{\text{Revenue} - (\text{Expenses} - \text{Pay and Benefits})}{\text{FTEs}}$$

In this case, we are looking at the profitability of the average employee. By subtracting all corporate expenses, except for pay and benefits, we obtain an adjusted profit figure. In effect, we have taken out nonhuman expenses. Then, when we divide the adjusted profit figure by FTEs, we produce an average profit per FTE. Note that this can be set up to include or exclude the cost of contingents, absence, and turnover. We'll look at it both ways using SamCo's figures—first, with only pay and benefits:

$$\text{HCVA} = \frac{\$100,000,000 - (\$80,000,000 - \$24,000,000)}{500}$$

$$\text{HCVA} = \frac{\$44,000,000}{500}$$

$$\text{HCVA} = \$88,000$$

If we include the cost of contingents, absence, and turnover, we would have an adjusted profit figure of $51,550,000 ($100,000,000 − [$80,000,000 − $31,550,000] − $100,000,000 − $48,450,000) divided by 600 FTEs, or $85,917 per FTE. The 600 FTEs include employees and contingents.

> With a minimum of effort you can have several views of the effects of people on financials. To contend that there is no valid and consistent way to do this is simply to admit one's ignorance.

You can see that with a minimum of effort you can have several views of the effects of people on financials. To contend that there is no valid and consistent way to do this is simply to admit one's ignorance.

Human Capital Return on Investment (HCROI)

Another relationship of human capital investments to profitability can be made visible through a ratio that follows from the formula for HCVA. HCROI looks at the ROI in terms of profit for monies spent on employee pay and benefits.

$$\text{HCROI} = \frac{\text{Revenue} - (\text{Expenses} - \text{Pay and Benefits})}{\text{Pay and Benefits}}$$

Again, by subtracting expenses except for pay and benefits, we have an adjusted profit figure. In effect, we have taken out only nonhuman expenses. Then, when we divide the adjusted profit figure by human capital costs (pay and benefits), we find the amount of profit derived for every dollar invested in human capital compensation (not counting training and the like)—in effect, the leverage on pay and benefits. This can be expressed as a ratio.

Applying the SamCo figures, we have the following equation with no contingent, absence, or turnover costs added in:

$$\text{HCROI} = \frac{\$100,000,000 - (\$80,000,000 - \$24,000,000)}{\$24,000,000}$$

$$\text{HCROI} = \frac{\$44,000,000}{\$24,000,000}$$

$$\text{HCROI} = \$1.83$$

In this case, the HCROI ratio is $1:$1.83. If we want a complete and true return on our direct and indirect human capital expenditures, we have to use the $31,550,000 figure as shown before, rather than $24 million. The HCROI ratio in that case is $1:$1.63. In effect, less of the total expense was for nonhuman costs because we transferred the contingent, absence, and turnover costs to where they belong—cost of human capital. For every dollar spent on human costs with no change in total expense, we got a smaller human capital profit ratio. Now that you see the logic, you can design additional metrics that include training and other employee-related costs to suit your special needs.

With the examples so far, we can see that the cost of human capital can be much more than is normally realized. However, the important point is that no matter what the costs are or in which direction they are moving, it is clear that the relationship of human capital to productivity and profitability has been definitely established.

Human Capital Market Value (HCMV)

Tobin's Q is a ratio that measures the relationship between a company's market value and its replacement value. It is a metric that is sometimes cited by the naive as a measure of human capital value. Economists or stock analysts may find it interesting, but as a management indicator, it is not very useful. In one sense, it is the market's view of the value of intangible assets. This can include not only human capital but also other forms of intellectual capital such as process capability, brand recognition, or marketing acumen. It is an interesting number, but it is subject to wild stock market fluctuations having nothing to do with the capability of the organization's human capital or the utilization of tangible assets. Thus, if it is going to be used at all, it should be tracked over a long period to smooth out external market machinations. For the intellectually curious, one variation on it would be to subtract book value from market value and divide that by FTEs. This gives us a market value premium per FTE. The formula would look like this:

HCMV = Market value—Book value / FTEs

As an example of the effect of market action on HCMV, let's say that Goldman Sachs is offering stock in its IPO at $15.72 per share. At the opening, the stock jumped, and at the end of the first day, it closed at over $50. On any given date since then, the share price could be anywhere. Does the fluctuation represent an increase in intellectual capital at Goldman Sachs since the opening? Tobin's Q would argue that it does. I leave it to you. Does Goldman Sachs's intellectual capital fluctuate on a daily basis, or are we really looking at the needs of investors (read gamblers)?

The *H* in Human Capital

We've discussed a set of financial-based human capital metrics. Now we have to balance it with a set of human-based human capital metrics. Most monitoring of employee metrics is basically a body count. How many employees do we have? What is the gender, racial, and ethnic mix? How many affected class personnel are in managerial positions? All that is fine, and it needs to be monitored for equal employment opportunity purposes, if nothing else. However, no one has yet shown that a given mix of people correlates with high performance. Before the diversity gods get me, I want you to know that I am married to a Latina so I wholeheartedly believe that all people, regardless of any demographic label, need to be cherished, supported, and helped to grow. And I believe that a diverse workforce is better than a homogeneous one. My interest here is to look for metrics that will tell us something about the effectiveness of certain human-financial ratios in our operating systems.

Workforce Demographics

It is useful to know things like how many exempt versus nonexempt people you have and what percentage of the work is being done with regular versus contingent personnel or is being outsourced.

Exempt Percent

The exempt percent is the number of exempt FTEs as a percentage of total FTEs. The proportion of your workforce that is exempt versus nonexempt tells you something about the nature of your organization. If your employees are predominantly nonexempt, you are probably in the processing business—building products, processing paper transactions, or running some type of logistics center. If your employees are predominantly exempt, you are probably more of a financial service, technology, or marketing business.

There are well-known examples of marketing companies. Nike enjoys a major share of the sneaker market and a significant piece of the sports apparel market. Yet it does not manufacture its products. It is principally a marketing company. Fidelity Investments has a mix of exempts and nonexempts. It offers both a variety of financial services, such as mutual fund management, and transaction processing through its benefits and payroll businesses. Predominantly professionals populate the investment advisory functions, whereas the transaction processing services have a higher percentage of nonexempts. Automobile manufacturers are heavily weighted toward production workers, who are mostly nonexempt. If one of them decided to sell its manufacturing facilities and focus on design and marketing, its mix would flip.

In conclusion, knowing your mix is useful because you can see it begin to move outside of acceptable levels. This is what happened to many U.S. businesses up through the early 1980s. The proportion of exempt to nonexempt staff in manufacturing firms got out of balance and created a breakeven point that made some companies noncompetitive. This led to the downsizing tsunami. If we had been watching the mix all along, we probably would not have experienced that pain.

Contingent Percentage

The contingent percentage is the number of contingent FTEs as a percentage of total FTEs. The growth of the contingent workforce has reached a point where it bears monitoring. We cannot keep adding contingents to the workforce without some type of plan. If we do not pay attention, one day we may find that contingent workers who have no company loyalty hold many of our core competencies. They can go at a moment's notice and leave us incapable of competing. It would be like the story of the camel who was allowed to put his nose into the tent during a sandstorm. After the nose came the head, and no one resisted. Then came the shoulders, trunk, and finally the hindquarters. At that point, the original inhabitant found himself out in the storm. When we don't pay attention to the key signals of our business, we will sooner or later find ourselves in the middle of a storm.

> One day we may find that contingent workers who have no loyalty to us hold many of our core competencies. They can go at a moment's notice and leave us incapable of competing.

A little side note about contingents: We tend to think that contingents are cheaper than regular employees. This can be true, but it is not axiomatic. Often in technical and professional ranks, contingents cost more on an hourly basis. Some companies that don't keep track may eventually realize that their contingents have been around for more than a year. In those cases, it might have made more economic sense to hire a regular worker. Contingents have a way of blending in and disappearing in large organizations. I know of cases in which both regular employees and contract workers were paid for more than a year after they had left. Some firms have found to their embarrassment that the courts considered their long-term contingents eligible for benefits, just like the regular employees.

Workforce Movement

Obviously, the workforce is not static. People come and go every day. Some are replacing terminated personnel, and some are taking newly created positions. It's not a bad idea to know how many are doing each, because movement is expensive. One company spent over $1 billion in a three-year period hiring, laying off, rehiring, and laying off.

Accession Rate

The accession rate is the number of replacement hires and hires for new positions as a percentage of the workforce. How many people did your company hire last year? The cost to hire a nonexempt person typically runs about $1,000. The cost of exempts averages closer to $8,000, with the top companies averaging $12,000 to over $20,000. None of these costs include onboarding or training the new hire or the effects on productivity or customer service.

Separation Rate

The separation rate is the number of voluntary and involuntary separations as a percentage of total head count. Turnover is a costly and disruptive event. Whether you fire someone or the person quits, it causes a break in routine. Surviving employees have to pick up the slack until a replacement is hired or if this is a downsizing, divide the work among themselves. The cost of turnover is detailed in Chapter 4. As you know, the retention of talent is a mission-critical activity. The first edition of this book came out prior to the dot-com bust, so turnover was not an issue. But today it is. Monitoring turnover is imperative. More important than a number is the issue of who is leaving and why. As I write this update, we are facing a recession. The price of gasoline is rising almost daily, the U.S. dollar is sinking, we have a major mortgage liquidity problem, and that's only the good news. One might think that getting rid of costly human capital is not a bad idea. But keep in mind, with the labor demographics forecasting major shortages by 2010, we need to be careful about how we handle turnover. If the separation rate starts to climb, you had better jump on what the rate is (a number) and find out why.

Cost Management

Although it is good to know about percentages and movement, it is even better to know about cost. The cost of an average employee's pay, according to most reports, is approximately $45,000. Add to this figure another 25 to 30 percent for benefits, and you are touching the $60,000 level. When you look just at professionals or managers, the figure is much higher.

Total Labor Cost Revenue Percentage

This figure covers all labor costs as a percentage of total revenue. TLC does not stand for tender loving care here. It includes the cost of pay and benefits for regular employees plus the cost of all contingent labor, including contract professionals. The best way to look at it is to see how much of each sales dollar is being absorbed by labor cost. Downsizing programs were launched to bring the percentage down. For every penny by which you reduce it, you add that penny to earnings, since expense reductions go directly to the bottom line. Rather than laying off people, you could consider how to leverage them into greater revenue. After all, this is an equation with two sides. When management truly believes that people create profit, it balances cost control with investments in skill building. Thirty years ago, quality guru W. Edwards Deming showed us that performance is affected more by managerial barriers than by employee effort. Research has confirmed for decades that executives who use the balanced approach to people management consistently outperform the reactive, feast-and-famine managers.

Investment Management

This is the other side of the cost management approach. We know from the human capital value added and the human capital ROI formulas from earlier that people do make money for companies. It only makes sense to invest in them and to monitor that investment.

Employee Development Investment

Employee development investment is the cost of all education, training, and development programs as a percentage of payroll. But there is a problem here. No one has figured out what constitutes employee development. Now we have *blended learning.* Does that change things? Tuition refund programs clearly qualify. Formal training classes in-house and public seminars also count. But what about coaching and counseling? What about the conference that was really a three-day vacation in Las Vegas to reward performance? Add to this uncertainty the ambiguous way in which training is accounted for, and you realize that we don't really know what we are spending on training. The CHRO of a major bank told me they spent about $250 million per year on development programs and have no idea what value it may be generating. The American Society for Training and Development has been working on this since the mid-1990s and it does not have a satisfactory, standard, and practical method yet, although it reports that U.S. businesses invest about $70 billion per year on L&D programs. This is up from about $55 billion in the late 1990s.

Nevertheless, let's not let ignorance stand in our way. We'll use it as a stimulant. There is a workable solution, even though its factual basis is suspect. Set your own standards for what constitutes a developmental expenditure. You can do it any way you like, because there is no generally accepted standard. Then, collect data according to your model and monitor those data every quarter. Pretty soon you will see movement, and you can begin to judge the value of that investment. Ask yourself, did we see quality, innovation, productivity, customer satisfaction, or sales increase as the training investment increased?

These are just a few of the things that can be tracked and managed at the enterprise level. Knowing how much is being produced and sold, what it costs, and whether you are getting a decent ROI is essential for corporate management. Ignoring human capital costs, or using only gross pay and benefit costs as your benchmark, is somewhere between simplistic and inexcusable. Of course, we all want and need to manage cost to stay competitive. But the real opportunity is in managing contribution to revenue and profits. We can cut costs only so far. But there is always room for more revenue generation. Human capital management takes us down that side of the path as well.

Human Capital Enterprise Scorecard

In 1996, the work of Robert Kaplan and David Norton culminated in their book *The Balanced Scorecard*.[6] It followed a series of articles by the pair that described their experiments with this method of management monitoring and reporting. Since then, the balanced scorecard has become a popular management tool. Lately, it has evolved into a strategic mapping device. Its premise is that standard accounting is too insular and focused exclusively on financial performance. They suggest that issues such as learning and growth, customers, and business process should be added to financial data. From their basic model, variations have appeared across the landscape. It is a refreshing and much needed break from total reliance on standard accounting.

To make some order out of all the indicators we've discussed so far, I suggest that an enterprise-wide human capital scorecard be developed. There would be two topical sections to start: financial and human. After some experience, others could be added, such as a learning or growth section or one on costs and ROI in workforce development. Figure 2-3 lists a set of recommended starters drawn from the metrics detailed earlier.

Norton made a key point about what differentiates the scorecard from other business performance measurement frameworks in the marketplace:

> The primary differentiator is that the balanced scorecard is based on organizational strategy. Many people will build a list of measures that are nonfinancial and think that they have a balanced scorecard, but in our view the scorecard has to tell the story of your strategy. The biggest mistake organizations make is that they think that the scorecard is just about measurement. Quite often they will get some lower-level staff in the organization to develop the metrics. To be effective the scorecard has to be owned by the executive team as only they are responsible for the fundamental corporate strategy.[7]

How to Marry Quantitative and Qualitative

So far, my focus has been on objective data. I did that deliberately. Executives live on numbers, although they sometimes act on feelings. We need the quantitative side as a consistent reference set. Still, there is value in the subjec-

Figure 2-3. Sample corporate human capital scorecard.

Financial	Human
Human Capital Revenue *Revenue divided by FTEs* Human Capital Cost *Cost of pay, benefits, absence,* *turnover, and contingents* Human Capital ROI *Revenue minus (expense minus* *total labor cost), divided by total* *labor cost* Human Capital Value Added *Revenue minus (expense minus* *total labor cost), divided by FTEs* Human Economic Value Added *Net operating profit after tax* *minus cost of capital, divided by* *FTEs* Human Capital Market Value *Market value minus book value,* *divided by FTEs*	Exempt Percentage *Number of exempt FTEs as a* *percentage of total FTEs* Contingent Percentage *Number of contingent FTEs as a* *percentage of total FTEs* Accession Rate *Replacement hires and hires for* *new positions as a percentage of* *the workforce* Separation (Loss) Rate *Voluntary and involuntary sepa-* *rations as a percentage of head* *count* Total Labor Cost Revenue Percentage *All labor costs as a percentage of* *total revenue* Employee Development Invest- ment *Cost of all training and develop-* *ment as a percentage of payroll*

Notes: FTEs include contingent workers unless noted otherwise.
Total labor cost includes pay and benefits plus contingent worker cost.

tive. Qualitative measures of leadership, engagement, readiness, knowledge management, and corporate culture balance the hard numbers. Whereas you can monitor volume and costs every month, you cannot take the pulse of the workforce that often. Semiannual or annual surveys of employee groups are common. If you need more frequent and detailed signs, you can sample different parts of the workforce monthly and cut it by level, function, job group, or geography. This way, you have a living tally of the state of wherever variable you need.

You can also compare movement in the qualitative indices against movement in the quantitative metrics. I'm not suggesting that you will find causation. If you see parallel movements, it might be coincidental. But at the very least, you will have insights to act on. There just might be some correlations buried in the data that you can test. The more of this you do, the more experience you gain, and your sixth sense will sharpen. Eventually, you will sense things that you didn't see or feel before. You'll look at data and know that something has changed, even though the data do not look that different. This is your reward for diligence. With this heightened sensitivity, you will be able to suggest preemptive strokes that cut off a nuisance before it becomes a problem or to take advantage of an opportunity that others have not seen. People will think that you are wise, and you are.

Benchmarking's Danger

Most alleged best-practice reports detail a particular process or project. The report usually describes how someone responded to a problem and found a solution that worked in that situation. This singular success is often extrapolated to an acclaimed universal solution. In fact, a follow-up inquiry usually finds that the process and the results were embellished somewhat. Furthermore, it is common to find that the process is no longer being used or is being confined to just one location. The object lesson is that one person's single, idiosyncratic success does not make for an organizational best practice applicable to other situations or organizations.

The Willy Loman Syndrome

My experience in nearly thirty years of collecting data worldwide is that the best performers usually don't self-nominate. They are too busy widening the gap between themselves and the pack, and they seldom feel the need to blow their own horns. In Arthur Miller's classic play *Death of a Salesman*, the main character is talking to his best friend. You need to know that Willy's sons have not done much since high school to distinguish themselves, but Willy puffs up their every little accomplishment. His friend mentions somewhat offhandedly that his lawyer son recently presented a case before the U.S. Supreme Court. Willy is dumbfounded and asks why the man didn't tell him sooner. His friend's reply is that when you do it, you don't have to talk about it.

Summary

Measurement of the effectiveness of human capital has been conspicuous by its absence in corporate financial reports. Only with the advent of the balanced scorecard has there been any attention paid to this most important of resources. The single typical measure—revenue per employee—is simplistic and out of date. Since human capital costs currently can absorb upward of 40 percent of revenue, they certainly warrant better attention. Couple that fact with management's belated realization that people can be viewed as an investment rather than as a cost, and it is absolutely imperative that more sophisticated metrics be devised to monitor human performance at the enterprise level.

This chapter has demonstrated with formulas and examples that human capital can be linked to economic value added, corporate productivity, cost structure, and profitability. Metrics have been placed into a scheme that includes quantitative and qualitative indicators of performance at the enterprise level. A human capital enterprise scorecard template shows how to view a set of financial and human metrics. Collectively, it displays for top executives a target against which functional unit performance can be judged. This performance measurement and reporting system has life breathed into it through eight enterprise-level practices that are common to top-performing companies: balanced values, long-term commitment, culture and system linkage, partnering, collaboration, innovation and risk management, communications, and competitive passion.

In the end, it should be evident, even to skeptics, that human capital's effect on corporate performance can be traced, analyzed, and evaluated. This base, along with the metrics for business units and human capital management (covered in the next two chapters), gives executives a method for managing their human capital in objective terms rather than relying on clichés, hunches, and unverifiable opinions.

References

1. "CEO Challenge 2007," The Conference Board, New York, 2008.

2. Betty Hintch, "Inside the CEO Mind," Humancapitalmag.com, October 2006.

3. "Five for Five," Human Resources Executive, 2006, pp. 50–56.

4. Gary Hamel and C. K. Prahalad, *Competing for the Future* (Cambridge, MA: Harvard Business School Press, 1994), pp. 141–142.

5. G. Bennett Stern III, *The Quest for Value* (New York: Harperbusiness, 1991).

6. Robert S. Kaplan and David P. Norton, *The Balanced*

Scorecard (Cambridge, MA: Harvard Business Press, 1996).

7. David Norton, "Keeping the Score," *Fast Track* (Spring 1998), pp. 14–15.

CHAPTER THREE

How to Measure Human Capital's Impact on Processes

"We have too many high sounding words, and too few actions that correspond with them."

—ABIGAIL ADAMS

Making Money Through Process Management

According to The Hackett Group's 2007 study of managing human assets:

"Typical Fortune 500 Companies net nearly $400 million annually by improving strategic workforce planning and other key talent management functions."[1]

This finding provides human resources organizations with a way to demonstrate the effect of their efforts on productivity, customer satisfaction, and employee commitment, and by extension, on sales, profits, and shareholder value.

The research found a strong correlation between improved financial outcomes and top-quartile performance in four key talent management areas: strategic workforce planning, which involves identifying the skills critical to a company's operation and how those needs match up against those of the existing workforce; staffing services, including recruitment, staffing, and exit management; workforce development services such as training and career planning; and overall organizational effectiveness, including labor and employee relations, performance management, and organizational design and measurement.

Companies with top-quartile talent management outperformed typical companies across four standard financial metrics. They generated EBITDA of 16.2 percent, versus 14.1 percent for typical companies. This gap netted a typical Fortune 500 company (based on $19 billion revenue) an additional $399 million annually in improved EBITDA. On average, top talent management performers also generated:

- $247 million annually via a 22 percent improvement in net profit margin
- $992 million annually via a 49 percent improvement in return on assets
- $340 million annually via a 27 percent improvement in return on equity

The most interesting point in the findings was that top performers in talent management operate very differently from their peers. Top performers spend 6 percent less on human resources overall than typical companies. This factor is driven by dramatically lower costs in key areas such as total rewards administration, payroll, and data management and also lower employee life cycle costs. These savings enable the companies to invest more in talent management processes. Top performers are also 57 percent more likely than their peers to have a formal HR strategic plan in place, more than twice as likely to facilitate strategic workforce planning discussions with senior management, and 50 percent more likely to link their learning and development strategy to their company's strategic plan. From these findings, we can develop a process management model that promises to outperform the competition.

Geary Rummler and Alan Brache draw on their experience in process improvement to state: "We believe that measurement is *the* pivotal performance management and improvement tool and as such deserves special treatment."[2]

They go on to point out that without measurement we cannot:

- Communicate specific performance expectations

- Know what is going on inside the organization

- Identify performance gaps that should be analyzed and eliminated

- Provide feedback comparing performance to a standard or a benchmark

- Recognize performance that should be rewarded

- Support decisions regarding resource allocation, projections, and schedules

The conclusion is simply that if we don't know how to measure our primary value-producing human assets and work processes, we can't manage them.

In the Beginning

Everything that happens in an organization is the result of a process. A process is a series of steps designed to produce an effect. All processes share a common pattern. They consume resources, and they generate a product or a service. This is as true for a social service program as it is for lead mining. The reason we want to study business processes is that an organization is only as effective as its processes, which is referred to as the ability to execute.

American businesses devoted a great deal of effort during the last two decades of the twentieth century toward improving process efficiency. To their credit, significant gains have been achieved. Despite the offshoring to Asia, the productivity of manufacturing processes has increased to the point where we have been able to recapture some market share and improve margins in international markets. Of course, the current low value of the U.S. dollar has had a positive effect on exports.

Unfortunately, the same improvements are not true in the staff side of the house. Since the 1920s, administrative costs as a percentage of sales have increased from 8 to 25 percent. *Fortune* magazine described this shift in pithy terms: "on the staff side of the house—which processes information—they have gotten worse, unable even to achieve economies of scale, let alone truly take out costs."[3]

The Return of Reason

The focus on processes stopped with the dot-com boom in the late 1990s. It was the rage to denigrate efficiency as the new grandiose idea that would be the new medium: WWW. The Internet as savior phenomenon lasted less than five years before it imploded in 2001. In the aftermath, many were stunned for a couple of years as they recoiled from the shock.

By the middle of the first decade of the new century, process efficiency rose from the dot-com ashes. Now, as we approach the end of the first decade, sanity prevails again. With it, the push for competitiveness has enlisted human resources as an ally. People are beginning to see how human resources can positively affect business processes in other units, which in turn support the goals of the enterprise.

Peter Keen made a compelling argument for processes as assets of the enterprise.[4] They are part of an organization's intellectual capital. He points out that traditionally, accounting has treated business processes as expenses. This ignores the fact that a process is more accurately an asset if it generates value. When we talk to managers about their most important resources, they seldom list balance-sheet assets. Instead, they point to items such as people, technology and the information it generates, corporate culture, brand recognition, management capability, and distribution systems. These are all intangible, off-balance-sheet assets. The way to look at processes is in terms of their ability to generate a return on invested capital. Processes that return more money than they cost are assets, and those that cost more than they return are liabilities. Reengineering an administrative process that is inherently a liability does not magically transform it into a valuable asset. At best, reengineering can only reduce the expense of running the process.

Others agree with Keen that a process should add value and not merely move something around. To the extent that processes are liabilities, they ought to be outsourced. Since it is difficult to see how to turn a process into a value generator outsourcing is usually the answer. Since 2000 outsourcing has become an industry unto itself. All the major consulting firms have outsourcing solutions. At last count, more than four thousand companies worldwide offer outsourcing.

Those processes that have the potential to add value should always show a direct link from the process outcome to an organizational goal. Rummler and Brache state unequivocally:

> Each customer process and each administrative process exists to make a contribution to one or more Organization Goals. Therefore, each process should be measured against Process Goals that reflect the contribution that the process is expected to make to one or more Organization Goals.[5]

Every discussion I have had over the past decade with practitioners of process management started with the same belief statements. Typical examples are:

"A process must always be linked to strategic, external, customer satisfaction, or retention goals."

"A process must be part of something bigger [the enterprise's objectives]."

"A process should support the achievement of the business's objectives."

Process values are not static. They change over time as the corresponding competitive issue becomes more or less important. However, if we decide that a given process does not affect our competitive position, then it is probably a liability, by definition. Yet tomorrow, something in the marketplace could change it into a potential asset to be improved. For example, if prompt delivery is not a competitive advantage, then there is no value to be gained from reengineering the order entry-to-shipment process. This would be the case in a monopoly. If we have such a strong market position that there is no competition, then speed is not an issue. When we had one telephone company, if the original AT&T could not deliver service or a new phone quickly, we had no choice but to wait. Now, there are many manufacturers as well as long-distance and cell phone companies, so everyone has to be competitive on speed as well as on quality and service. Process value is the foundation of the discussion in this chapter. Our concentration is on the effect of human capital on the value added of processes.

Positioning Business Unit Processes

Processes are the link between human capital management and the enterprise's strategic goals. Human capital, often called *people*, is an asset. Through processes, which are activities, assets are put to work. The investment of human and other forms of capital in the process propels it on a course of contributing, or not, to the imperatives of the enterprise. If the imperative is to reduce operating expenses, processes can be streamlined, automated, eliminated, or outsourced in support of the imperative. The decision and cost-reducing action give us a way to measure one of the three basic objectives of an organization: *productivity*. If customer satisfaction or that current cutesy phrase—*delight*—is the goal, customer-oriented processes can be improved and measured in terms of another objective: *service*. Last, if it is imperative that we reduce the number of errors or defects in product manufacturing or administrative processes, they can be overhauled in pursuit of the third objective: *quality*. In every case, my agenda in this book is to look at how the role or deployment of human capital in the process affects outcomes in a measurable way. The outcomes will be defined within productivity, service, or quality terms.

To gain leverage and ensure that our in-house processes are truly assets, we have to engage both types of capital investments: human and structural. The first investment can be improved by doing a better job of acquiring, supporting, engaging, developing, and retaining the human capital. Simply put, we need to generate better strategies and tactics around hiring, compensating, training, and caring for our human talent. The second investment can be improved by

> Processes are the link between human capital management and the enterprise's strategic goals. Human capital, often called *people*, is an asset. Through processes, assets are put to work.

shaping, organizing, and positioning the various elements within our structural capital base. This means more effective acquisition and deployment of materials, equipment and technology, information, and systems.

One of the more pleasing discoveries one makes when improving a process is that it yields gains in more than one objective. When we improve quality, we naturally reduce production or service costs as a by-product and usually make customers happier in the end. Naturally, this practice leads to customer retention. Happier customers also buy more and refer other potential customers. This improves a company's market reputation. In turn, that saves the marketing expense required to obtain new customers, which in turn improves profit margins, and so on. If we were to add up the dollar value of each of those outcomes, we could test it against the cost of running and improving the process. This tells us whether a process is a value-generating asset or a liability with little verifiable, tangible value. Figure 3-1 is a sample of three such cases. After we have the dollar values on the right side, we can compare them to the cost of running the process. We might find that it is more cost-effective to outsource the process.

Figure 3-1. Process value analysis.

Process ⟶	Change ⟶	Impact ⟶	Values ⟶
Time to respond to calls for customer service and to repair product was too long	Shortened response time and time to repair through new phone system and training for service technicians	Customer complaints dropped, and survey showed customer retention increasing	Reduced marketing expense to gain new customers: average cost to obtain a new customer = $XXX saved Satisfied customer continues to spend: average sales per customer = $XXX Customer referrals: each customer typically refers X new customers, who spend an average of $XXX Uncalculated: improvement in market reputation, leading indirectly to new customers
Time to fill key professional and technical positions was increasing	Shortened time to fill positions through new recruiting program without denigrating quality of new hires	Key jobs filled an average of 14 days faster; new product release and production schedules met; customer service phones covered	Each day a job is filled, the estimated average value (revenue−pay) = $XXX Better customer service values
Accounts receivable invoice errors were intolerably high	Computer invoice screen redesigned and accountants trained	98% of invoices mailed within 48 hours of receipt and error rate decreased to 1%; less rework	Receivables aging dropped 10 days; cash flow increase = $XXX; less rework saves $XXX; fewer calls from customers' accountants enhances reputation, perhaps attracting applicants for accounting positions and reducing cost per hire

Process/Talent Case

A concrete example of how human capital data can be combined with operating needs and facilitated through IT is labor scheduling at Louis Vuitton, as reported by IBM.[6]

There is a direct business benefit from better labor planning and scheduling. Gains come from cost reduction, revenue enhancement, increased customer and employee satisfaction and retention, and improved managerial control and responsiveness. Being able to match actual labor usage to labor forecasts reduces unnecessary hiring, overtime expenses, and outside temporary employment services. HR's ability to work out forecasts with managers using past data, current trends, and future expectations depends on IT's ability to design the appropriate programs.

Louis Vuitton North America reduced costs and focused staff on customers by upgrading its labor schedule practices. By improving time and attendance software and by integrating with HR's employee data, operations customer counting, and marketing's point-of-sales technology, management was able to shift more staff to higher traffic periods. Simultaneously, these lowered costs associated with manual data entry for the payroll process by 50 percent and reduced the time for managers to perform payroll and labor schedule tasks from two to four hours down to twenty to thirty minutes each week.

The ultimate objective is to trace possible linkages between process improvement and the enterprise goals. If there is a driving connection, then there is potential, measurable value added. This was a prime example of human resources as a business partner. There was no need to argue over who gets the credit for the improvements. Everyone recognized that it was a very successful collective effort wherein several functions contributed.

Supply Chain Management

In recent years, supply chain management principles have started to creep into staff processes. Although it is not a major wave of change, there are signs that it is being tested and is sometimes working. We can expect that, like any new valid idea, its time will come and human resources will see it.

Sunil Chopra and Peter Meindl, authors of *Supply Chain Management*, provide a simple definition of supply chain management: "A supply chain consists of all stages involved, directly or indirectly, in fulfilling a customer's request."[7]

John Mentzer and his associates offer a more comprehensive explanation:

> **The systematic, strategic coordination of the traditional business functions and tactics across these functions within a particular company and across businesses within the supply chain as a whole.**[8]

Alexander the Great used supply chain management to give himself an advantage. Rather than have supplies moved laboriously and expensively in terms of pack animals and support staff, Alexander made his soldiers carry their own supplies. This was an unusual burden at the time but it gave his army great mobility and quick strike capability. Now he was free to devise innovative strategies that gave him competitive advantage over slower moving enemy forces. So, you see, nothing is new.

Components

There are five major supply chain drivers that should be considered when running a human resources function.

1. *Production.* What, how, and when to produce. HR produces human capital for the organization through sourcing, hiring, and development.

2. *Inventory.* How much to make and how much to store. The current workforce inventory produces products and services for customers.

3. *Location.* Where best to do what activity. Deploying people quickly and efficiently helps meet production and customer service needs.

4. *Transportation.* How and where to move product. The hiring process delivers human capital to where and when it is needed.

5. *Information.* The basis for making these decisions. Data from the Human Resources Information System (HRIS) and from HR's operating metrics supports decision making.

HR's supply chain works best when it is integrated across functions. Planning, hiring, supporting, and developing need to work smoothly for both lost cost efficiency and optimum effectiveness. Supply chains must respond to the needs of their customers. Consider how this differs between a convenience store like 7-Eleven and a discount warehouse like Costco. Customers who shop at convenience stores are looking for a quick in-and-out experience and are willing to pay a little more for the convenience. At a Costco or Sam's Club the customer is looking for the lowest price and is willing to drive a distance and buy in large quantities. The supply chain reacts accordingly. At 7-Eleven, the emphasis in on responsiveness. At the discounter, cost-efficient operations are a must.

Human resources can look at supply chain management from two standpoints. First, it can be viewed by its own efficiency, responsiveness, and quality. What can you do to be the most cost-effective operation? Second, how is HR part of the larger corporate supply chain? What is the dominant business model that human resources must serve? Is it product quality, time to market, product cost, customer service, or what? The on-demand marketplace requires human resources to think of itself as a critical component of the corporate supply chain. To operate that way, human resources needs to align itself to serve the business processes as shown in Figure 3-2. Supply chain responsiveness or efficiency derives from decisions made about the five supply chain drivers. The choice is to emphasize responsiveness or efficiency depending on the demands of the enterprise.

Operating Divisions

Supply chain management in human resources parallels that of the organization. Instead of planning, sourcing, making, and delivering products, human resources plans, sources, selects, and delivers human capital skills. This is best done through a coordinated program of planning staffing and development.

Figure 3-3 on page 80 is an outline for an exercise in forecasting or predictability. Once we understand how supply chains work in human resources program management, we can more easily see and empathize with how it works in the larger organization.

Human Capital in Processes

Human, material, equipment, facilities, and energy capital are invested in a process. At the end, we want to know with some degree of certainty how much human effort affected the outcome. At one level, this is obvious, because all other

Figure 3-2. Supply chain alignment and strategic positioning.

PREPARATION

A. Understand the customers' requirements
B. Define core competencies and roles
    HR will play in serving its customers
C. Develop integrated supply chain capabilities
    to support the roles chosen

ACTION ALTERNATIVES

	Responsiveness	Efficiency
Production	Excess staff available Flexibility Mobility	Lean, low-cost operation Narrow focus Not able to travel
Inventory	Well-stocked labor pool Broad capabilities	Minimum staff plus contingents Dominated by specialists
Location	Many locations	Central location
Transport	Quick hires Broad range of skill	Cheap hires Narrow band of skills
Information	Can share wide range of data on hiring, training engagement, performance	Reliable, minimal information at low cost

forms of capital are passive. It is only the action of the employee that causes an outcome. Practically speaking, what we are trying to ascertain is how much more value the employee leveraged from other capital investments, such as computerization. A basic question is, if we invested in the automation of a process, how well did the worker leverage that investment? An economist might make the argument that the marginal improvements of automation have nothing to do with how the human leveraged that piece of equip-

Figure 3-3. Four phases of the HR supply chain.

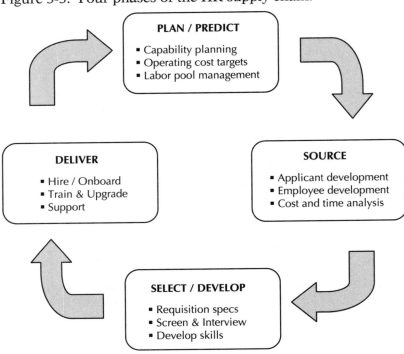

ment. However, if we get down off the economics horse for a moment and put our hands on the process, it becomes clear that the person contributed the knowledge and skills to fulfill the promise of the machine's specifications. Some people like to ignore that fact and claim that the human element was not critical. But when the promise of the structural capital investment is not fulfilled, they quickly turn to the operator as the source of the problem. So, one more time, the machine is potential. The person is the catalyst.

Assume for the sake of example that if the work output doubles, we will believe that the combination of automation and human capital created it. Can we prove what percentage of the change resulted from human effort? Pragmatically speaking, we cannot separate the person from the machine in a business setting. It would be like trying to separate the computer from the software in terms of relative value. Proof is the stuff of the laboratory. Degree or amount of improvement from invested capital is the concern of the business executive.

Can a person add value beyond the capability of the machine or the work process? Of course! There are thousands of stories of how the human element turned around a deficient situation without the addition of new equipment. Nobel laureate Richard Feynman, who worked as a physicist at Los Alamos on the Manhattan Project that built the A-bomb, recounts one of the best ones.[9] The short version of his story goes like this:

> I was asked to stop working on the stuff I was doing and take over the IBM group. Although they had done only three problems in nine months, I had a very good group. The real trouble was that no one had ever told these fellows anything. The army had selected them from all over the country for a thing called Special Engineer Detachment. They sent them up to Los Alamos. They put them in barracks. And they would tell them *nothing*.
>
> Then they came to work, and what they had to do was work on IBM machines—punching holes, numbers that they didn't understand. The thing was going very slowly. I said that the first thing there has to be that these technical guys know what we're doing. Oppenheimer went and talked to the security and got special permission so I could give a nice lecture about what we were doing, and they were all excited.
>
> "We're fighting a war! We see what it is!" They knew now what the numbers meant [they were pressure and energy readings]. They knew what they were doing. *Complete transformation!* They began to invent ways of doing it better. They improved the scheme. They didn't need supervising in the night; they didn't need anything. They understood everything:

they invented several of the programs that we used. [They physically rearranged the machines and got better output from them through a new process flow.]

So my boys really came through, and all that had to be done was to tell them what it was. As a result, although it took them nine months to do three problems before, we did nine problems in three months, which is nearly ten times as fast.

That is an illustration of the central point of the process question. Human value is found through the leverage it applies to structural capital. What we measure is the marginal improvement that occurs when a person picks up a tool and makes something happen. It

> What we measure is the marginal improvement that occurs when a person picks up a tool and makes something happen.

can be rightfully claimed that in the truest sense, all leverage is a function of human effort. A machine is not a machine in the hands of everyone. For some, it is an incomprehensible combination of metal, plastic, wood, or rubber. To others, it is a tool in the true sense of the word—a productivity lever. People make the difference through how effectively they employ other forms of capital. In effect, the result is the value added of human capital.

Anatomy of a Process

Figure 3-4 shows the position of the person, the human capital, within a process. Everything starts with the desired outcome of the process, which is allegedly linked to the goals of the enterprise. But here we run into the first of several problems with process management, or, I should say, mismanagement. Quite often, particularly in the administrative processes found in marketing, advertising, accounting, in-

Figure 3-4. Anatomy of a process.

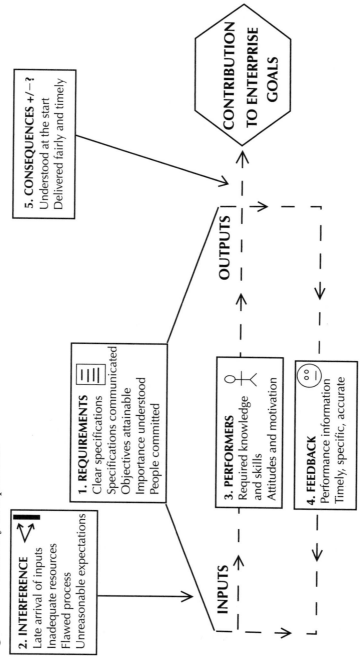

formation services, human resources, and other support groups, process management is nearly nonexistent.

Nearly forty years ago, Robert Mager and Peter Pipe led the human performance management analysis process by asking the fundamental question, "If their life depended on it, could they do it?"[10] This put people squarely in the middle of the value-adding game.

These questions set up the requirements of the process:

- Is there a clear, specific, quantitative outcome?
- Do the people involved know what it is?
- Are the expectations easily attainable, or are they a stretch?
- Do the people understand the importance of the outcome?
- Are the people committed to its attainment?

These questions may sound naive, but more often than not, I've encountered vague or incomplete answers, or even no answers at all. The following discussion draws on my studies with Rummler and Brache on process improvement.

The first external element impinging on the process is the interferers. These are forces or factors that get in people's way as they try to perform the tasks within the process. They are:

- Inputs from the preceding unit or person that don't arrive on time or are unworkable
- Resources that are inadequate to perform the tasks
- A flawed process, making performance difficult
- Unreasonable expectations of output speed

The central element, the person, is next. This is the one element that makes all the difference. It can make up for weak points elsewhere or break the process. Key questions are:

- Do the people have the knowledge and skills to perform up to expectations?

- Are they psychologically capable—emotionally and motivationally?

The other inside element in the process is feedback. The questions are:

- Do the people receive information of their own making or from others as to how effectively they are performing during or at the end of the process?

- Is the information relevant, accurate, timely, understandable, and specific enough to prompt an appropriate response?

After the fact, there are consequences surrounding the results. These include, basically, rewards or punishments. The relevant points are:

- Do the people understand the consequences?

- Are the rewards or punishments delivered in a fair and timely manner?

What stands out in this schema? It is the performer! Several of the factors in the five issues in Figure 3-4 deal with the personality, skills, and behavior of the people carrying out the work. Take these factors out, and what we have left is a static shell of a procedure. Now, let's take a look at how we locate and measure the effects of human capital in a business unit process.

Process Performance Matrix

Every function should have an ongoing set of operational metrics. Production, sales, and service units normally do.

> Just as there is an accounting system to tell us what is happening on the P&L, there is a basic methodology for process management: the performance matrix.

But when we move to staff groups, we often find a lack of metrics to tell us how efficient or effective the unit is. There is a solution to this deficiency. Just as there is an accounting system to tell us what is happening on the P&L, there is a basic methodology for process management. It is called the *performance matrix*.

Figure 3-5 illustrates the performance matrix. It is the fundamental template to lay over any function or process. Down the left-hand column, you see cost, time, quantity, errors, and reaction. These are the five ways to evaluate things in organizations and in life.

1. How much does it cost?
2. How long does it take?
3. How much was accomplished?
4. How many errors or defects occurred in the process?
5. How did someone react to it?

This is as applicable to shopping for groceries, taking your child on a picnic, having your car serviced, or working in an organization. It even applies to making love. You figure it out. Granted, each of the five measures is not equally important in a given situation. In some cases, you may use only one or two of the measures. Nevertheless, these are the five possibilities.

The matrix gives us the four basic criteria for judging in-

Figure 3-5. Process performance matrix.

	QUALITY	INNOVATION	PRODUCTIVITY	SERVICE
COST	Warranty Cost	R&D Investment	Unit Cost	Contact Cost
TIME	Repair Time	Time to Market	On Schedule	Response Time
QUANTITY	Meets Six Sigma	Scalable	No. Orders Filled	Number Served
QUALITY	Scrap Rate	Best in Market	Rework Rate	First Call Solution
REACTION	On Spec	Customer Delight	No Flaws	Problem Solved

termediate value added: quality, innovation, productivity, service—QIPS. These are the essential elements of business. Researchers call them dependent variables. We call them objectives. They are the steps along the way to competitive advantage and, eventually, the profitability of the enter-prise's goal. Although we treat them individually, they are interdependent. It is hard to imagine good service based on overly expensive products of low quality. Likewise, improve-ments in quality reduce the unit cost of the product or ser-vice because it doesn't have to be recycled. Everything that everyone does at all times can be dropped into one of these columns.

Quality

The customer defines quality. There are concrete measures of both product and service quality. The customer usually judges quality in terms of a combination of factors. The cost of the product and its utility and durability are the criteria that underlie a subjective judgment of quality. The quality movement of the 1980s focused on cycle time to produce the product and the error or defect rate. GE and Motorola became famous in the quality field for their Six Sigma pro-grams. This was a measure of the defect rate that was six standard deviations above the mean. In concrete terms, it meant that there were no more than three errors per million items processed. This applied to manufacturing, shipping, and any other high-volume operation. The company be-lieved not only that it had to aspire to this level to compete in international markets but also that customers were rais-ing their level of expected quality to this range.

Innovation

The advent of dot-coms raised consumers' expectations. Fu-eled by unsustainable claims around the "next great idea," prospects and buyers continually pushed providers for more and better whatever. Established brands were overwhelmed by highly touted new products, many of which failed to fulfill their promises. Nevertheless, the bar was raised forever. To meet this new standard, providers must continually introduce the latest and greatest. Have you noticed how many things are advertised as being "all new"? One of the oldest ways to track innovation came out of Silicon Valley. Electronics firms measured innovation in terms of the amount of revenue generated by new products or services in the market within the previous twelve months.

Productivity

The most concrete of all measures is productivity. The most common metric is unit cost. Manufacturers strive to reduce the average cost of producing each product in their lines. Whether it is paper cups or locomotives, the basic measure has always been unit cost. As international competition increased in the 1960s, U.S. businesses started to worry about production costs and delivery times. The volume-oriented phrases "do more with less" and "lean and mean" became mottoes behind the great downsizing of the 1980 and 1990s. Error rate reduction was a way to reduce unit costs and meet delivery schedules. Finally, reaction to the product became a key way of looking at production success. But behind that was the reaction of the people doing the work. Stress levels increased and employee complaints became more prevalent with the speedup of manufacturing processes. There was a famous case in the 1980s of an automobile assembly-line rebellion. The assembly-line workers revolted against the continual increase in line speed demanded by management. This attracted other management's attention, and the drive for productivity improvement took on a more humanistic tone.

Service

Taking care to satisfy the needs of people is service. Usually, we think of customers as the prime target of service. Although that is true, we also have to serve employees, people in the community, government agents, strategic partners, and, of course, stockholders. In effect, all relations with other human beings are measurable in service satisfaction terms. In Figure 3-5, satisfaction is found in the reaction cell, at the bottom of the service column. Other ways to measure service include the cost of the service event, the time to deliver it, the amount delivered, and the rate of errors made in its delivery. When a customer service person takes a call at a service center or makes a call at the customer's site, each of those measures can be applied. Despite the fact that the customer defines the level of satisfaction, and even though each customer is different, we can measure service on the five dimensions in the matrix.

I've filled in some of the cells in Figure 3-5 with a few of the typical process and outcome metrics. The degree or amount of change in the sample outcomes that could result from any improvement effort is measured by some combination of the cost, time, quantity, error, and human reaction indicators. In all, there are fifteen possibilities to find positive change. The caution is to remember that a positive change does not necessarily mean that it contributed to the corporate goals. This has to be recognized at the beginning of the process. The question is, if we improve this process, what difference will it make to the customer and therefore to enterprise value? Assuming that we have figured this out ahead of time and we are right, at the end of the day, we should be able to give specific examples of the improved metric and how that contributed value—as well as find the human capital contribution.

James Cortada and John Woods provide a guideline for

deciding what to put into a business unit's performance measurement system:

> The preference in the development of measures should be for those that aid improved understanding of customer preferences, employee motivations, or investor expectations, rather than those that offer only precision, convenience, or low cost.[11]

Finding Human Capital Effects

We've looked at processes per se, where they fit in the enterprise-to-human capital continuum, and the issues that need be addressed regarding people's ability to perform within the process. Now we come to the part that stymies most people: It is how to find the effects of HR's work on a business process and second, how to isolate human intervention in a process. Specifically, we want to tease out the human contribution within the general effects. This can be accomplished with a four-step analytic process called *process value analysis*. The steps are situation analysis, intervention, impact, and value. The critical step is the first one. If we thoroughly understand the situation in which we intend to intervene, it is not that difficult to find the value added at the end. Most failures emanate from this point. If we aren't diligent in laying out the situation, we have little chance of answering specific value-added questions at the end.

Step One: Situation Analysis

1. *What is the business problem: quality, innovations, productivity, service (QIPS)?* There seems to be a natural tendency in business to throw a solution at a problem, which is often no more than a symptom. Consultants, trainers, and

even managers all have their pet panaceas. They are solutions in search of a problem. The proper first question is not, What shall we do? It is, What is the business problem?

If someone is upset because of

> The proper first question is not, What shall we do? It is, What is the business problem?

the way employees are acting, I suggest they gulp down some Maalox or Prozac and chill out. So tell me, how does what is bothering you affect QIPS? Which of the four basic business goals is suffering? Often it is more than one. But whatever it is, you have to locate it before you can try to fix it.

2. *What is the current performance level in terms of QIPS indices?* Once you have defined the arena, give me the evidence in hard and soft data. Are there cost, time, quantity, error, or human reaction problems? It is helpful to have as much historic data as possible so that you can see how long this deterioration of performance has been going on and how far performance has slipped. At the very least, you need it described in one or more of the five indices.

3. *How is the current performance affecting competitive advantage?* Again, if you just believe that you ought to be doing better, don't bother me. Come back when you can see how your company is being disadvantaged in the marketplace. For example, if this problem continues, will it eventually affect your ability to compete? Will the competition be able to offer a better-quality product at a cheaper price? Will they be able to deliver faster than you can? Will they be servicing customers better? Why aren't you able to match the competition's QIPS? Answers to these types of questions take us to an element we can fix one way or another.

4. *What are the critical work processes in this situation?* First, is it a manufacturing, service, or an administrative

process? Are you making a product, providing a service to a customer, or both? Who and what are involved: first-level employees, technicians and professionals, supervisors, materials, equipment? What about the process itself; can you outline its steps for me?

From these four questions we should be able to understand all the important elements that define a situation. As we proceed, we will look for causes. When we have intervened and monitored ensuing changes, we will have a good idea of the source of and reason for change. This will tell us how and where an investment in human capital will contribute to the process improvement. It is this degree of preparation that unlocks the mystery of human value. Perhaps for the first time we will really understand the process and its effect on enterprise goals.

Step Two: Intervention

1. *What is the source of the problem?* You have made a list of all the elements in the process. As we review these elements and begin to discuss how they interact, it will become clear what is causing the breakdown or holding you back from making improvements. The source of the problem will be found within or among the following elements: people, equipment, material, the process, or, if it is a manufacturing situation, sometimes the product itself, which is designed in such a way that it is difficult to produce in quantity and quality consistently.

2. *What is the best solution?* At this point, it always becomes obvious what at least one of the interventions should be. With practice, people learn to ferret out all the possible problem sources and assign priorities to their solution. Sometimes we don't know whether an issue is really part of

the problem or just a possibility. In those cases, we have to send someone with technical skills into that area to study the process in action. This could be anyone from a materials engineer to a psychologist. Before acting, we might want to go outside the organization and benchmark the process elsewhere. We might decide that training, counseling, reengineering, or providing incentives is part of the solution.

3. *Agree on a solution, plan the action, and do it.* It is hard to believe that people will go through a lengthy analysis and never act, but every consultant has faced this problem. Clients sometimes get cold feet when they discover the source of the problem and the people involved. This is when they claim that discretion is the better part of valor and slip quietly back into the shadows. As Scott Adams reported in *Dilbert*, "I was part of a 'Quality' initiative where the only tangible change was to our notepads."[12]

Step Three: Impact

1. *Did performance change? If yes, was the change in a positive or a negative direction?* We have defined the problem, found the cause, and acted. After an appropriate time lapse to let the solution take effect, we want to know what happened. If nothing changed, the reason is usually so obvious that no analysis is necessary. Frankly, I have seldom gone through the intervention stage and seen no change whatsoever. When that does happen, it is because someone did not do what he or she was supposed to do. Assuming there was change, what was it?

2. *What and how much change occurred?* Here we go back to the basic indicators: cost, time, quantity, error, and human reaction. Perhaps you see now how this framework makes value analysis rather easy. The key again is thorough analysis in Step One. From that, we know the situation so

well that any later deviation is easy to spot, along with its cause, direction, and amount. At the end of the day, we can see whether we are saving money or time, increasing throughput with the same or less input, reducing errors, and making someone happier.

3. *What caused the change? Was it the action we took or extraneous factors?* This is the moment of truth. This is where we answer the question that many people believe cannot be answered. I'm sure that at this point you see that it is not a sleight-of-hand trick. We have analyzed and observed this process for some time. We know it inside and out. We've monitored its rhythms. We've watched it operate within the larger organization and seen inputs from other areas. We've witnessed unforeseen forces impacting it and watched it either absorb and rebound from the blow or be laid low by it. We know this baby. Now we are able to say with a high degree of certainty that the change amounted to *this much* in *these areas* (percentages or dollars). It was driven principally by *these actions* (training, reengineering, automation, counseling, and the like) and was or was not affected by *extraneous forces*.

Step Four: Value

1. *What are the* internal *effects on quality, innovation, productivity, or service levels?* Using the five change indicators, we can show how, where, when, and how much QIPS have changed in the business unit in question. We may also be able to trace changes and improvements outside the unit to other stakeholders of the process. Did we cause any problems on the input side? Did we deliver an improvement that helped on the output side? In all cases, we can quantify much of the change. Some effects will be perceptual, in that employees may report reduced levels of stress or fatigue or

attitude improvements as a result of the change. In these cases, we don't need to put a dollar value on the scale responses to a survey. Keep in mind that we are not doing a doctoral dissertation. We are just trying to figure out where the improvement is coming from and whether it was worth the investment.

2. *What are the* external *effects on competitive advantage?* If we were correct at the start (see Step One, question three), we knew where we were being hurt in the marketplace. We knew that if we didn't fix the problem or exploit an opportunity, eventually we would probably see lower sales and margins, declining customer relations, or other negative effects. Now, we can turn around and add the changes back in as gains in a competitive advantage. As we said at the beginning, if the problem that started this action was affecting the organization's key goals, it qualified as an area of concentration. If we were right then, we can see the value gained for the enterprise now. And we will have convincing qualitative and quantitative data regarding the ROI in human and structural capital.

Figure 3-6 is a form that can be used to do the process value analysis.

A Test Problem

Figure 3-7 is a list of basic process and function metrics for eight functions. If you look closely, you will see metrics for cost, time, quantity, error rates, and human reactions (customer satisfaction). Here is the problem:

1. Take one of the time measures, such as mean time to respond and repair, percentage of filings on time, average time to process a requisition, or work order completion time. Although these come from different functions, they

Figure 3-6. Process value analysis (form).

Situation Analysis

1. What is the business problem: service, quality, or productivity (SQP)?

_____

2. What is the current performance level: SQP indices?

_____   _____

_____   _____

3. How is current performance affecting competitive advantage?

_____

_____

4. What are the critical work processes in this situation?

_____

_____

Intervention

1. What is the source of the problem?
   _____Equipment   _____Material   _____People   _____Process
   Describe: _____

   _____

2. If people or process, what is the best solution?
   ___Benchmark ___Reengineer ___Provide incentives ___Counsel ___Train
   Describe: _____

   _____

3. Agree on a solution, plan, and act.
   Describe: _____

   _____

Impact

1. Did performance change?   _____Positively   _____Negatively

2. How much change occurred?
   Cost: _____
   Time: _____
   Quantity: _____
   Error: _____
   Human reaction: _____

(continues)

3. What caused the change?
   Your action: _____
   Extraneous factors: _____

Value

1. What are the *internal* effects on service, quality, or productivity?
   _____
   _____
   _____

2. What are the *external* effects on competitive advantage?
   Sales: _____
   Margins: _____
   Customers: _____
   Time to market: _____
   Other: _____
   _____
   _____

have one thing in common: They are processes that involve employees, equipment, supplies, a procedure, and supervisory management.

2. What are the consequences of these processes falling out of a tolerable range of performance?

Process Deficiency	Possible Consequence
Mean time to respond and repair	Dissatisfied, potentially lost, customers
Percentage of filings on time	Penalties levied by government
Average time to process a requisition	Production slowdown and late delivery
Work order completion time	Employee safety

3. Choose one problem to work through the process value analysis. Assume logical causes and effects. I'll demonstrate using the first possible consequence, which is that a dissatisfied customer may leave us and cause a loss of sales.

4. In going through the process value analysis, you can speculate on what could cause a delay in mean time to re-

Figure 3-7. Process and function metrics.

MARKETING	**CUSTOMER SERVICE**
Marketing costs as percentage of sales Advertising costs as percentage of sales Distribution costs as percentage of sales Sales administration costs as percentage of sales	Service costs as percentage of sales Mean time to respond and repair Service unit cost Customer satisfaction level
INFORMATION TECHNOLOGY (IT)	**FINANCIAL**
IT costs as percentage of sales Percentage of jobs completed on time and within budget Overtime costs Backlog hours Value of regular reports (use paired comparison)	Accounting costs as percentage of sales Aging of receivables Accuracy of cost accounting Percentage of filings on time Percentage of on-time closings
FACILITIES	**SAFETY & SECURITY**
Work order response time Work order completion time Level of employee complaints Maintenance costs as percentage of sales Recycling percentages	Safety & security costs as percentage of sales Accident rates Lost days level Worker compensation costs Security incident rates
PURCHASING	**ADMINISTRATIVE SERVICES**
Purchasing costs as percentage of sales Average cost to process a requisition Average time to process a requisition Inventory costs Percentage of purchases defective or rejected	General & administrative costs as percentage of sales Outsourcing cost/benefit Average project response time Internal customer satisfaction level Percentage of projects completed on time and within budget

spond and repair. It could be a communications problem, in that the customer's request was not given to the service department promptly. It could be that the process of assigning service people over time has become cumbersome or inefficient, causing them to drive back and forth across the service area, incurring travel expense and slowing response time. It could be that the service people are not properly trained. It could be a breakdown of equipment.

5. For each of these causes, there is a logical remedy. If it is the service people's skill deficiency, we can train them and see if the problem goes away. If that solves the problem, what is the value in saving a customer? The marketing or sales departments can give us a figure, and we now have a dollar **ROI** from upgrading human capital skills. If it is a combination of better skills and better communications, perhaps we can see that it was more of one than the other and simply report that the dual action solved the problem.

Go back and briefly look at the other three problems and consequences:

1. *Late Filings and Penalties.* What could cause the finance or legal functions to be late in filings with the government? It's not likely that there is a skill problem. We're relying on highly trained professionals here. It must be some combination of slow assembly of required data, a flawed process, a lack of commitment to on-time performance, a computer software bug, or something else. So what is the remedy? When we fix the problem, the value is obvious. We save the late fees and penalties previously imposed. What is the human component's contribution?

2. *Missing Material and Late Delivery.* It is not uncommon for this to happen. Sometimes the problem rests within the purchasing or procurement function. Sometimes it is the

fault of the person requesting the item or the vendor supplying it. What can cause purchasing to delay processing a material or equipment requisition? It could be insufficient staff for the workload. It could be an inefficient process, wrong instructions to the vendor, or an error on the requisition. If we fix the problem, we know that material shortages will not cause future delays or missed opportunities. The value of getting to market on time with a new product or serving a customer can be computed. What is the human component's contribution?

3. *Late Work Order and Inconvenienced Staff.* This could be either a trivial or a serious problem. The path of analysis is similar to the purchasing case. An internal process fails to deliver on time. Is it a failing due to human skill or motivation? Is it a miscommunication? Is it workload or timing of the work order? Are the priorities straight? What is the effect? Is it only an inconvenience, like a burned-out lightbulb? Or does it affect the ability to work, like a power outage? Is it a safety issue? Does it adversely impact employee productivity? The value of the solution is directly proportional to the seriousness of the shortcoming. What is the human component's contribution?

In all these examples, time converts to cost or savings. When there is an insufficient quantity produced for the amount of resource invested, the service or product cost can be excessive. If the problem is one of errors or defects in performance, recycling of the process adds cost. Lost customers obviously cost money. Any way you cut it, if you want to have a valid and reasonable

> If you want to have a valid idea of the value of human effort, you have to convert the problem to cost increase or decrease and ask what the human component is.

idea of the value of the human effort, you have to convert the problem to cost increase or decrease and ask what the human component is. Sometimes it is very specific and clearly attributable to an investment in human capital. At other times, it is a combination of human and structural capital investments. Either way, the process value analysis method makes clear the visible, measurable values.

Summary

Organizations are collections of processes. Processes run across business units, making for a complex management problem. Because they are so pervasive and complex, we might need to view them in a different light to find better ways to manage them. Peter Keen, author of *The Process Edge*, offers us such a perspective when he talks of business processes as either assets or liabilities. Processes that contribute to enterprise goals are at least potential assets. Those that are purely compliance based are liabilities. Most approaches to process improvement overlook the nature of processes as real capital. Clearly, a process consumes resources and should be assessed from that standpoint. In short, economic value added is the best measure of process worth.

Chris Ashton offers some important insights from another angle.[13] He supports the notion of linking process to organization and valuation by pointing out that effective process measurement is driven by the principle of continuous improvement against critical success factors and performance goals. There are different dimensions or levels to measurement, from strategic to operational to task detail. Systemic deployment of goals, targets, and indicators is the key issue. Processes must be planned and managed from an integrative perspective. Finally, Ashton suggests that the integration of process measurement with business planning and management is a critical success factor in itself.

Processes offer five points for adding value.

1. *Setting Requirements*. By giving clear, complete instructions, we reduce the probability of misinterpretation leading to costly mistakes.

2. *Interference from Outside the Process*. Through partnering with the other units that impact the process, we can ensure that things arrive on time and in proper condition.

3. *The Person Performing the Process*. Training, communication, supervision, and incentives help the person perform at an appropriate level.

4. *Feedback*. Prompt, accurate information on outcomes reduces errors and shortens time to correct deviations from acceptable levels.

5. *The Consequence*. By delivering rewards or corrective actions in a fair and timely manner, we teach the performers the value of meeting or exceeding expectations.

Value is all around us. We only have to look for it. Every time we find value added, we can ask and answer these two questions:

1. Did the person add value by improving his or her performance through training or other personal inputs?

2. Did the person add value by leveraging the tools that were provided by the organization? With a little practice, the answers become evident.

Improving a process typically yields multiple values, not the least of which is learning and personal growth. This is because when we save time, we save money. When we eliminate or reduce errors, we cut costs. If we increase the output from a given input, we decrease the cost of a unit of product or service. And when we satisfy customers, we keep them and help them buy more, and they refer others to us. Fixing a process generally yields two or more of these values. The process value analysis guides us in isolating the source of a problem and leads to the logical, value-adding solution. It shows us how the internal components of the process have changed and produced an improvement in innovation, quality, or productivity. This is then translated into external market and financial values. Throughout the analysis, we can see the qualitative and quantitative effects of human capital investments.

Supply chain management provides both a fresh view of HR process management as well as an insight into where human resources fits and contributes to process optimization.

Finally, all business units should maintain a set of metrics that describe their ongoing efficiency. Periodic reports of cost, time, quantity, error, and reaction act as both an early warning signal and a signpost indicating the source of the problem. Clearly, finding the effects of human capital is not a mysterious task. It just takes dedication to the belief that people are the primary profit lever.

References

1. "Companies Can Improve Earnings Nearly 15 Percent by Improving Talent Management Function," The Hackett Group Research Alert, 2007.

2. Geary A. Rummler and Alan P. Brache, *Improving Performance: How to Manage the White Space on the Organization Chart* (San Francisco: Jossey-Bass, 1990), p. 141.

3. Thomas A. Stewart, "Yikes! Deadwood Is Creeping Back," *Fortune,* August 18, 1997, pp. 221–222.

4. Peter G. W. Keen, *The Process Edge* (Cambridge, MA: Harvard Business School Press, 1997).

5. Geary A. Rummler and Alan P. Brache, *Improving Performance* (San Francisco: Jossey-Bass, 1990), p. 47.

6. Eric Lessor, "Creating Value from Investments in Labor Scheduling," *IHRIM Journal,* May/June 2006, pp. 20–26.

7. Sunil Chopra and Peter Meindl, *Supply Chain Management: Strategy, Planning and Operations,* (Upper Saddle River, NJ: Prentice Hall, 2001), Ch. 1.

8. John Mentzer, William DeWitt, James Keebler, Soonhong Min, Nancy Nix, Carlo Smith, and Zach Zacharia, "Defining Supply Chain Management," *Journal of Business Logistics* (2001).

9. Richard P. Feynman, *"Surely You're Joking, Mr. Feynman!"* (New York: W. W. Norton, 1985), pp. 127–128.

10. Peter Pipe and Robert F. Mager, *Analyzing Performance Problems: Or You Really Oughta Wanna*, 3rd ed. (Atlanta: Center for Effective Performance, 1997).

11. James W. Cortada and John A. Woods, *The Quality Yearbook* (New York: McGraw-Hill, 1997), pp. 410–411.

12. Scott Adams, *Seven Years of Highly Defective People* (Kansas City: Andrews and McMeel Publishing, 1997), p. 37.

13. Chris Ashton, *Strategic Performance Measurement* (London: Business Intelligence, 1997), p. 136.

CHAPTER FOUR

How to Measure Human Resources' Value Added

"We can have facts without thinking but we cannot have thinking without facts."
—John Dewey

Whither HR?

In the never-ending discussion of human resources' role, position, and value, the profession is treated as though it were a monolith. In fact, like any large population, there is a wide distribution of people from the most to the least capable. The evolution of human resources will be led by a very small group and supported by a slightly larger group. In my forty years in and around human resources management, I see the profession divided into the following four groups:

1. *Innovators.* The leading group is made up of the innovators. These are the people who create new ways of managing the function. More important, they are the ones who

focus on managing human capital with the goal of improving business management and generating value for stockholders. This group is only about 10 percent of the total. Almost all improvements start with them.

2. *Early Adopters.* The second batch is those who watch the innovations and when they see which ones are going well, they step in and build on them. They don't lead but they make a major contribution in rolling out better ways to manage human resources because they make second-generation improvements. A few of the early adopters will cross the thin boundary and become innovators. These people are about 20 percent of the total population.

3. *The Pack.* By far, the largest group is what I call *the pack*. They make up about 60 percent of the total population. These people come to work every day and do their job. Without them there would be no human resources function. Most of them are career HR staffers who settle into a unit and spend their lives as recruiters, benefits administrators, compensation analysts, field unit generalists, technology specialists, or trainers. Some, usually the aspiring youngsters, grow out of the pack and become early adopters. A few make it all the way to the top and replace retiring innovators. This group constitutes about 60 percent of the profession.

4. *Problems.* The final group might be called dysfunctional or challenged. I do not mean people who have physical handicaps. I'm identifying folks who struggle with life in general. They have a problem getting up every morning, getting to work on time, and playing by the rules. Their outputs are marginal to unacceptable. Fortunately, most of them depart either voluntarily or involuntarily. They are what I call the poor in spirit and they make up about 10 percent.

Measurement systems are built by the Innovators and Early Adopters. They are staffed largely by the Pack. Measurement projects fail for one of three reasons: They focus on HR's program costs, time cycles, or quantity. This is all about internal activity, which is expense, rather than external effects, which are potentially valuable.

If I were to ask you which of HR's services make the greatest contribution to your organization's success, what would you say? The second question is, if I asked C-level executives, middle managers, or frontline supervisors, what do you think they would say?

Therein lays the issue of value added. Value is subjective, isn't it? What is value to me might have no value for you. When it comes to an organization, where do we find human resources adding value? Certainly, the most obvious place is in supporting the organization's initiatives where they are cost related, innovation focused, quality based, or service driven. So value is found in an organization's outputs, not in human resources programs.

Measurement of the return on human capital starts with an understanding of the tasks involved with managing human capital from the workforce planning stage onward. Many measurement projects fail for one of two reasons: They start in the middle of the process, or they don't take into account how all the elements of the process interact. Figure 4-1 is the human capital management star. It displays the six tasks involved in managing the most important and the most elusive entity of the organization: the human capital.

Collectively, the six management activities encompass the work conducted within a typical human resources function, with the following exceptions: Human resources information systems produce the data needed to conduct the activities and to evaluate performance. As such, that function can

Figure 4-1. Human capital management star.

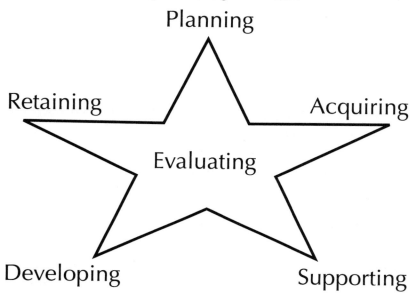

be judged internally in terms of its ability to provide specific, accurate data on a timely basis. Measures of cost, time, quantity, and quality can be established for practically any human capital management activity. Some human resources executives supervise functions such as security, medical, cafeteria, and even janitorial and groundskeeping. When that is the case, we are looking not at human capital issues but at the general administration of corporate services. This is not the focus of our study.

In the center of Figure 4-1 resides the task, or challenge, of evaluating the effectiveness of managing human capital. This is the least practiced of all six tasks. Human resources departments and line managers must hire, pay, develop, and keep human talent. They don't have to plan and evaluate, and, for the most part, they don't. There is a long list of excuses for ignoring planning and evaluation. But the central, irrefutable truth is that without the data that flow from planning and evaluation, a manager is at best an unconscious competent.

Evaluating

Evaluating the management of human capital is not a separate task. It is integral to the efficient and effective exercise of the other five tasks. There are ample opportunities to evaluate those five. The only question is, what is worth measuring? If HR is to add value, it must start with planning.

Planning

Before there can be effective action in an organization, there must be some amount of planning for human capital. Workforce and succession planning were widely practiced until the mid-1980s. Then, with the onslaught of corporate downsizing, the idea of planning for the acquisition of talent found no support. In 1990 companies were in a rush to get rid of people. Few human resources professionals looked beyond their daily problems to when the economy would pick up and large numbers of people would have to be hired. Yet, a check of workforce demographics at the time revealed diverging curves of economic growth and shrinking birthrates. An expanding economy and a declining birthrate told a chilling tale. I wrote about this and found no audience.[1] Today, things have changed. The demographics are so clear that everyone down to the dullest realizes where we are headed.

Workforce planning, or, as I like to call it, *capability planning*, is resurfacing. Workforce planning is an Industrial Age practice of filling holes in the company workforce with interchangeable bodies. Given then that we are thinking capability, we find the first opportunity to link human resources' functions into an integrated operation.

Once planning learns what will be needed in the future, it passes this on to staffing. Staffing's knowledge of the labor pool uncovers talent shortages that should be passed on to L&D for development planning. It also needs to be shared with compensation and benefits so that an attractive total rewards package can be designed.

Planning is responsible for passing on intelligence about the labor market as well as internal factors such as projected growth rate and the introduction of new technology. Attrition records and forecasts also go into the future capability mix. Planning going into the future is a much richer exercise than in the industrial era.

Acquiring

After there is a capability projection for either the short or long term, human capital must be acquired through hiring or renting from an agency or contracting with individuals directly for part-time or full-time work. Traditional hiring sought people who wanted full-time, permanent work. Late in the 1990s, the term *permanent* was dropped, as companies would no longer claim to offer permanent positions. In its place, the term *regular* was introduced to designate hires who were intended to be continuous for the foreseeable future, but with no guarantee of permanence. Eventually, the labor pool developed a subset that has come to be called the *contingent* workforce. This group represents people who are purposely hired for a short term. These are temporary and contract workers. They might fill in for a day while someone is sick, or they might work for more than a year on a project. A new body of labor law has emerged regarding the point at which a so-called temporary worker legally becomes an employee.

New employment contracts are surfacing. More home-bound people are telecommuting and working as call center service personnel. The new airlines such as JetBlue use these people almost exclusively. Job sharing, something as old as the 1980s, is becoming more prevalent as people try to balance work with family life. Older, able workers and early retirees are opting for part-time jobs. The practice of accommodating and hiring persons with disabilities is increasing. Vocational training with scholarships and internships is increasing. Immigration is helping, but periodically it becomes a political football between blinded selfish interests.

The biggest trend since 2001 has been the explosive increase of outsourcing. Despite some problems companies are learning how to work with outsource providers for many services including people. The bottom line is that there are people available, but they might not be the traditional types.

Effective recruitment is often assessed in terms of hiring costs and the time to fill jobs. Fortunately, some staffing departments are stepping up from transactional numbers to look at the effects on the business. In those cases, quality of hires is the most important metric. Surveying the hiring managers can be helpful to obtain their reaction to the process and the result. Eventually, the proof is in the performance. However, once you release the new hire into the organization, many forces act on it to make it successful or unsuccessful. Sometimes a great hire is lost through poor supervision, job change, lack of opportunity for growth, or other factors having nothing to do with the selection process or the individual.

Supporting

Once the precious human asset is in-house, it must be supported. This is done principally through pay and benefits—

the remuneration system. Nonmonetary reward and recognition is becoming more of an attraction, retention, and motivational effort than a support program. From a hierarchy-of-needs viewpoint, people seek basic safety and security first from their employers. Paying a fair wage and providing a reasonable degree of security through benefits programs are accepted as de rigueur for maintaining a skilled workforce.

> People seek basic safety and security from their employers. Paying a fair wage and providing a reasonable degree of security through benefits programs are accepted as de rigueur for maintaining a skilled workforce.

Very slowly the concept of total rewards is emerging. For all but a few companies, this is still more theory than practice. However, I believe that within the next few years compensation directors will wake up to the fact that compensation or remuneration encompasses not only traditional benefits but development opportunities as well as newer benefits affecting the associates' total work-life experience.

Measures of support effectiveness naturally focus on money spent. Wage and salary levels, pay and benefits as a percentage of revenue or expense, and average compensation for nonexempts, supervisors, managers, and executives are all captured and published by different sources. Operationally, we want to know what effect changes in compensation programs have on productivity and separation rates. This is a complex question, but there are answers for managers who are willing to commit time to studying it.

Developing

Having acquired and maintained a viable workforce, the next step is to develop it to its fullest potential. Human capital is unique in that it is the only asset that can be developed. You can send a bicycle to training classes forever and it will never learn to fly.

U.S. industry spends over $75 billion annually on employee development, according to *Training* magazine. This is a 10 percent increase in the past eight years. That includes only formal training that the human resources development group has a role in or can identify. Human capital development is accomplished through various forms of education and training and by on-the-job experience. It is fair to state that the best development comes from on-the-job experience.

If you have data on the relative costs of acquiring, supporting, and retaining a given set of skills, it is much easier to justify development investments. Useful data include cost per hire, average compensation expense, and the rate and cost of turnover.

Development takes many forms. Every action from supervisory coaching to self-paced training to formal classroom courses to job rotation to external programs is a form of development. The irony of development programs is that nine times out of ten, their payback is virtually unknown. The foremost source of training evaluation methods and data is the ROI Institute. Jack Phillips has developed a valid and reliable process for measuring the effectiveness of all types of training as well as other interventions.[2] Another method is the process value analysis model we looked at in Chapter 3. It was designed and tested in the 1990s by a consortium of thirteen companies that wanted a generic model for measuring the ROI of any type of human development intervention. The effect was described in *Training* magazine.[3] It is as effective today as it was then.

The value of training and development goes well beyond cost payback. If you spend time and money helping people learn and grow, you make a deposit in their loyalty bank. This is part of engagement. They notice and appreciate how an organization goes about helping them attain their goals. This includes fair pay, security through benefits, and, most important, assistance in personal growth and career development.

Training effects are measured best through changes in trainee job performance and the ensuing improvements in quality, innovation, productivity, or service. Asking people how they felt about the training after the fact has value only in terms of program modification and instructor ego. The company invests in development programs to achieve business goals, not just to make someone feel good.

Engaging

After the dot-com bust, the concept of engagement emerged. It grew out of the disenchantment engendered by the many failures of dot-com ventures. The absurd promises that people swallowed left them with a bad taste regarding leadership. If there is no respect for leadership, there can be no engagement. The two are tightly linked.

Retaining

The last step in the human capital management game is to retain talent. Employee-relations programs, engagement surveys, and various other means are used to learn what it takes to keep talent in the organization. Improving retention generates many values of which these are just a few:

- Reduced recruiting costs
- Reduced training costs
- Less supervisory time required

- Improved quality, innovation, productivity, and service (QIPS)

In public contact jobs, the maintenance of customer service leads to referrals by satisfied customers, thereby reducing marketing costs. The referral of job applicants by long-term employees reduces recruitment costs.

Many organizations conduct exit interviews with employees who have quit in the hope of learning the reasons behind their decision to leave. In-house exit interviews rarely yield the truth. Extremely disgruntled employees and people who have won the lottery or inherited a bundle are the only ones likely to reveal the real reason. People are smart enough not to burn their bridges. They know that it might come back to hurt them. Only when an external service conducts the interviews and maintains the ex-employees' anonymity can the organization hope to find the truth.

Top Reasons for Employees Leaving

According to Leigh Branham, who specializes in employee turnover and engagement, there are seven major reasons for employees wanting to leave their employer. They are:

1. Job or workplace not living up to expectations

2. A mismatch between job and person

3. Too little coaching and feedback

4. Too few growth and advancement opportunities

5. Feeling devalued and unrecognized

6. Stress from overwork and work-life balance

7. Loss of trust and confidence in senior leaders[4]

The essential question is, before you lose someone, what can you do to keep the person in the company and in a productive state of mind?

Clearly, the main measure of retention efforts is the separation rate. Beyond the raw percentage, the key questions are: Who is leaving? Why? At what point in his or her career? What drove the person to consider employment elsewhere? Where is he or she going? Finally, the most intriguing question is: What in a competitor's offer appealed to the former employee that he or she thought was unavailable with us? If you want to get someone's attention regarding turnover, the answers to these questions will help. But the pièce de résistance is showing what it costs to lose a valued employee. We'll go through that calculation later.

Engagement is not a function of the human resources department. It is an activity usually carried out by employee relations. However, it is so essential that it cannot be left out. Engagement is measured principally through employee surveys. There are a number of survey vendors whose products range from highly reliable to just a bunch of disconnected, invalid questions. Keep in mind that just because someone has a questionnaire, it does not mean it is a survey of anything.

We should expect that when a vendor provides feedback from a so-called engagement survey, that is only the beginning. The vendor should also be able to tell us, based on research, how to respond to the data. Engagement is measured in terms of emotional commitment to the organization, initiation of improvements, support of coworkers, and the like. It is different from job satisfaction, which might be labeled contentment. Figure 4-2 shows the comparison between satisfaction and engagement at two levels: feeling and behavior. At present, engagement is receiving a great

Figure 4-2. Satisfied vs. engaged.

FEELING

Satisfied Employee	Engaged Employee
Pleasant	Passionate
Content	Energized
Gratified	Involved
Satiated	Committed
Safe	Trusting

BEHAVIOR

Satisfied Employee	Engaged Employee
Low absenteeism	Persistence
Low turnover	Helps others
Low substance abuse	Goes beyond expectations

deal of attention and I expect that this will go on for some time.

Given all of the above, we know now the issues and some key trends that affect our human capital from an asset management standpoint. Within these activities, we can find ample data on which to act. Once we have taken action, we will also have plenty of data to measure and evaluate the return on our investment.

Human Capital Performance Evaluation

As you saw earlier, all performance can be evaluated using a matrix. I have been applying this matrix for both internal performance assessment and external market impact for nearly thirty years. We have yet to find a case in which a performance measurement and reporting system couldn't be built around the matrix. Figure 4-3 shows the components of the matrix when it is applied to four core human resources functions: acquisition, support, development, and retention. Engagement is an activity often conducted by employee relations or sometimes development and it can also be measured.

The Matrix Metrics

Cost

Cost is the one variable that always gets management's attention. It is direct. You can usually count business issues in monetary terms. People talk readily about the cost of serving a customer, the cost of rework, and the unit cost of a product. Management seems to want to manage cost first. In one sense, this is good news, because it is the easiest metric to understand, present, and describe.

As the matrix shows, we can track the cost of individual services and programs. The cost of hiring can be broken down into its major elements to understand where the opportunity for reduction lies. We have developed and tested a formula for cost analysis that severely reduces the effort needed to track the ongoing cost. Six elements account for 90 percent of the cost of hiring, plus or minus 10 percent. Obviously, in any given situation, they can change when relocations are involved. The point is that you can set out on a new staffing strategy or employ a new tactic and track your ROI by element or in total.

To learn and be able to predict the most cost-effective method for selected job groups, you have to look not only at input and throughput costs and time cycles but also at the performance of the new hires over time. In Chapter 10 I will

Figure 4-3. Human capital performance matrix.

	ACQUIRING	SUPPORTING	DEVELOPING	RETAINING
COST				
TIME				
QUANTITY				
ERROR				
REACTION				

show you a detailed example of how to do source analysis with an eye toward predictability.

Costing processes in compensation and benefits management is relatively easy. We have conducted studies of the cost of processing paychecks and found tremendous differences among companies. The range was from one dollar per check to over twelve dollars. Clearly, in the latter cases, there is a considerable unnecessary expense. Benefits administration has focused on rising premium costs and on the cost of processing claims and other program transactions. Most companies consider the provision of benefits as a necessary expense that should be conducted at as low a price as possible. This accounts in large part for the surge in outsourcing.

When we move to other activities, such as those involving employee relations, the history of cost management is somewhat spotty. Granted that most programs are budgeted, but not many are reviewed for ways to reduce cost without losing the value of the service. Employee assistance programs are often outsourced, and costs are monitored in the contract. Recognition events and ad hoc problem counseling are usually managed only from an overall cost standpoint. Some companies track the cost of counseling employees as well as the effects. This was detailed in my book *How to Measure Human Resource Management, 3rd edition.*[5] Basically, a simple grid can be constructed that shows the number of counseling sessions conducted by topic and the total amount of time spent on counseling. This tells us where the counseling time is being spent if we track it by department or level. Those data are a signpost pointing to the business units with problems. Today's computer programs make tracking a much easier task than it was twenty years ago.

Development program costs can be measured in several ways. They include cost per:

- Hour
- Delegate
- Program
- Total development budget

The more important question for the learning and development staff is, what is the ROI?

Finally, we can measure the cost of turnover (or lack of retention). There are four costs associated with turnover: termination, replacement, vacancy, and productivity loss. The costs are calculated like this:

1. *Termination.* Typically, someone must process out the departing employee. This may take a few hours to collect badges, keys, and company equipment. The person must also be taken off payroll and any security lists. There may be benefit program extensions involved. In total, the cost is usually about $1,000 to $1,500 in staff time to process the termination.

2. *Replacement.* In most cases, the departing employee will be replaced. The cost of hiring and onboarding a nonexempt employee is usually no more than a couple thousand dollars and often less. For an exempt person, the cost varies widely depending on level, possible travel, and relocation costs. The minimum cost is often at least $10,000 and sometimes much more.

3. *Vacancy.* Assuming that all jobs add value or we would not have them, we incur a loss of revenue for every day a position is vacant. The amount of loss depends on the position. A cost can be determined in the following manner: Take the total annual company revenue per employee and

divide it by the number of workdays in the year—usually around 240 to 250, depending on vacation and holiday programs. Multiply this number by the number of workdays that the job is vacant. Subtract the cost of pay and benefits for those workdays (they weren't paid out), and you have the general cost of vacancy. If you choose, you can inflate or deflate this figure for different job levels.

4. *Productivity*. The new employee is seldom as productive as the departing one, so there is a denigration of performance for some period until the new person's productivity at least matches the productivity of the former employee. You can get very detailed on this measure or just develop a rule of thumb. The detailed route involves calculating the revenue per employee per day and then deciding how many days it takes to reach the level of performance of the previous incumbent. In the case of sales jobs, the average daily or hourly sales level can be calculated. During that time, there is some productivity or value. The question is how much. Our experience over hundreds of cases is that the absolute minimum loss is the equivalent of three to six months' pay and benefits. For professional positions, it is more likely a year's worth. Other research has shown that the true cost of losing a salesperson is as high as $300,000.[6]

Time

Time has become more important as the pace of life and business has increased. With the Web, e-mail, cell phones, and computers, we can do things faster, but we are also expected to respond more quickly. To paraphrase an old cliché, time truly is a surrogate measure for money. Managers manage response time, cycle time, delivery time, and many other times. Like cost reduction, if you can do something faster than your competition, you have a differentiating competitive advantage. The race may not always be won by the swiftest, but it is seldom won by the slowest.

> Like cost reduction, if you can do something faster than your competition, you have a differentiating competitive advantage. The race may not always be won by the swiftest, but it is seldom won by the slowest.

Time has other effects as well as direct costs or savings. Delays frustrate people. They affect morale and thereby negatively impact productivity. Delays in filling jobs can put extra stress on the incumbents. Failure to deliver information on time can stop the wheels of productivity of a whole function. Taking too long to fix an employee's performance problem can cause other employees to despair and quit. The hidden effect of time lost can be devastating.

Quantity

Quantity is the third most common metric. It is easiest and most obvious, because you can physically count the items under consideration. Whether we want to know how many applicants were hired, customers or employees served, paychecks or legal claims processed, or people trained, there are many ways to tally it up. To me, one of the more ironic facts is that although many HR software packages automatically count the number of items processed, human resources professionals almost never use that capability to understand even this simple performance indicator. Consequently, when they go to management to ask for more resources, they can't tell how much they are doing, much less what it costs or the average cycle time of the current process. By itself, knowing the quantity processed is not very useful. But it is the starting point for asking this important question: What difference did it make that we produced this much with a given amount of resource input? By matching quantity with effects, we can obtain the first indication of an efficient staff loading.

Error

Error and defect rates became popular with the advent of the quality craze of the early 1980s. Thanks to W. Edwards Deming and Joseph Juran, U.S. businesses learned how to measure quality.[7] An error or defect is simply something that did not meet expectations or requirements. With the publicity around quality programs, consumers began to demand better product and service quality. Eventually, employees picked up the chant inside their companies. Employees expect the company to make fewer errors as it relates to their records, benefits claims, training requirements, and communications needs. Acceptable error rates are a very individual issue. Some people would like perfection. For them, life must be an unending series of frustrations. What constitutes an error or defect is sometimes a subjective issue. One person may feel that something is "good enough," whereas another individual flies into a tantrum over the same level of treatment. Having spent many days and nights as the recipient of earnest attempts by airline, hotel, and restaurant personnel to please, my observation is that a good spanking early in life might have given the adult customer brats a more tolerant viewpoint. Unfortunately, the measurement of quality has seldom become an HR program performance indicator. Usually HR waits until someone complains.

Reaction

Human reaction refers to the physical, psychological, or emotional response of individuals to events around them. Here, we drop into the purely subjective realm. Some people are more demanding, have higher expectations, or want more of something. These folks tend to react more negatively than the average bear. Customers and employees have values and attitudes that determine their reactions to services and products. These are measurable through a wide variety of tools, from galvanic skin responses and blood pressure readings to psychological tests, survey questionnaires, interviews, and focus groups. Scores can be produced and sorted by any demographic set we need. The most important issue is response. If we don't want to deal with what people tell us, then we shouldn't ask them. The worst and most common mistake is for companies to poll employees about something and then fail to acknowledge the responses or act on them.

In summary, the five indices of change give us ample opportunity to monitor, measure, and report change. These apply to personal and organizational issues within any functional unit. They can be used for establishing internal measurement and reporting systems and for benchmarking outside entities. The first, last, and only important question is whether the change is for the better. That is, did it add value? To answer that question, we need a context. The primary context is the immediate effect on internal service, quality, or productivity levels. The secondary and more critical context is the effect those internal improvements had on key external success factors such as customer retention. The final context is the economic value added to the enterprise. This is the most important because this is our raison d'être in organizations.

Figure 4-4 shows examples of human capital management measures using the matrix. These are a small sample of the many ways that staffing, compensation, benefits, development, and retention can be viewed from an objective perspective.

Figure 4-4. Human capital performance matrix examples.

	ACQUIRING	SUPPORTING	DEVELOPING	RETAINING
COST	Cost per Hire	Cost per Paycheck Cost per EAP Case*	Cost per Trainee	Cost of Turnover
TIME	Time to Fill Jobs	Time to Respond Time to Fulfill Request	Cost per Trainee Hour	Turnover by Length of Service
QUANTITY	Number Hired	Number of Claims Processed	Number Trained	Voluntary Turnover Rate
ERROR	New Hire Rating	Process Error Rate	Skills Attained	Readiness Level
REACTION	Manager Satisfaction	Employee Satisfaction	Trainee Responses	Turnover Reasons

*EAP = employee assistance program

Predictability

As I promised earlier, to know the effectiveness of the hiring process we need to look at the results of the process. Indices could include performance, salary progression, potential rating, responsiveness, and tenure. Basically, the criteria in performance management serve as valid indices of hire. However, we must keep in mind that job conditions can change and drive a good hire out of the organization. From here we can review our sources and methods to determine which are most effective. This will be detailed as part of the total predictive management process in Chapter 10.

Change Measurement

In organizations, measurement is usually about the degree or amount of change. Managers don't measure absolute points so much as they manage change. They monitor the amount of change that takes place from one period to another. That being so, the most important thing about measurement is to be consistent. Pick a methodology, define your terms tightly, and do it over and over using the same process. Seldom in management do we have to prove anything with statistics. Management simply wants to know:

- How are we doing?

- How does this compare with someone else or with a previous period?

- What can we do to get better?

Having said that, several functions have been introducing business intelligence tools into their work. It won't be long before top management is going to expect statistical analysis from human resources. That is why we developed the model and operating system described in Chapter 10. As business intelligence software becomes more common, eventually someone will turn to human resources and ask why can't you do this? The answer is that you can. So I suggest you start looking at business intelligence (BI) software packages that are applicable to HR issues. Statistical Package for the Social Sciences (SPSS) programs have been in use in some human resources departments for several years. They are simple, reliable programs that help you identify problem sources and suggest solutions.

The only way that HR can aspire to business partnership or to deal with strategic issues is through statistical capability.

Human Capital Scorecard

The arrival of the balanced scorecard model opened a new path to organizing and monitoring human capital information. We can take the concept behind the balanced scorecard and create a human capital version. The human capital scorecard consists of four levels, each devoted to one of the basic human capital management activities: acquiring, supporting, developing, and retaining. Planning is not part of the scorecard, since at its inception it was not practical to monitor the effects of planning on a regular basis. By its nature, planning deals with the future. The human capital scorecard is focused on recent and current events. There are no generally accepted accounting principles that must be adhered to at this point. In fact, the scorecard concept

> We can take the concept behind the balanced scorecard and create a human capital version. The human capital scorecard consists of four levels: acquiring, maintaining, developing, and retaining.

was developed to deal with factors that are ignored in standard financial statements. It was realized that standard accounting was not sufficient for presenting data that were necessary to manage large organizations in times of great change, intense competition, and rapid growth. Nevertheless, this is changing as leading indicators and intangibles are becoming more susceptible to measurement. In the metrics chapter you will see that emerging.

Figure 4-5 is an example of the types of metrics that can be used in the scorecard. Ideally, the choices made should provide a basic yet thorough look at the investment and utilization levels of human capital. Each of the quadrants should contain cost, time, quantity, and quality measures to the extent practical and possible. Across the bottom, a base can be added to cover reaction factors. The reactions of managers and employees to human resources programs are important. A measure of manager satisfaction is useful for the human resources department. An employee engagement measure can be added to the base if it is carefully crafted.

Acquisition

The first activity after planning is to acquire human capital for the organization. This can be done with a combination of three tactics: hiring, renting, and developing. Our focus in the acquisition quadrant is on the results of hiring or renting. The term *renting* is a catchall for contingent workers. It includes paying an agency or a person directly for a period of work without the person being on the company payroll. This form of human capital is, in effect, being rented or leased and then let go after the requirement is satisfied. The rental period can be anything from a few hours to fill in for someone who was delayed one morning to as long as a year or more to complete a project. The legal and

Figure 4-5. Sample human capital management scorecard.

PLANNING	
Delivered on Time	Meets Specifications

ACQUISITION	SUPPORT

Cost per hire
Time to fill jobs
Number of new hires
Number of
  replacements
Quality of new hires
	Total labor cost as percent
	  of operating expense
	Average pay per employee
	Benefits cost as percent
	  of payroll
	Average performance score
	  versus revenue per FTE

RETENTION	DEVELOPMENT

Total separation rate
Percent of voluntary
  separations: exempt
  and nonexempt
Exempt separations by
  service length
Cost of turnover
Reasons for quits
	Training cost as a percent
	  of payroll
	Total training hours
	  provided
	Training hours by function
	Training hours by job group
	Training ROI

Engagement Scores	Attitude Scores

ethical question of when a *rental* really becomes a *buy* is not at issue here.

Support

This function covers a broad base of activities focused primarily on paying salaries and providing benefits. Every asset needs to be maintained in good condition in order for it to retain its value and, in the case of a human being, continue to contribute value to the goals of the organization. Pay and benefits are monitored through a combination of cost ratios. We want to monitor the effects of managing salaries and wages. Therefore, we can look at pay in terms of average pay of employees, distribution across levels, cost as a percentage of operating expense, or other macro measures. The decision of what to put in the maintenance quadrant is left to the user.

Development

Tracking and monitoring the development of human assets or human capital is the most difficult of the four quadrants. It is a complex problem. First, what is training or development? We have already noted that it can be anything from daily coaching to external formal programs. Where do we start and stop? Second, from a practical standpoint how do we capture the costs? So much of development is invisible and even unrecognized that it is truly impossible to know the total cost. Everyone realizes that some portion of so-called external training expenses is a surrogate for other expenditures. The easiest task is to track inputs such as costs and number trained. The more difficult challenge is to measure effectiveness. Having said all that, we must create a set of measures that give us some general sense of resources being committed in the name of development. It is a practical matter in which something is better than nothing.

Retention

Keeping talent will always be an important activity. Even in the severest times, when a company plunges into a negative earnings position, it still must retain a critical talent core.

In a merger or acquisition, human capital is a key issue. By far the vast majority of mergers and acquisitions pay scant attention to the talent of the organization. Typically, only in the highest technical buys does the acquirer focus on key talent in the acquired company. I have lived through two acquisitions; in one, the buyer poured half a billion dollars into the game before writing it off as a failure. The other was where the buyer simply didn't know what to do with the acquisition. In the first case, it was largely a matter of letting the wrong people go. In the second, it was bringing in people who were ill suited to the task. Experience has proved time and again that when people and people-related issues such as culture are ignored, the potential for failure is well above 50 percent. It follows that separation rates and costs are important and must be part of any human capital scorecard system.

At this point, employee-relations staff members may be wondering where their work fits. The effects of their labor are found most often in productivity, engagement, retention, and problem resolution. Through employee assistance and social and recreational programs, they contribute to keeping employees. Beyond that, they also make contributions to all other quadrants, since they are constantly moving about the organization working with employees on personal and interpersonal issues. As such, when they are functioning as they should, they are an intelligence unit that contributes to the plans and designs of many human resources programs. Ultimately, their work affects organizational effectiveness.

Human Capital Accounting

In 1965, Roger Hermanson proposed a method for determining the value of a human being to an organization. This, along with work at the Institute for Social Research at the University of Michigan, became the foundation for what was then called human resources accounting (HRA). The first attempt by a public company to publish pro forma financial statements that included human assets was the R. G. Barry Corporation, a small manufacturing company in Columbus, Ohio. Interest grew slowly through the early 1970s, and in 1975, Eric Flamholtz published the seminal text on the topic.[8] As more people became involved, articles appeared in various personnel and accounting journals. However, it gradually became apparent that this was a complex problem requiring expensive long-term research, without any assurance that the problem could be solved. Over the next decade, interest waned and waxed until the topic finally withdrew in favor of more pressing business issues.

The principal failure was an inability to agree on how to put a monetary value on people. Several models were proposed but never widely adopted. Accountants are never comfortable with something they cannot "buy" or "sell" at a given price. To put a value on a person within a business organization, one has to be able to calculate the variability of a person from four current perspectives and potentialities:

1. Productivity
2. Promotability
3. Transferability
4. Retainability

The human resources value depends on the value of each of the four factors during a fiscal year. The likelihood of an individual being in any of those positions—or service states, as they are called—is subject to the law of probability. Flamholtz argued that by using a *stochastic rewards valuation* model, one could determine the following:

- The mutually exclusive states a person might occupy
- The value of each state to the organization
- A person's expected tenure in the organization
- The probability that a person will occupy each state at specific future times
- The expected discounted future cash flows that represent their present value

As intriguing as this problem is, so far there has been no support from business or professional groups to take it on. Having said that, I have been approached a few times lately by people interested in valuing a person or a job. To my mind, the problem has been attacked from the wrong angle.

The first issue is that we can't know the value of a person based on efforts to be made in the very uncertain future. This is potentiality. Right there, it turns an interesting model into an impractical solution. Business is too variable. As a person who started his own company and ran it for almost two decades, I can testify that the true value of any tangible asset is unknown until someone gives you money for it. You can forget the so-called value that is carried on the books. Everyone knows that depreciation and amortization are artifacts of the deliberations of the Financial Accounting Standards Board, and human beings, not God, sit on the FASB. A more practical angle is to look at what really happened, as accounting does, and then calculate the value added by human effort after the fact.

I can tell you with a reasonable degree of accuracy what it costs to hire, train, and lose an employee. I can also calculate the average value per employee based on sales and net income before tax. You saw it in the human capital value added and human capital ROI formulas in Chapter 2. Admittedly, these are gross numbers, but they are factual as

opposed to probable. Business executives are held account-
able for results. Only the most enlightened and secure are
going to fund complex research.

At the time of the first edition of this book, there was a
groundswell of calls for the reform of standard accounting,
such as including nonfinancial data and reporting in so-
called real time. There are demands for the Securities and
Exchange Commission to open its mind to a parallel system
that will evolve over the next decade into a system that reflects the realities of 2000 and beyond. Unfortunately, nothing has come from this proposal, despite the efforts of
Baruch Lev and others, and the passion for reform has
cooled—at least for now.

A Human Capital P&L

Granted, the accounting establishment has not yet accepted
human capital accounting because dramatic changes and
new methods seldom come from within the establishment.
Amazon, Southwest Airlines, and Apple Computer all came
from an outsider. Innovation almost always comes from
outside the established institutions. This is because institutions concentrate most of their energy on fighting a rearguard action to protect their *assets*. I dare to suggest that
there is another way to think about this issue. In Chapter 2,
Figure 2-3 contains the metrics that could be used to make
up a human capital profit-and-loss statement.

Benchmarking, Best Practices, and Other Fairy Tales

When the topic of benchmarking or best practices comes
up, the question focuses on what difference these practices

made in an organization. Did they help reduce operating expense and thereby product cost? Did they shorten the cycle time of an important process? Were people able to do more with less through this method? Is a customer or an employee more satisfied than before? Is retention up? The vast majority of so-called best practices are seldom subjected to stringent quantitative analysis. In the case of benchmarking, we usually don't know very much about the culture, leadership, initiatives, or financial viability of the companies reporting. Those issues drive everything that happens. A close study shows that most reports evade the issue or dance around it with simplistic, partial, and inconsistent measures. An incident that is not repeatable is not a generic best practice and should not be called that. One should never take a best-practice report at face value. It should be checked with the author for logic and demonstrable data. Adoption of an unverified practice can be embarrassing or worse.

> The vast majority of so-called best practices are seldom subjected to stringent quantitative analysis.

A central issue in any data-sharing project is the guarantee that data definitions, data quality, and data terminology are reliable and valid. When we introduced benchmarking in 1985, the marketplace was much more stable than it is in the twenty-first century. Today, comparability is extremely limited and therefore benchmarking is passé in my view. The only exception is when you have thorough knowledge of the internal issues above.

Truly Effective Practices

There are several practices that the most effective companies exhibit in the management of their human capital.

Planning

Workforce planning has begun a slow comeback since the dot-com bust. The new generation of workforce analysis must focus on capability development rather than filling holes. This approach puts less energy into manning tables and more into developing a cadre of personnel with certain skills. The more common model for the study of planning practices has been that one or more large firms sponsor and bear the expense of inviting others of similar size to join a short-term project usually run by a third party such as The Conference Board or the American Management Association.

Staffing

Some people believe that costing staffing is not useful, since the most important issue is the quality of talent attracted. It is true that quality is the prime issue. However, our experience shows that those who manage cost also obtain better quality. The reason is that they are truly managing the process, not just responding to job orders. By monitoring cost sources, they also monitor quality simultaneously. Traditionally, the basic tool has been source analysis as described earlier. More recently we've introduced process optimization. This is the practice wherein sources and selection methods are matched in the search for the most effective new hire performance factors. Traditional and experimental sourcing is analyzed. The question is: What is the most cost-effective source for a given job group? At the end of the day, the staffing manager knows which source produces the most cost-effective applicant flow. Then he or she must look forward and ask if the process is adequate for the future.

Compensation

Pay programs can be set up in response to the market, or they can be configured as a strategic tool. In general, the distribution of pay between top and bottom performers is barely differentiated. Everyone knows it, and the salary increase scales prove it. I believe that viewing pay as an investment to motivate performance needs a good deal of work.

In 2007, I partnered with SuccessFactors in a study of pay for performance. To make a long study short, we found that where companies tied personal objectives to organizational goals, quantified them, and paid based on the achievement of the goals, there were orders of magnitude different in revenue growth, margins, and return on assets.

Rather than viewing pay as an ongoing process, we recommend that the pay of all employees above entry level be more flexible both upward and downward. Management philosophy, ability to pay, competitor's actions, organizational structure, and other factors come into play in establishing compensation programs. It is not a mechanistic game with rigid rules.

Benefits

Employee benefits are the background. No one thinks of them except when they need them. Traditional benefits such as health care and 401(k) programs should be outsourced. There is no value to be added by keeping the administration of them in-house. As long as someone manages the vendor and responds to employee problems promptly, the benefits program will yield what it was meant to do, which is security at a reasonable price.

Finally, *total rewards* is a concept that should be introduced as the underlying base for pay, benefits, and other rewards that organizations hand out in return for employee labor.

Development

Paradoxically, employee development is one of the most important issues for the foreseeable future and one of the worst managed. In fact, it would be an overstatement to claim that it was badly managed. Our experience is that it is unmanaged. No one knows how much money and time are spent on even formal training programs. And very few have any idea of their ROI. ROI in training can be calculated with a sufficient degree of accuracy as demonstrated by the work of the ROI Institute as well as my own. Despite this fact, surveys have consistently shown that less than 5 percent of the United States' $75 billion training effort is evaluated. An officer of a major financial institution told me last year that the company spent about $250 million on training and did not measure its effects. When effectiveness is unknown, how can anyone claim that training is managed?

Retention

As the impact of aging boomers and insufficient numbers of young people rises, managers have become sensitive to the need to retain talent. There are points in a person's career when he or she is most susceptible to the siren call of the outside opportunity. About two years in, at four to five years, and again at seven to eight years of employment, people see themselves as prized commodities. These are the points when we should be especially attentive to their career needs. Almost all turnover research shows that the principal reason people leave a company voluntarily is the behavior of their supervisors. The secondary reason is perceived lack of growth opportunities. Accordingly, effective retention programs focus on supervisory training and career management. Finally, when we lose a person, a systematic, thorough exit interview conducted by a firm specializing in that can be extremely illuminating.

Summary

Human resources and human capital ROI begin with a thorough scan of the capacity of the organization to deal with the outside world. This scan is followed by a review of internal factors that may enhance or inhibit the ability of the organization to respond effectively. The data obtained in the scan is the basis for capability planning. Once we know what we need, we review our ability to handle hiring, paying, developing, engaging, and retaining talent. Significant changes in costs, time cycles, volumes, error rates, and human reactions flow through the organization. In most cases, these changes are absorbed downstream within the organization's processes. Because they are submerged, they are unseen. Accordingly, the unenlightened tend to ignore or discount emerging signals.

However, when the cost of hiring decreases, the volume of human resources' output over input increases, or employees acquire practical new skills, which is an added value. Factors such as the quality of new hires and the satisfaction of hiring supervisors can be tracked. These are first-level returns on investment in human resources' programs. If you need a detailed description of the pros and cons of human resources department measurement, I suggest my book *How to Measure Human Resource Management, 3rd Edition.* It contains more than fifty formulas and many graphic examples taken from my experience managing human resources in three companies and consulting with dozens of others. By developing a human resources department measurement system and monitoring changes monthly or quarterly, the ROI of initial human capital management becomes clear. These become part of the mix when customer service, product quality, or unit costs are measured later. It is only through the actions of these human capital assets—people—that anything happens downstream.

The performance matrix is the basic assessment model that can be laid on any business operation. It is as applicable to the administrative units of human resources, accounting, and information services as it is to manufacturing. When evaluation problems are encountered, it is usually because the objective of the process is unclear. Quite often, people or units are given objectives that are specific in terms of delivery date but nonspecific in relation to cost or quality. The best measures are those that incorporate as many of the five indices of change as possible. Failure to look at all of them leaves the producers vulnerable to criticism that they didn't get the most important factor right.

The lesson is obvious: Know exactly what the outcome should look like, and be able to specify it in terms of the desired amount of change in service, quality, or productivity.

Top executives fool themselves into thinking that they have an effective human capital management program when, in actuality, they have no idea what they have or what one looks like. Their criteria for effectiveness seem to be: Come quickly when I call, and keep me out of trouble.

Consider for a moment that total labor costs typically consume anywhere from 20 percent to 70 percent of sales revenue (depending on the industry)[9] and that the productivity of human capital is the only profit lever. Doesn't it make you wonder when top management will catch on to the lost opportunity cost and the profit potential that exists? The objective of this book is to give managers a model that they can apply to draw a better ROI from their expensive and valuable human capital.

References

1. Jac Fitz-enz, "Getting and Keeping Good Employees," *Personnel Journal,* August 1990, pp. 25–28.

2. Jack Phillips, *Return on Investment* (Houston: Gulf Publishing, 1997).

3. Jac Fitz-enz, "Yes, You Can Weigh Training's Value," *Training,* July 1994.

4. Leigh Branham, *The 7 Hidden Reasons Employees Leave* (New York: AMACOM, 2005), p. 29.

5. Jac Fitz-enz, *How to Measure Human Resource Management,* 3rd ed. (New York: McGraw-Hill, 1994).

6. Frederick F. Reichheld, *The Loyalty Effect* (Boston: Harvard Business Schools Press, 1996), pp. 102–103.

7. W. Edwards Deming, *Out of the Crisis* (Cambridge, MA: MIT, 1986); Joseph M. Juran, *Juran on Quality by Design* (New York: Free Press, 1992).

8. Eric Flamholtz, *Human Resource Accounting,* 2nd ed. (San Francisco: Jossey-Bass, 1985).

9. This range comes from the many studies by many organizations about labor costs. Typically, in capital intensive businesses, i.e., factories or refineries, it is low and in people intensive services, i.e., software, professional services, it is high.

CHAPTER FIVE

End-to-End Human Capital Value Reports

"The greatest obstacle to discovery is not ignorance—
it is the illusion of knowledge."

—DANIEL J. BOORSTIN

Up to this point, you have seen how to measure the value of human capital at three levels, from the enterprise or corporate level targets down through the functional business unit processes to the activities of the human resources department. You've seen how management of human capital supports functional processes in pursuit of enterprise goal fulfillment. And you've had a taste of HCMetrics, the next generation of human capital measurement, in the first four chapters. Now it is necessary to bundle all the components together in one cohesive system so that you can see the connections and interdependencies. As you might presume, this is a complex package that requires some degree of concentration.

Although there is a general pathway from human capital

investment to enterprise value, there are many routes that are somewhat specific to each organizational function. As with any asset—whether material, equipment, facilities, or energy—there are a multitude of links and drivers that vary with each case. Figure 5-1 shows the basic pathways. Within each cell there are measurable actions and results. Starting at the bottom of the diagram, the result of an action in hiring, paying, training, or keeping talent affects the activities and outcomes of the functional units for which the provider is performing the human capital management service. Human resources may not directly deliver the service; for example, it may come from an outsource vendor. Nevertheless, HR often contracts for and/or manages the service. Either way the human capital service uploads from the HR level to the functional level.

In turn, since organizations are collections of processes, the work within one functional unit affects the ability of related functions to fulfill their commitments. Whereas objectives run vertically through an organization, processes run horizontally and diagonally. The collective outcome of all functions largely determines the level of enterprise performance. So a positive or negative action in one function or process can ripple throughout the organization. And it all starts with and is dependent on the behavior and skills of people. Such is the power of human capital.

I realize that an organization, be it a commercial business or a not-for-profit institution, is not a closed system. In a commercial situation, management can screw up and still beat its competition if the competitors screw up even worse. It can also go the other way. That is, superb performance does not always guarantee goal achievement, because the actions of other stakeholders—most of all the customers—can change. If the economy takes a sudden downturn, even the best-run company may not be profitable in the short term because customers stop buying. All that notwithstanding, the pathways outlined in Figure 5-1 essentially describe the natural model.

Note that there are arrows running horizontally within the functional and human capital processes. These are an illustration of the natural interaction among groups and activities. I called it *collaboration* in my study of the practices of exceptional companies.[1] The top performers achieve their preeminence through internal partnering in a common cause. Collaboration is one of the many platitudes that the mediocre espouse but don't practice. For the best of the best, it is not a platitude. Richard Kovacevich, the CEO of Wells Fargo Bank, called it *integration* and was very explicit about how important it is. He explained:

> The first thing we had to do was not to have silos. We had to design our culture and systems to focus on the customer, not on the product line. We reward the behavior we want, which is getting all of our customers' business.[2]

It worked for Wells Fargo because that bank sells two to three times as many products to its customers as do other major banks.

One Sure Path to Profitability

We'll look at three examples of enterprise goals and how human capital management links with and supports the functional processes that achieve those goals. Most improvement programs focus on cost reduction. That is too simple a challenge. Many turnaround specialists have showed how fast one can cut out waste. I would not begin to make a case for that approach. Massive employee layoffs and asset sell-offs don't take a lot of intelligence. If you cut

Figure 5-1. Pathways.

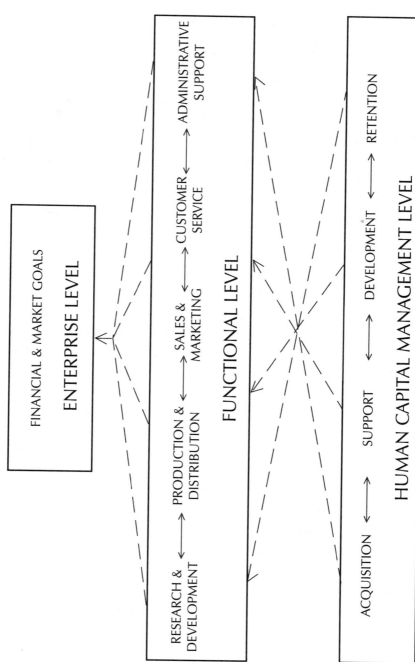

out extra employees and sell off assets, your income statement and balance sheet are bound to look better—for a while. Any first-year MBA student learns that. In the end, that approach guts the business.

Overall, U.S. businesses did a credible job of reducing their bloat and improving their efficiency during the 1990s. Downsizing, total quality management, and reengineering all contributed to general cost reduction and competitiveness. Unfortunately, less attention was paid to the revenue-generating side. Eventually, managers looked around at the aftermath of reductive efforts and asked what they could do next. About that time came dot-com with its ridiculous assumptions and outlandish projections. After the bust of 2001, we have come back to reality. Most managers realize that the surest pathway to sustainable profits is through people—the only asset that can add value.

We accept that the investment bankers can arrange mergers and acquisitions that create synergies, some of the time. Their record is rather spotty, in that more than half of all acquisitions fail to achieve their initial financial projections. Nevertheless, after the new management team is in place and the palace coups have run their course, someone has to do the damned work and keep the beloved customers happy. Business is, in the final analysis, a people game. The path to long-term success is through the effective management of internal human capital, which in turn finds, services, and retains customers.

Beyond cost reduction, there are many pathways we can trace from the enterprise goals downward through organizational functions to human resources. When the human resources department is truly supporting the enterprise instead of just filing and smiling, it becomes the host of human capital. It leads management in acquiring, supporting, developing, engaging, and retaining the precious commodity without which nothing happens. I deliberately use the word *lead* to emphasize that human capital management is not the sole responsibility of the human resources department. It is everyone's job from top to bottom in the organization. Human capital investment is optimized only when all parties from the board of directors to first-line supervisors and the employees themselves play a role.

> When the human resources department is truly supporting the enterprise instead of just filing and smiling, it becomes the host of human capital.

Staff departments such as information services, finance, or human resources presumably develop systems, design processes, and offer services aimed at supporting corporate goals. It would be absurd and wasteful for them to do otherwise. However, in all my years in and around staff groups, I have often found it difficult to locate the connections. Most often, it is a case of a general enterprise goal and a general staff response devoid of direct, verifiable, point-to-point links. This is okay if you want average returns on your staff investments. That is what probability theory predicts— general response and average results. In our case, we are building direct, visible links all the way up and down the pathway from the enterprise level to the human resources– led response and back up again. With direct links, it is possible to assess results in explicit terms and thereby make improvements that yield above-average results.

Three Examples

Let's look at three examples of specific pathways between enterprise goals and human capital management. The cases I've chosen are important issues for any commercial endeavor. They are also points on which government and education should focus. Moving more quickly, serving the constituents, and operating in a more flexible and humane way internally would be a great improvement for many public institutions. The three key issues are:

1. Time to market

2. Customer service

3. Great place to work

Each has a different focus: time, service, or employee retention. They represent the basics that give us a number of different angles from which to understand the multitudes of connections along the pathway. Figures 5-2, 5-3, and 5-4 display the pathways of the three cases that follow. They reveal only a small number of the many connections between human capital management outputs and various functional units. They show a mix of activities and possible measurable outcomes. Space (and mental exhaustion) precludes showing all the possibilities of all three cases. It would be overkill, and soon you reach the point of diminishing returns. By applying your experience with each of the line and staff functions listed, you will be able to think of many more relationships. But a few excellent connections are better than numerous mediocre connections. Of course, the outputs from the functional units relate to and support the specific enterprise imperative.

Figure 5-2. Sample human capital-to-enterprise pathway for time to market.

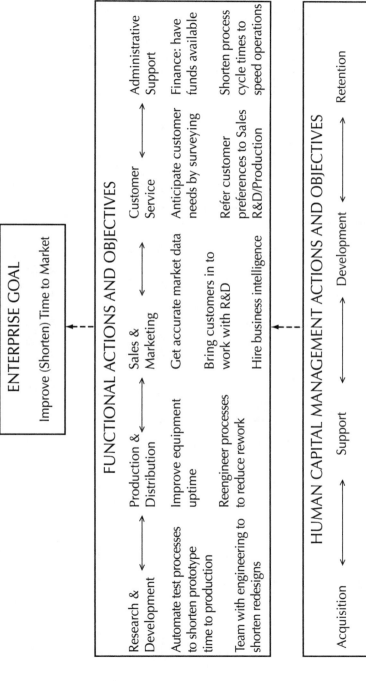

Figure 5-3. Sample human capital-to-enterprise pathway for world-class customer service.

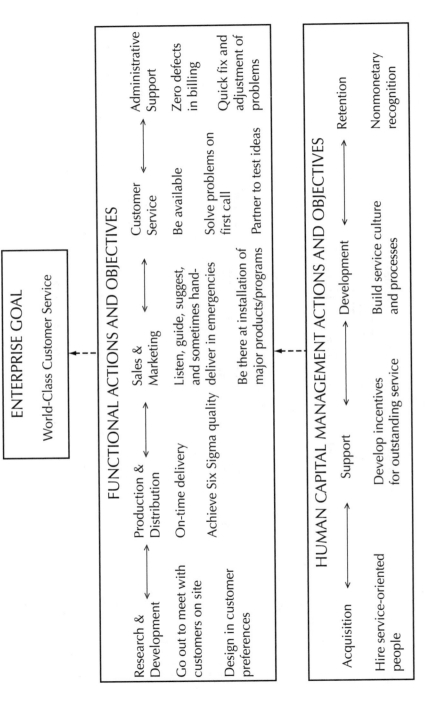

Figure 5-4. Sample human capital-to-enterprise pathway for employer of choice.

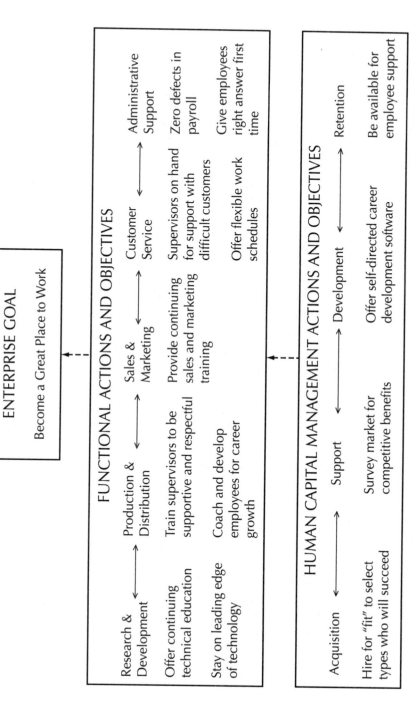

Cases

Case 1: Enterprise Goal: Improve (Shorten) Time to Market

Value: Being in the market ahead of the competition enables us to stake out a position and gain market share before competitors preempt the space.

Imperative: Each function—line and staff—must focus on the primary issue of timeliness within its arena without negatively affecting cost, quality, or service.

Human capital management applies the time criterion to acquisition, maintenance, development, and retention of human assets (employees).

- *Acquisition.* Reduce the number of days required to obtain a quality hire for the requesting department. Ensure that jobs are filled promptly and production is not adversely affected.
  Measure: Average number of days for time to start. You can assume that quality is constant or periodically test for it.

- *Support.* Improve process efficiency and accuracy in compensation, benefits, and payroll so that it does not interfere with operating imperatives. Processing salary increases and benefits claims promptly supports employee morale and reduces time wasted by employees tracing their missing pay or unpaid claims.
  Measure: Average time to complete selected key processes, error rates, and employee satisfaction with processing and results.

- *Development.* Shorten time to respond with appropriate training, development, mentoring, or consultative services. Upgrade skills, enabling employees to produce at the required level.
  Measure: Time to deliver program. Later, measure the effect of the acquired skill on business unit performance to validate the program's value.

- *Retention.* Engage employees through leadership with the enterprise time imperative by communication and counseling programs (quickly), thereby bonding them to it. *Measure:* Time to implement the programs. Later, assess the impact on employee commitment to timeliness.

Summary

If human capital services are provided as outlined above, quantitative connections can be made between some of the human capital management results and the outcomes of the affected functional departments. One way to do this is to apply the process value analysis model described in Chapter 3. As we move from one imperative to another (e.g., time to service), we need to ask which is more important. Michael Treacy and Fred Wiersema argue that companies have to have one primary imperative: product leadership, customer intimacy, or operational excellence.[3] Their position is that no one can be number one in all three areas. Companies must choose their primary competitive edge and do the best they can in the other two. Not everyone agrees. Many argue that a company can eagerly pursue two or three simultaneously. Yet the evidence is relatively consistent that most great companies are great because of focusing on only one of the three imperatives. In its heyday, IBM dominated the market with customer relations, even though competitors offered equal or better technology. Hewlett-Packard was always the engineer's company. Its products were top of the line. Wal-Mart's initial rise came out of operating excellence, specifically inventory management.

More recently, Amazon succeeds through operational performance, by offering quick, high-quality service. Nokia took market share from Motorola by product innovation. Ritz-Carlton's customer service is unparalleled. This is an argument with no winner, although it seems in the end that one imperative will eventually emerge as the prime driver.

Case 2: Enterprise Goal: Increase Customer Satisfaction

This is a case where validated new hire assessment services have made a great contribution in the past decade.

Value: Customer satisfaction can be assessed through surveys and interviews. More important, it can be measured through customer retention, account penetration, and account profitability indices.

Imperative: Management realizes that the customer truly is king. Competition—domestic and international—has forced all firms to focus employees on customer service. Human capital management applies the service criterion to human resources department services.

- *Acquisition.* Develop a hiring profile through assessment technology to identify applicants who have a service mentality and value system. *Measure:* Service-oriented interviews and questionnaires as well as the assessment model can be scaled to yield scores that tell how closely we are hiring to the desired profile.

- *Support.* Design incentive programs for excellent customer service. For example, in units that have a direct impact on customer satisfaction and retention, monetary incentives can be offered. *Measure:* Satisfaction and retention-level improvements can be weighed against the amount of incentives paid.

- *Development.* Determine the elements inherent in a service-oriented culture. Communicate that to other human resources units and to managers and supervisors by incorporating it into all training programs, no matter the topic. *Measure:* In time, employee surveys will tell how far the culture has moved in the desired direction. This is a slow-moving, long-term change.

- *Retention.* Design nonmonetary recognition programs for excellent customer service. Also, support development's culture program through engagement leadership, employee counseling, and supervisor coaching. *Measure:* Track the number of individuals who receive recognition awards and the effects of the improved customer service.

Summary

Human capital management is critical to sustained customer service excellence. Incentives typically yield short-term effects. It is necessary to inculcate service into the workforce as everyone's primary responsibility. This is directed by customer service management and supported by human resources programs. Finding a way to engage people around customer service is not difficult once you have hired people with a service orientation.

The system starts with the service of internal customers. Since processes flow horizontally and diagonally through organizations, the output of one department is the input of another. In effect, every department has internal customers. Measures of customer satisfaction can be taken across the company as well as externally. One way of promoting good internal service is to put cross-functional teams together. These teams not only get work done but also teach everyone on the team, through personal experience, the value of collaboration. Organizations that practice good internal customer service become highly efficient and set themselves on the road to becoming great places to work. This is one of many human capital management truisms that most people know intuitively but forget to practice daily. It's also another example of the interaction among organizational activities and functions.

Case 3: Enterprise Goal: Be a Great Place to Work (GPTW)

Value: The ability to attract and retain top talent is reflected in organizational effectiveness and eventually in financial performance.

Imperative: The talent shortage in the United States is not going away. Those who wish to be in the top echelons of their industry must focus on making their workplace as attractive as possible.

Human capital management focuses on the issues that drive people to apply to, join, and stay with an organization. This is a more complex problem than the previous cases. Since a great place to work is a multifaceted, idiosyncratic issue for each organization, no single, direct service or program will achieve the goal. In essence, you are looking at culture change. GPTW is more than pay, special benefits, and recreational programs. It demands actions on the part of all employees from the CEO down to entry level.

- *Acquisition.* Conduct research to learn what makes an employer attractive to the type of talent your organization seeks. The Great Place to Work Institute has developed the essential qualities that differentiate such organizations. Most employees share common basic interests, but once you move beyond those, there are diverse needs. A fast-paced versus a stable environment, a technological versus a marketing orientation, a cooperative versus a competitive atmosphere, company size and location, degree of flexibility, and many other variables attract different types of people. Profiles can be drawn and a staffing strategy launched to draw your type. An efficient and empathetic hiring process tops off the program. *Measure:* Degree to which you are attracting the people who score high on your profile.

- *Support.* Survey people regarding their benefit needs. Day care, work-hour flexibility, telecommuting, work-family balance, recreation, time versus money, and healthcare plans all have their customers. Selecting a flexible set of benefits that people can choose from to fulfill their needs helps the recruiting and retention process. *Measure:* Surveys of employee needs, focus groups, and interviews yield satisfaction data.

- *Development.* Offer career development services. Professional-level employees are very interested in career paths. Lower-level employees can also be shown that there is no ceiling for ambitious types. Self-administered career planning software and counseling follow-up is a cost-effective way to show people that you care about them. Mentoring and executive counseling are gaining as part of upper-level development services.

- *Measure:* Promotion rates, performance scores, and turnover rates are all prime indicators of how employees are moving through the organization and how they see the organization as a place to work. Focus these on mission critical people as a group. Measures of diversity also indicate how attractive your organization is to all segments of the workforce.

- *Retention.* Find out what it takes to engage people in your organization. Survey general employment needs. This can be anything from pay to supervisory support, corporate leadership, advancement opportunity, tolerance for change, coworker relationships, physical work environment, and so forth. *Measure:* Degree to which the organization can comply with the needs expressed in the engagement survey.

Summary

All visible actions are susceptible to measurement. The only question is how deep do you want to go? A GPTW program is not a single profile. According to the Great Place to Work Institute, there is a general profile that is effective in most organizations. There is a need for large-scale, longitudinal studies of what GPTW really implies. The prime question is whether GPTW means the same thing across industries and geographic regions. Is it the same profile in an economically depressed area as it is in a hotbed of commercial activity? Another question that has yet to be answered definitively is how it affects financial results. This type of research cannot yield definite answers in six months. It may need a year or more before we can say that we truly understand this phenomenon's complexity.

An Integrated Reporting System

Now that we have established the pathways, you understand how to move deductively from the enterprise level down to functional objectives and human capital management responses, and then move inductively back up the levels. Assume for the sake of example that you have set up such a process. Now, you can track selected high-priority activities and watch the change in the metrics at each level. The bad news is that when you stretch such a system across a total organization, monitoring the outputs can become an onerous chore. You need to proceed with caution. After setting up measurement systems around the world for more than thirty years, I can tell you that there are three things that eventually kill them:

1. The amount of work involved in collecting the data on a timely basis

2. Not finding a way to report the data that makes them easy to understand

3. Not sustaining staff and management's commitment to the system

Taking these factors in order, the only way to solve the first problem is to automate. We do not have a scarcity of data, but we do have difficulty collecting it easily. Fortunately, there are a number of data extraction tools on the market as well as many software applications that naturally collect some of the data you will need. This will greatly reduce the manual labor involved in data collection. It will be the first blow in breaking through the wall of apathy or resistance around data management for staff functions.

Second, automated reports have to be designed that are simple and explicit and focus the readers on the key issues without burying them in mountains of secondary data. Again, available data is not the problem. Cutting the mountain down to bedrock is the challenge. Graphics are helpful, so long as they are used wisely and not as a substitute for focus. A graph that is irrelevant or not clear is no help. Fortunately, data display software is abundant. Displays are important, because at heart we are all still impressed with color and movement. Software programs use color to signal tolerance levels. So-called dashboards come in many variations in form, but the principle is the same. If performance is within tolerable levels, the light on the dial is green. If it is moving a bit in the wrong direction but is not too far off, the light turns yellow. And if the performance level is way off, the light goes to red. Furthermore, extraction tools give us the ability to instantaneously hop from one set of variables to another and show us in green, yellow, and red when the results have moved from acceptable to unacceptable levels.

Finally, top management has a short attention span for anything that is not tightly focused and explicitly displayed. This is understandable, because the higher one rises in the organization the more entities one has to manage and the more complex are the issues. This puts a premium on specificity and brevity. To maintain management's support for human capital performance metrics, we need to show managers issues that are important to them and not bury them in data for the sake of data. Consistently, I see reports coming out of human resources departments that are waaaaay too big. Because many human resources people don't know what their audiences want to see and because HR people prefer narrative over numbers, they tend to publish a volume of text with a minimum of quantitative displays. It must go in the opposite direction by using lots of graphics with a minimum of annotation. I always caution clients to publish only the most important as-

> Top management has a short attention span for anything that is not tightly focused and explicitly displayed. We need to show them issues that are important to them and not bury them in data.

pects of the most important issues. If your audience wants more, it will tell you.

Figure 5-5 is an example of the dashboard idea. Using the time-to-market example, I have laid in a model of three blank metric lines and circles per function. The lines represent the metric title, while the circles need a color indicator. I am not prescribing three metrics for each function. Every company is different, and imperatives change over time, making it necessary to add or remove certain metrics. Essentially, this is a sample template that needs filling in. Dashboards can be set for monthly or quarterly snapshots by using the lighted dial method. For progress reporting against targeted objectives, a thermometer-type graphic can be designed. You can even run the thermometer horizontally if that suits your needs better. The choice of graphic representation depends on the preferences of the readers.

Leading Indicators

We have made a good deal of progress in developing and showing leading indicators since 2000. We have long had a workable system for measuring the impact of current human capital management on intermediate functional objectives and the ultimate enterprise goals, so what about the future? Given the rate of change in today's market and the continual increase in competition, windows of opportunity open and close rapidly. By definition, financial measures are lagging indicators of an organization's past and current state. Looking backward through accounting lenses is not sufficient, since they restrict our view to internal happenings of the past. It is imperative that we have some sense of how prepared we are to meet the challenges of the future. Part of being prepared is to have flexible policies and structures that can be shifted rapidly to meet emerging customer

Figure 5-5. Enterprise dashboard template.

Enterprise Goal: Shorten Time to Market by 12 Months

Functional Objectives

R&D	Production	Distribution	Sales	Marketing	Customer Service	Information Services	Accounting
1. —— ○	1. —— ○	1. —— ○	1. —— ○	1. —— ○	1. —— ○	1. —— ○	1. —— ○
2. —— ○	2. —— ○	2. —— ○	2. —— ○	2. —— ○	2. —— ○	2. —— ○	2. —— ○
3. —— ○	3. —— ○	3. —— ○	3. —— ○	3. —— ○	3. —— ○	3. —— ○	3. —— ○

Human Capital Objectives

Acquire	Support	Develop	Retain
1. —— ○	1. —— ○	1. —— ○	1. —— ○
2. —— ○	2. —— ○	2. —— ○	2. —— ○
3. —— ○	3. —— ○	3. —— ○	3. —— ○

demands and exploit the opportunities of the marketplace. One of the imperatives that The Conference Board found in its 2007 survey of 769 CEOs worldwide was the need for agility. That implies a management team that is skilled and stable and can move quickly to adapt to market changes. There are enterprise, functional, and human capital metrics that show how well the enterprise is prepared for the unforeseeable. These are described and shown in Chapter 6.

References

1. Jac Fitz-enz, *The 8 Practices of Exceptional Companies* (New York: AMACOM, 1997).

2. Greg Farrell, "CEO Profile: Richard Kovacevich," *USA Today*, March 28, 2007.

3. Michael Treacy and Fred Wiersema, *The Discipline of Market Leaders* (Reading, MA: Addison-Wesley, 1995).

Human Capital Analytics: The Leading Edge of Measurement

"In these matters the only certainty is that nothing is certain."
—**PLINY THE ELDER**

In October 1996, doctors predicted that Lance Armstrong would be dead from cancer in less than six months. In July 1999, he won the Tour de France. Over the next six years, he won every time for an unequalled seven victories.

Prediction is a fine but dangerous art. If anyone really knew with certainty what was going to happen tomorrow, much less a year or more from now, that person's advice would be prohibitively expensive. I don't claim for a moment to know with certainty what will happen tomorrow around human capital management; however, I do know something about organizational variables and how they interact in predictable ways most of the time. From this, we can risk projecting future events with a better-than-average degree of success. The goal is not to change the world over-night. It is just to decrease the variance and increase the certainty a bit at a time.

In general, people do not understand simple probability statistics. Let's use gambling as an example. The casinos in Las Vegas make billions every year on just a percent or two in favor of the house. However, when we apply that concept to organizational improvement programs we can find simi-lar incremental gains but not the same type of success. The reason is that a couple percent of improvement in quality or productivity in one part of the organization does not accu-mulate to the same percent corporate-wide. In fact, in some cases, the effect is only in the local process with no effects elsewhere. To obtain that percent gain across the organiza-tion and drop it to the bottom line we have to work holisti-cally.

A Model and System

Consider that each year, barring some national or global economic anomaly, most companies have anywhere from a financial loss to a small profit. That leaves no more than about 20 percent that have a good to better-than-average year. Every population has only 10 to 20 percent on the top end of the traditional bell-shaped distribution curve. It is a law of distribution that never changes under normal condi-tions. To be on top, all we have to do is to beat two out of ten competitors. If we can increase our return on human capital a couple of percent a year more than the competi-tion, we will be in the top 5 percent of our industry. The best way to do this consistently is to manage our greatest lever-age point, which is people, more effectively than the other two competitors. The secret is not to focus on transaction efficiency. To attain this position we need the following:

- Clear vision from the CEO
- Brand and culture that are coordinated
- Capability plan
- Effective processes
- Integrated delivery
- Predictive analytics

Relationships and Patterns

Many of us unconsciously follow an instruction or example without thinking about the rationale behind it. There are several reasons for this. Among them is fear of contesting an authority figure, whether it is our boss or a so-called expert. Another is resistance to change. It is easier to do something the accustomed way than to spend energy thinking of another way. How many times have I done something the old way rather than take the time to reset or revise the process so that I could do it more easily in the future? And if you think I am going to read the bloody manual, you are crazy. Frustration is another barrier. Maybe we tried to do it a different way and were told, "That isn't the way we do things around here." Then there is apathy. Some people simply do not care. In business, the common retort of employees when asked why they are doing something a certain way is, "I just work here. They don't pay me to think." Or, "We've always done it that way." Or, "We're doing pretty well and you can't argue with success." The litany of excuses goes on. These sad but all too common retorts are examples of doing without learning—and obviously doing without caring. If we apply that to managing and measuring human capital performance, we learn nothing through mere repetition. There is a better way, which I call *looking for patterns*.

Pattern Recognition

We've established in previous chapters that there is a connection, an interdependency, between and among human
capital activities, between and among functional processes,
and between human capital management outputs and functional process outcomes. Logically, we should expect to see
correlations between and among some of the many variables inside those activities, processes, and outcomes. If we
look for them, we will find them. Once these correlations
have been established at any consistent rate of occurrence,
we should be able to make tentative predictions.

Now comes the problem: Things are not always what they
seem to be. Just when you thought I was going to be profound, I fall back on a cliché. I'm sorry if I've disappointed
you, but clichés are often an effective way to startle us into
peering through our biases or misperceptions. As my
mother once told me after I explained in great detail all the
things I was learning in a psychology seminar, "It seems like
common sense to me."

Fallacies in Trend Identification

In the research business, we are always looking under the
covers of data for patterns. This is what we have to sell. If
we can find a valid trend, we can package it and sell it to
people who want to understand their company, market, or
region better. This inner drive of researchers often leads
them to espouse a directionality that does not exist. It also
pushes them to infer causality that is not sustainable.

Stephen Jay Gould, a paleontologist who wrote so beauti-
fully that I read his books for the language as much as for
the content, wrote a marvelous treatise about data analysis
that a layperson can understand.[1] An interesting side note

that is relevant to my point is that Gould and Ed Purcell (a Nobel laureate in physics), both of whom were baseball fanatics, once conducted an exhaustive study of baseball streaks and slumps. They found that all such runs fell within reasonable probability except for one solitary instance: Joe DiMaggio's fifty-six-game hitting streak in 1941. According to probability statistics, it should not have happened at all. Thus, it is the greatest achievement in baseball, if not all sports. What few people know is that the day after his streak was broken, he started another that lasted seventeen games. Imagine a seventy-four-game streak! That is almost half a season. Before that, he had a sixty-one-game hitting streak in the minors. Thank you, Joltin' Joe. I am indebted to Gould for the following dissertation on the complex but fascinating issue of data analysis, to which I have added my views.

Finding Meaning

We are prone to reading patterns into sequences of events because we are looking for meaning in our lives. Yet, to the untrained eye, there is little sense of how often a pattern will or should emerge from random data. Gould illustrated this point with coin flipping. Since the probability of heads is always one in two, or one-half, then the chance of flipping five heads in a row is $\frac{1}{2} \times \frac{1}{2} \times \frac{1}{2} \times \frac{1}{2}$ or one in thirty-two flips. This is rare, but it happens occasionally simply through randomness. No one can predict when that rare sequence might occur, but when it does, we might think that we are on a hot streak if we are betting heads against the flipper. If, after a couple more trials, the flipper produces a run of five tails in a row, we might think that the person was cheating somehow, even if he wasn't. As Gould pointed out, people have been shot over such innocent occurrences.

Another fallacy about trends is perpetrated when people

correctly discover a directionality in events but then assume that something else moving in parallel must be the cause or the effect. Mistaking coincidence or correlation with causality is the stuff of the naive, of charlatans, and of demagogues. Politicians, religious fanatics, and consultants are masters at this tactic. As a consultant friend says, "Anything that is not provably wrong is arguably right." In any system there is variation. The apparent trends can be nothing more than random expansions or contractions of the natural variation within a system. Nothing runs in a straight line, or along a predictable curve, for long. To add even more unpredictability to the mix, two things running in the same system will occasionally coincide for no apparent reason. This is why we cannot ever *prove* anything. Even in the controlled atmosphere of the laboratory, we don't try to prove our hypothesis. We only try to disprove the null hypothesis—that is, that the effects we observed are apparently not caused by forces other than our treatment 95 percent of the time (.05 level of confidence). This is as close as we try to get in the lab. So imagine how much less proof there is available in the field, the so-called real world, where nothing is controllable. (I must add that in medical or pharmacological research, which deals with matters of health, the level of confidence must be much higher—in the neighborhood of 99 percent or greater during repeated trials.)

> Mistaking coincidence or correlation with causality is the stuff of the naive, of charlatans, and of demagogues. Politicians, religious fanatics, and consultants are masters at this tactic.

Extrapolation

One of the common misuses of trend data is extrapolation. When we have a data set that covers a period of time whether it is for weeks, months, quarters, or years, we usually want to know what it will look like going forward. If something is on an upward or downward slope of, for example, 5 percent over the past three years, is it safe to say it will be 5 percent next year? We do this with benchmarking all the time.

Assuming or extrapolating a past trend into the future is risky. A straight line extrapolation would assume that the future will be a mirror of the past. You could do that with some confidence in the 1970s and 1980s, but since then it has become highly unlikely. Volatility and constancy are polar opposites. This is why I believe that benchmarking has lost most of its value since the arrival of the dot-com industry. The dot-com phenomenon rewrote our thinking about organizations. It was a highly disruptive technology, which although it was disastrous for many people, did launch U.S. business in a new, more unpredictable direction.

The Importance of Context

If we want to use data from the past to tell us about the future, we have to add context. As I write this book, I am preparing a benchmarking survey for a client. We will talk to thirty companies about seventeen human capital variables. If we bring back the data and simply present it without any contextual questions, we do a disservice to the client. First, we know that the data from the thirty companies will not be identical even though they are all in the same industry. What will make it different are their individual idiosyncrasies, or their context. So we are developing more than a dozen questions having to do with financial, technological, organizational, and human capital issues that affect the human resources activities we are surveying. A few of these issues are listed in Figure 6-1.

Figure 6-1. Contextual questions for benchmarking.

What were your company's strategic initiatives during the period just concluded? (The period matching the data set.)

What is your company's financial record over the past two years?

What external and internal elements are you tracking for effects on HR strategy?

Do you use a validated pre-hire assessment, if so for which jobs?

Do you have a formal onboarding program?

Is compensation linked directly to quantifiable performance?

What (how much) effect is turnover having on your ability to compete?

How is learning and development linked to the business plan?

Collectively, the answers to these types of questions will give insight into the quantitative results. As we match the context with the quantitative we should understand why there is variance. We might even obtain some ideas about generalizable effective practices. Notice, I did not say "best practices."

Charlatans

Over the decades, I have witnessed the arrival and departure of many products in the business management market that allegedly claimed correlations, if not also causation. One of the most popular exercises has been the attempt to find causation between employee activity and human resources programs with financial results. I admit to being part of this practice at times. The best-practice craze lent support to the search for this holy grail—namely, the value of people in business. Published stories of isolated events claimed to be revealing generalizable paths to financial performance. I am hard-pressed to remember any that has ever been proven to work beyond chance over the long term.

One of the more blatant ruses I've seen is to recommend a set of mixed, arbitrary, often overlapping, subjective issues, while simultaneously ignoring quantitative performance records, and then promise to draw correlations with the creation of shareholder value. Even if a set of opinions about programs, employees, applicants, systems, and what have you did match to some degree with the movement of shareholder value, it is ludicrous to claim more than coincidence without analysis. Carrying this ruse to the ridiculous, to take one sample in time and make claims of general validity is almost criminal. It certainly could not claim to hold over a long period through market changes. There are so many reasons why this is bogus that I won't even attempt to list them. Opinions do not correlate with anything other than the opinion-giver's own biases. So, let's call it what it is: a very thinly veiled attempt to sell consulting services.

Business Applications

Taking business events as examples of correlations and causation, there are a multitude of variables that coalesce in sales, operating expense, and profitability. All the people and things inside the enterprise plus the people and things outside of it that can affect sales, expense, or profit are in constant movement. At any moment, there can be an aligning of two variables, such as increasing pay and increasing sales. Although both might be moving in the same direction—coincidence, possibly correlation—there may be absolutely no causality involved. Sales can rise for many reasons that have nothing to do with the incentive pay plan for salespeople. To infer that the new pay plan caused sales to increase is premature until we check out and eliminate the other possible causes. Among those other drivers that must be examined are our product compared with that of the competition in terms of price, performance, reliability, deliverability, and service, plus the personal relationships of seller to buyer. The movement of any single variable or combination of variables could affect sales in either direction.

Congratulating the sales force without checking other possibilities can cause problems. We might even go so far as to give an extra bonus for outstanding performance only to learn later that the increase was due to a competitor's inability to deliver while its plant was on strike or burned down. Suppose the competitor subcontracts production to a third party and next month is back in business, perhaps with an even more reliable product, and our sales decrease accordingly. If we did not take the time to research the cause, our conclusion might be that the salespeople were coasting after receiving a big bonus. Having spent nearly ten years as a salesman and sales manager, I have personally witnessed this type of executive disappointment many times. The typical response is, "They're not as hungry as they used to be." This is the classic rationalization of executives who won't invest the time and expense to understand what is really happening. As a result, they continue to make the same mistakes over and over in sales and other functions as well.

Performance Valuation

An example in another direction is the way in which we set standards of performance. Nearly everyone dislikes having to do performance appraisals. We know that accurately judging another human being's performance is an extremely difficult task that is filled with room for error. Despite all the advances made in this technique, the situation of having to defend a rating in court is very difficult. In an attempt to reduce the error rate, we set supposedly objective standards of performance. For the simplest tasks, this is not too difficult if we have enough observations of a given performance. For example, assume that we want to know how long it should take warehouse staff to move a number of boxes a certain distance in the warehouse by hand. This would allow us to forecast how many workers we will need as the volume of boxes increases with increasing sales. If we observe the one-time movement of one 10-pound box that is 2 by 2 by 1 foot a distance of 20 feet, we can say that it takes 7 seconds (my wife just timed me doing it). So, we set the standard at 7 seconds. What are the variables: my strength, my agility, or my motivation? Am I the model for all men? What if the box size, shape, and weight change? What if the material in the box varies? If the box is filled with paper and the humidity is very high, the weight of the box can change significantly. What about the fatigue factor, boredom, and breakage if we have to move two hundred boxes versus twenty? Forecasting performance is a subtle and complex task.

To make a long story short, you can see how complicated it is to set standards of performance for even the simplest tasks. When we move to the work of salespeople, systems analysts, loan officers, nurses, or a hundred other professional occupations, you get the point. So, how do we rate and forecast human performance if we cannot step away from our prejudices and sometimes flat-out mistaken notions? Obviously, if it is important, we have to study the variables within the system to reduce our estimation errors. To end with another cliché, you get back what you put in. If we want to understand the correlation and causation of our business in pursuit of competitive advantage, we have to put some effort into it or continue to follow the pack. To use a graphic model for being in the pack: If you are not the lead animal in a sled-dog team, you spend your career looking at the rear end of the guy ahead of you.

We are indebted to W. Edwards Deming for showing us how to reduce variance and set valid performance standards in factories. After his explanation, we could see that it made sense and was comprehendible by the average person. Carrying the same concepts into other areas such as human capital management greatly reduces the mystery and exposes true correlation and causation.

Data Sensors: Forecasting and Predicting

There is a phenomenon I call *data sensors*. These are data that tip you off to the emergence of a problem or opportunity. They are early warning signals. They are not evident to the amateur. It takes time and many observations to perceive the signals. The following are examples drawn from my experience:

- An increase in absenteeism is often a sign of unrest among employees. Employees are telling management that they are unhappy by staying off the job. If this signal is ignored, it is highly predictable that turnover will begin to rise in about six months.

- Increases in processing errors of any type are a precursor of employee and later customer dissatisfaction. Employees respond to their unhappiness by slowing down their productivity, turning out sloppy work, and staying home. Customers respond by complaining and eventually finding another supplier.

- Reductions in any voluntary activity, from suggestion programs to company picnics, are signs of employee unrest. People are signaling with their abstention.

- Sharp increases in employee requests for transfer, even when there is no problem with the current supervisor, might be a sign of general malaise or boredom.

- High levels of employment-offer rejections tell us that we are not treating applicants properly. Offers are seldom turned down for pay reasons. More often, it is due to the employee's perception that this is not a good place to work.

- A change in any metric presages effects in others. Increasing turnover means more hiring and training to come. An increase in employees coming to talk to employee-relations staff indicates problems with supervision, coworkers, or work conditions, which leads to employees quitting. Decreases in attendance in training usually signal employee frustration or supervisors who won't let employees take time to be trained. Either one will lead to requests for transfers or quits.

All the above factors negatively affect quality, innovation, productivity, and customer service. So, what can we predict with some degree of confidence? What leads to what? This was implied in Chapters 2 through 4. I stated that there were clearly predictive connections between the human capital management tasks of acquiring, supporting, developing, and retaining employees and the outcomes of the various functional unit processes. Let me note that I'm not talking about causation, only some level of connection. To quickly review linkages, consider the following:

> If human resources, in collaboration with the hiring supervi-
> sor, delivers a high-quality candidate faster than normal, the
> business unit supervisor should be able to maintain or even
> increase productivity. Hence, there is probably a correlation
> between the time to fill jobs and productivity, all other things
> being equal. But as Hamlet said, "Ay, there's the rub."[2]

The nonbelievers have a standard objection: What if this
or that happens during the same time period? What about
all the things in the environment that pop up and affect the
outcome? The obvious answer is that when you change the
circumstances or an intervening event occurs, you get a different result. The only way at the beginning you can judge
or forecast anything in any function or at any time is to assume that surrounding conditions are constant (even if they
aren't). This principle is called *ceteris paribus* or "other
things being equal." This constraint is not unique to social
science. It applies to all judgments we make in life. In the
morning we mentally forecast that if we take a certain route
to work, we will arrive in a certain number of minutes, give
or take a small variance. That is a ceteris paribus assumption
that normal conditions will prevail. The same thing applies
in business for attempts at evaluating and predicting. Budgets, sales plans, and production schedules are based on ceteris paribus assumptions. In effect, we say that if things
go according to our assumptions about the cost of goods,
competitor actions, product development, the weather, customer tastes, and so forth (ceteris paribus), the following
should be attained (probability).

If something happens during the course of the study, we
can identify it and account for it. Previously, we played out
the process value analysis model and saw that at step three,
the impact stage, we would be able to account for significant
external events and make statements of apparent correla-

tion, if not causality. This can be done without running a field experiment. At the very least, using that model would allow us to be more confident of our conclusions than most managers can be of theirs. So, let's get on with it.

The following is a set of examples of actual problems, actions, and events and their predictable results compiled over the past twenty years.

Issue	Result
Time to fill jobs increasing	Productivity and/or customer service in the hiring departments negatively affected at a predictable level leading to lost customers
Absenteeism increasing	Turnover will increase within six months leading to negative effects in QIPS*
Introduction of flextime and telecommuting	Turnover will decrease as applicant pool increases, positively effecting QIPS
Introduction of employee referral bonus program	Quality of candidates improves, hiring cost decreases, and turnover drops
Employees cite poor support and communication from supervisors in exit interviews	Incidence of employee-relations problems and absence increases, performance decreases, then turnover and customer dissatisfaction increase, especially in public contact units
Introduction of employee assistance program	Absenteeism decreases, performance increases, turnover slows, eventually cost of healthcare benefits decreases

Issue	Result
Training increased	Internal replacement pool increases and turnover decreases
Training staff and budget cut	External aplicant pool shrinks as market learns we have reduced development support; eventually, voluntary separations increase
Consistent college recruitment program with internships	Higher job-offer acceptance rate, lower cost per hire, improved hire quality, increased longevity, enhanced reputation

* QIPS = quality, innovation, productivity, service

Over time, you will see patterns that are common, as well as ones that are unique to your situation. The more you study your data, the more your predictive capability will improve. The key to improving that capability is to ask yourself why when you see any phenomenon. What could have caused this: problems with people, material, process, or equipment? People can be employees, supervisors, managers, customers, vendors, and even executives. Here is a true story that makes the point of predictable results.

Company X had a very successful year. The following February, the CEO assembled everyone through an electronic town-hall setup. He went on at great length about what had occurred last year and what was coming this year. In the next month, morale dropped like a lead balloon, turnover started to increase, and customer service slipped noticeably. What happened at that meeting? If we knew, what would we have predicted?

> The key to improving your predictive capability is to ask yourself, Why?

The CEO's remarks can be boiled down to two statements.

1. "We had a great year last year with record profits (read between the lines, I got a hell of a bonus)."

2. "This year will not be as good, so we are cutting the salary increase budget in half and might have to have some layoffs."

Do you have any idea why the people responded as they did? Could you have predicted their behavior after that communication? Of course you could. These things happen, and people—managerial personnel, especially—have to think ahead to the predictable response. Most important, they have to get out of their skin and put themselves in the place of their audience with *its* values, needs, and viewpoints. As an example, a single parent, male or female, who is barely making ends meet, has a different view of life than does a high-income male executive with a wife or nanny to care for the kids. In the end, you can watch data over time and begin to improve your forecasting capability. You can also view planned actions and suggest probable responses of customers and employees.

Toward a Human Capital Financial Index

Indexes are a common and effective trending mechanism. They provide an effective base from which to risk forecasts. Since it usually takes a good deal of study, definition, and consideration of variables and relationships to set up an index, we can count on its reliability. The only caution we need to observe involves semantics. Calling something an index doesn't make it one. Sometimes the term is applied to any unconnected set of data. Making an alleged random selection of variables into an index because they "feel right" is invalid. The dictionary offers several definitions of an index. The one that most closely suits our situation is the following one: "Something that serves to direct attention to some fact, condition, etc."[3]

Underscore the word *fact*. I think of true indexes as valid and reliable sets of data, all of whose variables are focused on a given concept and are maintained over an extended period. The index must have internal validity as the central point. This means that it represents a true relationship among components. The most familiar examples of long-standing, reliable indexes are the government's cost-of-living index and the consumer price index. These are well-established data sets that give us a good idea of how these two issues are moving. It might not have much effect on you depending on your lifestyle. So, the government does not claim perfection, and through criticism and modification, it has improved the indexes over time. An index does not purport to *prove* anything. Rather, it gives us a consistent, legitimate view of the movement of a complex phenomenon over time.

If we study the components of an index, we can understand what drove the index number up or down. Then, if we understand what affects each component, we can look into the future and plan accordingly. For example, if the cost-of-living index is rising and we see that one of the components, the price of petroleum products, is rising more than other components, how can we react? Turning to the commodities market, we can look at the futures contracts for petroleum and decide for ourselves whether the price is likely to continue to rise for the next twelve months. Then, we can look at long-range weather forecasts for the Midwest (if that is where we live) to learn if we are in for a cold winter. Coincidentally, if the weather is going to be unseasonably cold, the cost of heating oil will rise even more. This leads to a decision about adding insulation to our homes to preserve ambient heat (or moving to Florida).

In business it is useful, if not vital, to know trends. Trends offer the astute an opportunity to view the future with a bit more certainty than their less insightful competitors. That is what separates the 20 percent at the top from the 80 percent who follow—a slight incremental advantage time after time. We read about the great leaps in the results of great companies, but we don't see and hear about the daily decisions that individually are a bit better than those of their competitors and that collectively blow them away. Managing a large-scale business is not a walk in the park. It requires great attention to detail. This means having reliable data and knowing what they truly mean. Indexes offer an advantage over single, unconnected data points in that they provide the collective result of a set of related variables. This gives us a broader view. Inside the index, we can look at the component movements.

The first hurdle in developing a human capital financial management index is the lack of longitudinal, quantitative business databases. For anyone who wishes to establish an index, the following examples may be helpful.

Human Capital Revenue Index (HCRI)

HCRI is revenue per full-time equivalent (FTE) employee. Revenue includes all sales and service income. FTE employees include all persons on payroll plus all contract, temporary, and other workers not on payroll (termed *contingent*). It does not include the personnel who work for outsource program providers. That human effort is considered to be part of general purchased services. This is an example of a productivity trend.

Human Capital Cost Index (HCCI): HCCI is the total labor cost per

FTE employee. Human capital cost includes the pay and benefits of persons on payroll, the contingent worker cost, and the cost of absence and turnover. The latter two costs are generally ignored in calculations of labor cost. However, it is logical and obvious that absenteeism and employee turnover are a cost of labor. You can include development costs if you like. This index shows movement of people costs.

Human Capital Profit Index (HCPI): HCPI is revenue less purchased services per FTE employee. Profit attributable to human capital investment is total revenue less all nonhuman expenses (everything except pay and benefits), divided by FTEs. The numerator is a standard form for calculating value added. This shows the leverage of human effort that resulted in profit. This is one of two metrics that show ROI in human capital. The other divides the numerator above by pay and benefits. That produces a profit leveraged from employee pay and benefits.

When I tracked these costs during the 1990s, it told me that the cost of people was tracking almost on top of the inflation rate. In short, job for job, there has been very little real dollar increase. This is one of the reasons why the U.S. economy through 1999 had been so robust. The cost of human capital, one of the two major costs of most companies, had barely risen in real terms. If this index had continued to the present, I believe we would have seen a significant difference with revenue outstripping costs.

The other interesting and surprising point was that human capital–leveraged profit did not track with revenue. Whereas there was an increase in revenue per FTE of nearly 29 percent over nine years, profit per FTE over those nine years increased only 16 percent. This means that either there were significant investments in technology or poor management of operating expenses other than employee costs.

Index Value

The value of having a human capital financial index is that it gives us the ability to uncover and understand the real story of human value in organizations, devoid of media or government hype. Given our knowledge of what has affected the trend, and looking ahead at those factors, we can begin to understand what the near-term future might look like. From there, we can do a much more effective job of planning a path to profitability. If we add to this type of index a human economic value-added index, we would understand in depth how much value, if any, was being added to the national economy by human capital as opposed to equipment and facilities. If a company spends $XX million on computerizing the workforce, how much does productivity rise, and therefore what is the leverage on that investment? Productivity is a human issue. Investment in sophisticated equipment does not guarantee productivity improvement.

Paul Strassmann has written extensively about the relationship of information technology and knowledge creation. He has shown that, generally speaking, the true cost and ROI of software, in particular, are largely unknown or miscalculated.[4] When management fails to follow up information technology investment with training, process improvement, and, most important, sound strategic moves, there is seldom economic value added.

Index Application

In what ways could the index teach us to be more effective in managing our human capital? Key questions might include:

- What contributed most to our sales and service income?

- What was the ratio of investment in equipment and facilities to people?
- What hard data evidence is there that each investment improved productivity?
- Were there visible interactive effects among the three?
- What is the competition doing to improve human capital productivity?
- How did the competition manage the ratio of contingents to regular employees, and how should we manage ours?

On the cost side, ask the following questions:

- What is the average compensation of our employees—pay plus benefits—in critical job groups (most salary surveys do not disclose actual average total compensation, only pay ranges)? How does that compare within our industry or to other human capital competitors (companies that hire away our people)?
- What is the ratio of benefits to payroll, and how is it changing?
- What are our absence and turnover rates, and where are they concentrated?
- How does our rate of compensation growth compare with revenue, productivity, and profitability?
- What is our leverage factor on human capital investment?

For the profit side, ask the following questions:

- How many dollars of profit per employee are we generating?

- Is profit per employee growing at the same rate as revenue per employee? If not, then why not?

- How does our economic value added (EVA) look compared with that of competitors in our line of business?

It should be clear that if you have the answers to these questions, you can do an effective job of forecasting.

Data Sources

Your efforts at prediction are strongly supported by the availability of public data. North American businesses are blessed with a plethora of data. In both the United States and Canada, the governments support extensive databases of population, economic, and business information. A few of the U.S. federal government sources include:

Congressional Budget Office

Department of Commerce: Bureau of Economic Analysis

Department of Labor: Bureau of Labor Statistics

Economic Reports of the President

Economic Research Service

Economic Statistics Briefing Room

Federal Reserve Board

Social Security Administration

U.S. Census Bureau

U.S. Government Printing Office

FEDSTATS (http://www.fedstats.gov) is a website for quick searches of these and other federal agencies with an-

nual research and publication budgets in excess of
$500,000. It lists over a hundred federal government data
sources. Many states also have research services. If you are
new to this type of research, you can get guidance from your
local public library research section.

In Canada, Statistics Canada is an excellent central
source of national population, workforce, economic, and
commercial data. In addition, the Canadian Conference
Board conducts and publishes ongoing business research.

A few of the commercial sources of quantitative business
data include magazines such as *BusinessWeek, Forbes, Fortune, IndustryWeek, InformationWeek, CIO,* and *CFO,*
among others. Some of the HR journals feature statistical
sections as well. They provide both hard data and articles
on trends and effective practices.

Prominent research organizations are:

American Productivity and Quality Center

American Society for Training and Development

Bureau of National Affairs

Corporate Leadership Council

Dun and Bradstreet

National Association of Manufacturers

Society for Human Resource Management

The Conference Board

U.S. Chamber of Commerce

In addition, there are many industry watchers, of which
IDC, Yankee Group, and Gartner are representative. Internationally, there are the several United Nations bureaus:
The Organization of American States in Washington, D.C.;
and the *World Competitiveness Report* published by IMD in

Switzerland, which provides data on forty-seven countries and lists over fifty other sources of data worldwide.

Finally, the Internet is spawning information websites faster than we can keep up with them. By merely listing a keyword, you are likely to find several sources. The point is that there is a great deal of information available from which to identify trends, build forecasts, and even attempt predictions. Just be ready to modify your original estimates with periodic updates. The marketplace is so volatile that today's truth is tomorrow's anachronism.

Summary

The business of data management is maturing. We have moved from a reliance on accounting as our primary source of business information to literally hundreds of government and commercial sources of objective and practice data-bases. Some require membership, but most are available to the public either free of charge or for a reasonable fee. The trick is to learn how to interpret data and to use data to look forward as well as backward.

Success will accrue to those who can see patterns and re-lationships among data. The objective is to turn data into information and ultimately intelligence. This takes experi-ence and practice. Through trial and error, anyone who has the energy to stay in the hunt can learn to improve his or her forecasting ability. There are four levels of data. One level is the general marketplace, which offers everything from international demographic and economic data to industry and technology data. Inter-nally, there are data at the enterprise, function, and human capital management levels. These naturally interact and are

> The objective is to turn data into information and ulti-mately intelligence.

interdependent. Actions at one level drive activities and outcomes at the others. Businesses are complex and dynamic
environments. The wealth of data generated by business activity can be overwhelming. We must learn how to identify
the factors and forces that make a difference.

Take care not to fall prey to the natural desire to draw
correlations where they do not exist. Data from one activity
may be moving in parallel with those of another. However,
this may be more coincidence than correlation. It very seldom shows causation. Isolated, one-time events are rarely
generalizable to a different population or situation. It is useful to understand the intention behind the publication and
the context behind the data. Is it a desire to share useful
information, or merely a thinly disguised attempt to sell you
something beyond the data?

Forecasting and predicting are difficult but not impossible. All attempts at explaining the future are made under
ceteris paribus conditions. That is, other things being equal,
if one applies our assumptions, the following will have a
high probability of occurring. Skill can be built and estima-
tions made more accurately if one practices looking behind
the extant data to what might be driving them. Context is
absolutely essential to understanding differences.

Indexes are valid bases from which to practice forecasting. A well-designed index offers a number of components
that are inherently related. This simplifies the task of prog-
nostication. But just because someone calls a data set an
index does not make it one. Look into it and ask yourself
whether the alleged connections are logical and consistent.
Caveat emptor.

References

1. Stephen Jay Gould, *Full House* (New York: Harmony
    Books, 1996).

2. William Shakespeare, *Hamlet*, act 3, scene 1, line 65.

3. *American Collegiate Dictionary* (New York: Random House, 1998).

4. Paul Strassmann, "The Value of Knowledge Capital," *American Programmer,* March 1998.

CHAPTER SEVEN

Predictive Analytics: Leading Indicators and Intangible Metrics

"When one admits that nothing is certain one must,
I think, also admit that some things are much more
nearly certain than others."

—BERTRAND RUSSELL

Toward Leading Indicators

Organizations have lived very well for five centuries with lagging indicators emanating from double-entry bookkeeping. Ever since Fra Luca Pacioli allegedly invented that process in the 1490s, accountants have churned out tons of data describing the outcomes of past work processes and investments. This served businesses well as the process became standardized. However, it does not generate data about the future, which is the only thing that can be managed.

As the turbulent twenty-first century emerges, it is clear that we need a peek at the future. We need data that gives us insight into what might happen if we make certain investments. It also should tell us what might be coming as the outgrowth of various economic conditions. I ask you, what is more useful, describing what happened yesterday or predicting what is likely to happen tomorrow?

When we plan a trip to a distant city, we need to know what type of clothes to wear. The normal thing to do is not study the weather history of that place, but to look up the weather forecast for the period we plan to be there. I grant you that a general knowledge of past weather patterns is interesting and somewhat useful as general information, but in the last analysis we need to pack clothes for a specific future date.

Leading Indicator Examples

In the management of human capital the value of leading indicators is very useful. By definition, a leading indicator purports to tell us something about the behavior of people and/or the return on an investment in people. It is an inference or a well-worked-out claim that a given metric or set of metrics forecasts or predicts a future likelihood. Of course, no one can truly tell the future. As the Greeks used to say, "When people make plans, the Gods laugh."

Nevertheless, decision science has reached a point where we can foretell future events with a high degree of probability. Examples are shown in Figure 7-1.

Intangibles

Most leading indicators are intangible. General business intangibles include brands, reputation, a great place to work, and innovation.

Nick Bontis of McMaster University has correctly stated the case of intangibles:

Figure 7-1. Sample of leading indicators.

Leadership. Scores on an employee survey of attitudes toward leaders tell us how employees value their leadership. Behind this is research that correlates employee attitudes with their likelihood of staying or leaving the organization.

Engagement. This is a relatively new topic that refers to the employees' emotional and intellectual commitment to their work and to the organization. As with leadership, positive feelings portend loyalty, higher productivity, and stronger commitment. Satisfaction does not connect with productivity or commitment.

Readiness. Having a given number of important positions with at least one person qualified to step in in the event of a vacancy predicts a continuity that relates to customer service and work quality. Our research has also shown a correlation between readiness and revenue growth. When at least 75 percent of mission critical positions have a replacement ready to step in, revenue per employee starts to rise.

Knowledge Management. Since the twenty-first century is a knowledge-driven market, it follows that there is a correlation between knowledge management programs or knowledge exchanges and revenue growth. One major consulting firm claimed that its knowledge exchange helped it win contracts worth several billion dollars in one year.

Loyalty. Turnover and engagement are affected by loyalty or lack thereof. Commitment to staying and working through difficult times is also a function of employee loyalty. Indicators of loyalty can be obtained through employee surveys as well as examples of positive attitudes and helpfulness.

Customer Satisfaction. Obviously, customer satisfaction is the result of quality products, kept promises, and employee service. Satisfaction leads to return business, a larger spend, and referrals. It can be measured through surveys and it is a strong predictor of future business levels.

"The intangible value embedded in companies has been considered by many, defined by some, understood by few, and formally valued by practically no one."[1]

Although still in its infant state, HRP work on leading indicators and measurement of intangibles is already producing value for management. As we blend these metrics into our new predictive management model and operating system, we are lifting human capital management out of the measurement era and into the analytic era.

Enterprise Futures

The future of the enterprise is the sum of the future of the functional and human capital levels. Top management can set future goals, but if the future capability does not exist below it, this will be an exercise in frustration. (An element of the future was embedded in Figure 2-3 in Chapter 2 when I presented the corporate human capital scorecard.)

> Top management can set future goals, but if the future capability does not exist below it, this will be an exercise in frustration.

The two principal enterprise-level futures are shown in the financial column. They are human economic value added (HEVA) and human capital market value (HCMV). First, if the company's balance sheet (economic value added is balance sheet–oriented) is in a free fall, we are in a heap of trouble. Our ability to fund short-term emergencies or long-term growth from borrowings will be severely if not totally diminished. Lenders will tell us by withholding funds that they doubt our ability to sustain a viable business. Our ability to offer commercial paper will be diminished, and our bond ratings will sink. If this goes on long enough, the operative word is *bankruptcy.*

Second, if our market to book value is dropping precipitously, the market is telling us that it is losing faith in our ability to perform in the future. The stock market is the biggest gambling table in the world. Smart gamblers (read *investors*) are not placing their bets based on what we did last year or last quarter; they are betting on the next turn of the economic wheel. Which way will the economy go? Which way will the stock market go? And which way will our performance go? If they do not like the looks of the future in general or our future performance in particular, they do not bet on us and our stock loses its luster. As our stock price falls, the value of stock option incentives declines, and their employee holding power diminishes. Typically, the top managerial, sales, and technical talent has stock options. The loss of those people can seriously undermine a company's ability to meet future challenges, even if it is profitable today. Income statement figures seldom display any direct links to the future unless they are in extremis, in which case they are a sign that the whole bloody enterprise is about to sink. This happened in several well-publicized recent cases such as Enron, WorldCom, Tyco, and others.

Functional Futures

The functional units depend on human capital to attain their objectives. As we already know, all nonhuman assets of the organization are inert (and so are some of the human assets). People leverage them to achieve their mission and produce profits. Therefore, leading indicators should be focused on the characteristics of the workforce. To the experienced eye, they paint a picture of how well we are positioned for the future. The metrics cover issues such as preparedness, competence, job satisfaction, commitment, and depletion. They can be viewed on their own merit or combined with financial measures of human capital at the enterprise level to create an enterprise scorecard. Use these to stimulate your imagination and generate others.

Be Prepared

There are two measures of preparedness: competence and readiness. The competence level is simply the percentage of people who have demonstrated the skill and knowledge that make them able to meet current and near-term future performance requirements in their current jobs. Competence became a much-talked-about topic in the last half of the 1990s. Because it has gained so much attention, I believe that it is useful to provide background and definition.

The concept of competence sprang from David McClellan's pioneering work for the United States Information Office in the early 1970s. He was charged with determining the critical competencies for the successful performance of a field service information officer, a position that functioned in a wide variety of geographic, political, and ethnic settings around the world. To make a long story short, he was able to accomplish the task by focusing on the behavior of the person in the job rather than on background factors such as education or aptitude test scores. From that came the first standardized definition of the term *competency:*

A competency is an underlying characteristic of an individual that is causally related to criterion-referenced effective or superior performance in a job or situation.[2]

Criterion-referenced is a fancy way of saying that a given competency actually predicts behavior and performance. When you cut through the jargon, this is what we want to be able to do in selecting and developing people for jobs in our companies. It is logical that if we could identify competencies for key jobs, we could test the incumbents to agree on how many are average and how many are superior. Target levels could be established and tracked.

This metric could be monitored as we work with people to bring them up to full speed. From it, we would know two things: where we stand today and how well we are prepared for the foreseeable future. So long as there is no drastic change in the character of a job, the required competencies should not change materially.

The competencies are also precursors and requirements for the next level of preparedness measurement, which is bench strength or succession. I call this the *readiness* level.

Readiness is the percentage of key positions with at least one fully qualified (competent) person ready to take over now. Applying the readiness criterion to all key positions yields a picture of the organization's general human capital health. Just as vital medical signs tell us how fit a person is, and therefore how vulnerable he or she is to disease, readiness tells us how vulnerable the enterprise corpus is to the onslaught of future competitiveness. If we have people who can step in and take over at a moment's notice, we will probably experience fewer slowdowns in the event of unforeseen emergencies. This cadre of qualified personnel can also be mobilized quickly for problem solving, team projects, or new market opportunities.

> If we have people who can step in and take over at a moment's notice, we will probably experience fewer slowdowns in the event of unforeseen emergencies. This cadre of qualified personnel can also be mobilized quickly for problem solving, team projects, or new market opportunities.

For readiness, it is again a case of the percentage of people who have demonstrated their capability to step into a position above them on short notice. The future is unpredictable. We never know when a key talent will decide to leave or will need to be transferred to support another initiative. Clearly, if we have backup talent ready to step in immediately, we are more ready for the future than if we have a void for any significant period of time. The one unequivocal demand is a clear description of the required capabilities. There is no sense fooling ourselves into thinking that we are ready when we actually are not.

The two preparedness measures—competence and readiness—are testable against a set of standards that you establish. If you detail the requirements for key jobs, it should be a simple matter to assess how close the incumbents are to attaining them.

Assessment

In recent years, there has been a resurgence in assessment tools. Assessment follows the same general route as competency except it is not interview based. Key job attributes such as skills, work preference, and potential are collected. Then, a questionnaire is designed and tested until high degrees of validity and reliability are achieved. A number of vendors have developed assessment programs. When used properly, they can be of great value to a company.

One case that I have seen up close when I was an adviser to Unicru (now Kronos) dealt with a major retailer. The application of the assessment tool made a dramatic change to turnover, sales, and the learning curve. In this case, turnover dropped by more than 30 percent and the time to standard performance was shortened by 25 percent. In addition, average sales per hour exceeded the standard by almost 7 percent. In total, including cost savings from reduced turnover and the revenue increase from a shorter learning curve and higher average sales, there was a gain of $45 million.

As a predictive tool, assessment helps management to forecast the turnover rate with greater accuracy and also future sales increases.

Employee Mind-Sets

Another set of predictors deals with the veiled attitudes and feelings of our workforce. Indicators of the mind-set of the workforce are important. They uncover a hidden view of what we might consider undercurrents or background concerns. It doesn't take a great deal of imagination to foresee that dissatisfied employees or employees who have concerns about the culture are unlikely candidates for longevity awards. Seldom do employees tell us directly that they are unsatisfied. They give subtle signals such as solemn faces, not volunteering for projects, being absent, or working at a slower pace than normal. One sure way of tapping into the mind-set of the workforce is to look around the office and see how many people are still there an hour after quitting time. If the place is empty and the parking lot has no cars in it, we have a problem. When people are unhappy, the easiest way for them to express their displeasure is to withhold effort. High levels of absenteeism are a concrete sign that something is on people's minds. These half-hidden concerns can be turned up through surveys, interviews, or informal discussion groups.

Surveys are useful because they produce structured data unfiltered by another person. Surveys of commitment, job satisfaction, culture, and climate yield data points that can be tracked periodically. Many companies tap this well once a year. Others have taken to surveying one group each month. This provides current data. During the time between surveys, keep your eyes and ears open. As you know from experience, problems do not occur overnight. There is usually a series of frustrations that build up over time. The cliché of management by walking around has a kernel of value in it if you pay attention to the subtle signs that employees are continually putting forth. Another absolutely critical requirement is that when you conduct an employee survey, you provide prompt feedback to the respondents. If you are not committed to dealing with uncomfortable information from below, don't ask for it.

Indirect Sign

There is another two-part indicator that is not necessarily a direct leading metric but is useful to monitor and stimulate action before a major loss occurs. It is the depletion rate and cost. I already discussed the separation rate in Chapter 2 as part of the human capital enterprise scorecard. Now I want to take another look at it as a leading indicator. I grant that the separation rate is an indicator of past action. The employees have voted with their feet already. But if the rate is increasing, it is a sure sign that trouble lies ahead.

Departures are called attrition, turnover, or separations. Bontis refers to voluntary terminations as depletions of human capital, which gives us a different perspective.[3] First, let's focus on voluntary separations rather than total separations, because totals include involuntary separations resulting from management's decision to cull unneeded or unsatisfactory labor. One could make the argument that downsizing to reduce fixed costs is depletion. But if we needed the people in order to be profitable, we wouldn't have let them go. The argument is that we did not deplete our human capital capability bank. In effect, every time the organization loses a person it would rather keep, its stock of human capital is depleted. There are at least two ways to avoid or reduce such depletions. One is to run surveys on a regular basis and to act on the results. That is the proactive method for handling it. The other method is to employ an outside professional firm after the fact to conduct exit interviews with departed employees. When these interviews are well done, they yield a wealth of information that can be used to avoid further losses.

The best way to become motivated to do that is to calculate the cost of turnover or human capital depletion. The loss of a competent exempt-level person typically costs the equivalent of at least one year's pay and benefits for that position. Note that these calculations do not include the effects on customers, which are potentially additional costs. The point is that at today's compensation level, if you lose ten professionals, it will cost you about $1 million, plus unknown outside losses. Ask yourself how much you have to sell to produce a pretax profit of $1 million. The bottom line on depletion rate and cost is that unwanted turnover not only costs you today but also leaves you vulnerable in the short run for tomorrow. Thus, it is a predictor of future problems of several types. If you are continually having to break in new people, there is no way that your company can be highly competitive.

Competitiveness

Think of leading indicators and intangibles as competitive benchmarks. In addition to the short list in Figure 7-2, a composite metric can be developed that can be described as a competitiveness measure. These are just a different way of looking at leading indicators.

Rather than give you a description of competitive benchmarks, let me pose a question. From a human capital standpoint, what would you have to do or have or be, to be able to claim a certain level of competitiveness? That takes a minute to establish, doesn't it? So, what does competitiveness consist of from a human capital standpoint?

I believe that it contains the data points listed earlier—competence, readiness, employee satisfaction, commitment,

Figure 7-2. Leading indicators.

Human Capital Competence Level
Percentage of key employees who have met competence standards

Human Capital Readiness Level
Percentage of key positions with at least one fully qualified person ready

Human Capital Commitment Level
Percentage of employees expecting to stay at least three years

Human Capital Satisfaction Level
Percentage of employees scoring in top quartile of job satisfaction survey

Corporate Climate
Percentage of employees who indicate concern with culture and climate

Human Capital Depletion Rate and Cost
Voluntary separations as a percentage of head count and the cost of separations

climate, compensation levels, separation rates, and perhaps something else that is unique to your company. If you and I were to sit down together, I am certain that we could come up with superordinate metrics that describe your ability to compete in the human capital marketplace. We could call it a competitiveness index. This type of metric shows how prepared your company is to compete in the near-term future. The last variable of company-unique factors is yours to develop.

The individual measures of competence, readiness, employee satisfaction, commitment, and climate cannot be taken every month or even every quarter. The same is true for a competitiveness index. Separation rates are objective and can be monitored each month.

Indexing the Problem

The world is a mix of the objective and subjective. Movement in any or all of these indexes helps to explain corporate performance trends. If we see negativism in any of them, it would probably be a precursor of problems to come in turnover, further damaging employee productivity and customer service. One of the shortcomings of accounting is that it deliberately does not include perceptual data. Accounting can alert management to impending cash shortages but not to foreseeable human capital problems, which are much more difficult to solve. We can go to the bank, borrow cash, and put it to full use immediately. It takes a good bit more effort and a much longer time line to acquire key talent, infuse them with new skills, acclimate them to our organization, and make them fully effective. Adding the perceptual element aids in focusing management on the more complex human side.

> Accounting can alert management to impending cash shortages but not to foreseeable human capital problems, which are much more difficult to solve.

You could make the competitiveness index a semiannual adjunct to your human capital enterprise scorecard. Collectively, these would tell you how you were doing financially, structurally, and competitively from a human capital management standpoint. Along with that, your data from the operating processes and human resources service levels would make you more knowledgeable than your competition by several light-years.

Human Capital Management Futures

At the bottom of it all are the foundation activities to support the functional units. As I pointed out in Chapter 4, the human resources department should be leading this activity. Working with its management and employee *customers*, human resources hires, pays, supports, develops, and assists in retaining the organization's human capital. There is plenty of data available, some inside and some outside, that the human resources department should be monitoring and placing on a futures board. Examples from human resources activities are as follows:

Talent Availability Trends (Acquisition Function): The Bureau of Labor Statistics and various other federal agencies and private organizations study and publish labor trends. Unemployment level, workforce population trends, absence and turnover rates, part-time versus full-time employment ratios, visa regulations, and other indexes provide a picture of what is happening and what may be coming. These types of measures could be tracked individually and then presented as an index number on the futures scoreboard.

Salary and Benefit Surveys (Support Function): Pay rate and benefit program comparisons and trends within an industry or region give you an idea of the movement of employee costs. This is factored into annual budget building, which is a crystal-ball exercise if there ever was one. With a workforce whose needs are dynamic, it behooves everyone to constantly monitor what types of benefit programs will support hiring and retention. Again, pay and benefits could be put into a single number and reported as total labor cost.

Investments in Training and Education (Development Function): The knowledge economy demands constant learning. Hence, a company's investment in all forms of employee development is an effective predictor of future human capital capability. This includes all types of training courses, career development services, and all outside education, including tuition reimbursement benefits. Arguably, supervisory coaching, mentoring, and on-the-job experience are the most effective development processes. However, it is difficult to extract and collect the cost of these activities. It is doable, but beyond the scope of this paragraph to describe. The easiest metrics to capture are training investment as a percentage of payroll or as a percentage of revenue. Because these activities are a mix of quantitative and qualitative, they should probably be reported as two separate data points. Mentoring program objectives might be a good catchall for the qualitative and investment dollars for the quantitative.

Workforce Values and Needs (Retention Function): Nothing helps retain talent so much as addressing people's personal issues. Spherion developed a standard method for assessing workforce values that was tested in two national surveys.[4] The study focused on the direction of change in employee values. It dealt with a number of variables that have a futures implication. The list includes attitudes toward loyalty, management style, job duties, performance and rewards, advancement, career opportunities, the work environment, and change, among others. As a rearguard action, exit interviews can be conducted by an objective outside party to find out why people became dissatisfied and why they eventually left. These values can be grouped into composites such as management and opportunity or culture and climate. Since this is a new idea, you can construct it any way that suits your needs. The important point is to have a valid and reliable telescope through which to view the future.

Figure 7-3 is a cutout example from the Figure 5-5 layout. It shows how the future's dashboard might look. In addition to the enterprise-level indicators of HEVA and HCMV, I've selected four of the eight functions and the four human capital arenas and put in examples of the topics that could be displayed. These are only basic suggestions to stimulate your imagination. I'm certain that you and your colleagues can come up with a set that serves your needs.

Scoreboarding Overview

Because accounting looks only backward, many managers are forced to operate more through a rearview mirror than through a windshield. This accounts for the fact that so many companies suddenly find themselves unprepared. They cannot fund a response to a competitor's unexpected

Figure 7-3. Enterprise futures dashboard template.

Enterprise

HEVA $ _____ ◯   HCMV $ _____ ◯

Function

Production	*Sales*	*Customer Service*	*Information Services*
1. Readiness _____ ◯	1. Readiness _____ ◯	1. Readiness _____ ◯	1. Readiness _____ ◯
2. Commitment _____ ◯	2. Commitment _____ ◯	2. Commitment _____ ◯	2. Commitment _____ ◯
3. Depletion _____ ◯	3. Depletion _____ ◯	3. Depletion _____ ◯	3. Depletion _____ ◯
4. Satisfaction _____ ◯	4. Satisfaction _____ ◯	4. Satisfaction _____ ◯	4. Satisfaction _____ ◯
5. Culture _____ ◯	5. Culture _____ ◯	5. Culture _____ ◯	5. Culture _____ ◯

Human Capital

Acquire	*Maintain*	*Develop*	*Retain*
1. Talent Availability Index _____ ◯	1. Total Labor $ Cost Index _____ ◯	1. Mentoring Index _____ ◯	1. Management Index _____ ◯
		2. Investment $ _____ ◯	2. Opportunity Index _____ ◯
			3. Climate Index _____ ◯

Note: Except where indicated, the values would be expressed in percentages or index numbers.

move, support new product development with people or facilities, or stop the outflow of talent whose stock options are suddenly underwater. The point is that the future is a lot harder to understand and prepare for than the past. That may sound like a non sequitur, but you get the point. Of course, you can add whatever suits your special needs. We are building a new method of accountability together, and as yet, there are no generally accepted accounting principles. When we reach a point where hundreds of companies are practicing this as an essential way of doing business, a standard system will develop so that people can benchmark themselves against the marketplace. Until then, you are free to be creative without the fear of violating some arbitrary standard. FASB is unlikely to get involved so long as the attitude is that if the asset is not a piece of real estate, inventory, cash, or equipment, it cannot be measured. One of the best arguments for the value of measuring intangibles comes from the early work on intellectual capital when someone said, "It is better to be approximately right than precisely wrong." Traditional accounting is precisely the wrong thing when one looks to the future.

Summary

The underlying theme of the book and this chapter is the connection between human capital management and organizational outcomes. This chapter shows the total outline, with the basic pathways from the human capital level, through the functional business units to the enterprise's goals. Step by step, we see examples of how an action at the first level should have a measurable effect on business unit operations. These, in turn, contribute to the strategic goals of the organization.

The process reaches its culmination with an example of

integrated dashboards and a futures dashboard template. These do not take the place of standard reports. Rather, their purpose is to provide management at middle and top levels with a sharply focused report on the state of key human capital and process goals and objectives. Since executives have a large number of units to supervise, they need a quick-look model that tells them at a glance where there might be trouble spots. By having both accounting's backward report on recent results and human capital measurement's forward view of what might be coming, management has a better sense of what to do next to develop or maintain a competitive advantage.

References

1. Nick Bontis, "Human Capital Valuation," working paper, 1999.

2. Lyle M. Spencer and Signe Spencer, *Competence at Work* (New York: John Wiley & Sons, 1993), p. 9.

3. Bontis, 1999.

4. "Emerging Workforce Values Study 1997–1998," Spherion, Fort Lauderdale, FL.

CHAPTER EIGHT

How to Measure and Value Improvement Initiatives Results

"I said to myself, I have things in my head that are not like what anyone has taught me so I decided to start anew, to strip away what I had been taught."
—ARTIST GEORGIA O'KEEFFE

Rebirth of U.S. Business

Although few people recognized it at the time, U.S. business was reborn in the 1970s. Coming out of World War II, the productive capacity of Europe and Asia was in ruins. As a result, the Untied States ruled the world market for the next ten years. However, by the 1960s, the more efficient new European and Asian factories, their relatively low wage rates, and their motivation to rebuild their economies brought fierce new competition. Only after we lost large segments of major consumer product markets did Americans wake up.

Our initial response was the productivity movement of the mid-1970s. This movement led to the first rebuilding of our manufacturing structure and the first cutbacks in staff. Two of the more prominent productivity service organizations that started in that period were the American Productivity Center (APC), later APQC, and Productivity Inc. APC obtained seed money and sponsorship from a number of major corporations. The center's mission was to carry out research and share information on productivity methods. Productivity Inc. ran productivity improvement seminars and conducted study trips (read *benchmarking*) to Japan to learn better manufacturing methods. A number of other organizations jumped on the bandwagon as U.S. businesses sought to regain market share.

That laid the foundation for the quality movement, which was initiated by an NBC television white paper titled, "If Japan Can, Why Can't We?" that aired in 1980. It featured the work of W. Edwards Deming, an American whose statistical process control methods had been rejected in the United States but adopted with great success in Japan. From this came the "quality is free" work of Phillip Crosby and the Six Sigma programs popularized by General Electric and Motorola. Toward the end of the decade, the first major downsizing of companies began. By this time, everyone was aware of the competitive nature of the marketplace. Nevertheless, some still did not comprehend that it was the end of the nineteenth-century manufacturing model from the Industrial Age and the beginning of a new order.

The New Age

Eventually, in the 1980s we came to recognize that we had entered the Information Age, a system dominated not by factories and hard goods but by computers, communications systems, and information services. Gradually, this new era came to be accepted as more executives stated with conviction, "People are our most important resource." Some, but certainly not all, meant it. This brought us to the threshold of the new generation of human capital management.

I submit that we have passed quickly through that period and are now in the Intelligence Age. This is the time when we need not only data but the tools and knowledge to analyze and predict. Accounting was fine as a measurement and reporting system when markets were stable and industry practices were consistent. That is no longer the case. Today, volatility and uncertainty rule. Those who can understand what is happening and can foresee the future will undoubtedly emerge as the leaders.

> Today, volatility and uncertainty rule. Those who can understand what is happening and can foresee the future will undoubtedly emerge as the leaders.

Measuring the New Capital

The term *human capital* introduced by Theodore Schultz in his 1981 book, *Investing in People: The Economics of Population Quality*,[1] didn't attract attention in business until the 1990s. Now it is a common label for the people who labor in organizations. I am not trying to determine the intrinsic value of humanity, rather I am confining my ambition to methods of assessing, evaluating, or measuring—whichever term you prefer—the effects of human behavior on organizational processes and therefore outcomes in economic terms. I use *economic* to include both financial and human value. In short, I am looking for valid and reliable procedures for determining what difference people make in the pursuit of organizational goals as well as learning how we can make management more effective for the human element of an enterprise.

Stumbles

The first attempts to evaluate services in this new world were crude. They tried to apply manufacturing process measurements. This worked for routine administrative transactions, but it wasn't suitable for professional work that was varied and whose output was often more qualitative than quantitative. An early classic case was measuring programmers based on lines of code produced rather than bug-free programs. The result was obvious; lots of lines, lots of inefficient programs.

Methods had to be found to measure white-collar work on its own terms. I had encountered this problem in 1969 when, after ten years in sales, I went to work for Wells Fargo Bank as a management trainer. I found almost immediately that the personnel and training function was not valued because it didn't know how to express its value added in financial terms. The function was viewed strictly as an expense center to be minimized and largely avoided. In fact, the people doing personnel work did not think of themselves as value generators. Over the next dozen years, at the bank and later at a computer company, I tried various assessment methods and eventually discovered the processes and rules that are described throughout this book. Today, we are faced with a different challenge. It is how to evaluate the major management imperatives driving businesses worldwide as executives try to reposition the new cohort of human capital for what I believe should properly be called the Intelligence Age.

The following examples are chosen from the most prevalent initiatives undertaken by management in general and by human resources specifically. They involve restructuring, employee engagement, managing contingent workers, mergers and acquisitions, and benchmarking projects. Each is different, yet all share common goals and can apply a consistent methodology to tease out the value added by the program. I outline some of the processes and experiences from each of these initiatives and then point out ways in which you can quantitatively evaluate the effectiveness of the endeavor.

Restructuring: A Fading Star

Call it what you will, restructuring is one of the oldest management gambits. Along with reengineering, which was the fad of the early 1990s, restructuring has been a tool of managers forever. I remember a quotation from a famous Roman general who said, in effect, "Every time we are finally prepared to act, we reorganize." As organizations have come under the gun to restructure themselves for greater competitiveness, all units inside have had to do the same. Typically, restructuring in manufacturing companies starts with production processes. Next may come information technology due to its mission-critical position and high cost. Marketing and sales are tapped shortly thereafter and bring the customer service and call centers into the game. Eventually other staff units—finance and human resources—join in.

However, since the publication of the first edition of this book, restructurings are not nearly as visible as they were in the 1990s. Admittedly, restructuring continues but not at the pace of the past decade. Still the topic is important enough that we need to address it from two viewpoints. One is human resources' role in restructurings. The other is how to value the results of a restructuring.

The Prime Question

Usually, the first question in restructuring is: What should be redesigned? I submit that the first question should be: Why are we considering redesigning anything? In this, all previous studies tended to find the same rationale. Restructuring is undertaken to gain competitiveness by:

- Lowering cost structures

- Improving service

- Taking advantage of technology advances

In the course of doing this, companies typically:

- Downsize

- Reengineer processes

- Shift controls by centralizing or decentralizing

- Outsource some noncore functions

So, the first question is: What is HR's role in restructuring? The more pointed question should be: What does HR have to offer a restructuring? If we really want to be strategic partners, here is our chance. Are we prepared to contribute something of value?

Typically, one would say that HR would add value by considering the effects on employees of a restructuring and that would be true. But, is there more that we might add? Don't we know something about process management, workforce planning from a capability standpoint, compensation structures and incentives, engagement, retraining, coaching and counseling, and performance measurement? Restructuring does more than move boxes on the organizational chart. It touches many aspects of organizational capital, such as structural, relational, and human.

The second angle focuses on restructuring the HR function itself. For decades, the question has been: What is HR's role in the organization? Research over the past ten years is consistent in claiming that human resources has a significant role. A summary of the studies of this question showed that for most HR departments, a new service delivery model is needed that simultaneously improves customer service, provides strategic consulting to line businesses, and reduces the costs of HR administration. The research is consistent in finding that many departments have yet to fully automate, outsource, or shift administrative and transactional responsibility to employees and managers.

It is not my responsibility to make the case for human resources in this book. I believe that it has a valid role when it shows that it adds value. I also believe, based on more than eight hundred presentations to HR groups in forty-five countries from 1978 to the present, that well over 50 percent of the HR departments in the world do not come near to fulfilling their potential. But hold on! Before we dump them—or nuke them, as has been suggested in several famous articles—let's remember who hired them and gave them their marching orders: the CEO. I estimate that only 25 percent of HR managers take hold of the job and proactively show top management how they can add tangible value. I will focus on how these 25 percent restructure their departments to meet changing circumstances.

Restructuring Issues

There are a small but critical number of issues that are central to any restructuring plan:

- *Service Expectations:* What are we supposed to accomplish?

- *Control:* Where will control and accountability reside?
- *Competencies:* Are we prepared to deliver?

All other questions and answers, problems and solutions, devolve from these three issues.

To make good decisions, it helps to know the landscape. Externally and internally, what are the forces at play? In short, what happened or will happen that has caused someone to launch this restructuring drive? Starting on the outside, there are marketplace forces that have driven us to believe that we need to change our organizations. In no particular order, they may include the availability of talent, the productivity of our workforce, advances in technology, the plans and actions of our competitors, mergers and acquisitions, entry into new markets, and, in some cases, the state of the national or regional economy. Each of these and other factors make up a complex issue with many ramifications. Suffice it to say that some combination of them is the most common external factor driving restructuring.

Internally, our studies uncovered eight factors that drove and still drive most HR department restructuring. Figure 8-1 shows the relative weight of each one. Service improvement, cost reduction, and the vision of the HR director were the main drivers. Quite often, we found that CEOs decided

Figure 8-1. Reasons for restructuring the HR function (%).

Service improvement	96
Cost reduction	88
HR director's vision	77
Benchmarking	69
Update methods	58
Downsizing	54
CEO's vision	50
Merged/acquired	35

that human resources needed to be run differently. Those executives hired new HR directors with the charter to change human resources into a value-adding function. Quite often, as pointed out in a recent *Wall Street Journal* article, CEOs are selecting people from outside the profession to run human resources. The reason is that they believe, with some justification, that HR people do not have a broad knowledge or appreciation for general business issues.

Success Factors

Studies of more than seventy-five restructurings in the United States and England uncovered a set of six factors that separated the successful from the unsuccessful. The magic six are as follows:

1. *Business Focus*. First, and most important, there must be a compelling business reason for the change. This requires an awareness of the vision, values, and mission of the organization. Along with that is implied a detailed knowledge of the workings of the organization. Human resources needs to be familiar with the operating processes of its internal clients. This leads to an understanding of the needs of the clients—both employees and management.

2. *Planning*. An effective plan includes several components. This generates a clear strategy for carrying out the change, along with an explicit set of goals and performance targets. A communication plan must be in place to articulate the reasons for the change and the values to be obtained. An often-neglected point is how the change will be phased in. In addition, there should be a program for dealing with the effects restructuring will have on the human resources department and its corporate customers. Finally, there needs to be a method for assessing and evaluating the outcomes.

3. *Communication.* This is so essential that it cannot be overemphasized. The best companies believe that you cannot communicate too much. This is doubly true in the time of upset, which is what a restructuring is. Power shifts, control changes, and processes are redesigned. Almost nothing is untouched. People must continually be kept up-to-date about what is happening. Failure to communicate breeds fear and fear leads to dysfunctional behavior.

4. *Teamwork.* Large-scale change requires involvement. Few organizational projects are done by individuals. Teams make most of the restructuring happen. Because restructuring affects everyone who is served by HR, as well as everyone who inputs data to HR, there must be a great deal of teamwork. Collaboration with persons outside the department builds support for the change, a sense of shared ownership, and perseverance through the difficult days of implementation.

5. *Commitment.* Top management must actively and visibly show support for and personal commitment to the change. When it doesn't, people believe the restructuring to be just another management game. Project leadership is absolutely critical. The organization must commit a superior individual to lead the project. This is someone who is respected, wants the job, and is creative, hard driving, and influential with others.

6. *Benchmarking.* Three out of four companies reported that they engaged in some amount of external benchmarking before launching their projects. Ideas, cautions, and effective methodology come from a sound benchmarking exercise. Both practices and metrics can be studied and incorporated as appropriate. The caution is to learn the fundamentals of the companies you benchmark. Then, make certain that whatever learning you adopt you adapt to your circumstances.

Human Resources Changes

The study found that restructuring resulted in one of two quite different results. In the first case, the department found new ways to manage transactions and to develop and administer programs. Value was usually found in cost reduction and ease of administration. In some instances, the restructuring also made it easier for employees to interact with the HR function. The second result shifted the department into a new modus operandi. Instead of being principally a service provider, it moved toward being more of a business partner to its management clients.

Some of the signs of change were that in about one-third of the cases, the staffing function underwent a major overhaul. Some recruitment and placement functions were outsourced to placement firms, some were delegated to line management, and others went into shared service centers. All this helped shift HR staff attention to strategic business matters. The other HR function that was severely impacted was training. Only about one-quarter of the responding firms planned to retain training in its present form. Corporate universities, self-study systems, and electronic networks have been introduced. Overall, the training function is slowly moving out of HR in favor of decentralization and utilization of contract trainers and consultants. The outsourcing of benefits, payroll, and some employee-relations programs is increasing. This is releasing transaction work and embracing strategic partnering.

Restructuring's ROI

When all is said and done, we need to know whether we have achieved our restructuring goals. Obviously, in order to assess that and measure the ROI of the project, we must have clear objectives at the outset. The basic question that assessment answers is what we set out to improve: service, quality, productivity, ease of administration, cross-functional processes and relationships, or what? Quantitative data can be obtained before and after the restructuring to determine whether we achieved those objectives.

Figure 8-2 is an outline of the elements in a spreadsheet report that provides an overview of how we are doing. The key points are:

- The driving issue
- Baseline performance at the time the restructuring started
- Target performance level
- Quarterly progress points

Plotting the results of the restructuring stimulates people to persevere. People need feedback on their efforts. They need reinforcement that says, "You're making it," or, "You

Figure 8-2. Performance measures of restructuring.

Issue	Baseline	Target	Progress per Quarter			
			First	Second	Third	Fourth
Service (hours)						
Response time	72	24	60	54	48	36
Cost ($)						
Exempt per hire	18,786	12,000	15,150	13,300	12,500	11,900
Nonexempt per hire	1,300	800	1,190	924	890	810
Per trainee hour						
Efficiency (number)						
Exempt requisitions per recruiter	18	30	28	28	26	20
Nonexempt requisitions per recruiter	35	50	35	38	39	45
Customer satisfaction (%)	70	95	85	90	90	94

need to do better." With this method, they can see how fast and how far they have gone. Some changes will occur quickly; others will take time. For example, requisitions per recruiter will not change until you have had time to reengineer the recruiting process and perhaps install an automated applicant-tracking system. As you see the changes from quarter to quarter, you can calculate the values. In the case of the recruiter-to-requisition ratio, if you reduce the number of recruiters needed for a given requisition load, you are saving staff time to apply toward more value-adding work in human resources; you can transfer the recruiters to other jobs or downsize the function. With cost issues, it is easier to see value added, because there is a direct reduction in the targeted hiring costs. Improvements in service to employees obviously help engagement, which in turn should positively affect productivity and turnover. It will take a quarter or more for the effect to be felt and acknowledged by the employees. So long as you have a tracking system to monitor your progress, you will be able to show the return on time and money invested in restructuring.

In summary, by studying restructuring projects, we can clearly see the focus shifting from HR specialties to business-centric services, from HR department management to human capital management, and from process and policy activities to planning and operating management.

Employee Engagement

Employee engagement is a recent management phenomenon. The premise is that it is a magnetic rather than a coerced approach to convincing people to want to do what is necessary to generate a competitive advantage for the company.

The Human Capital Institute reports that engagement is generally marked by:

- High levels of effort

- Persistence at difficult tasks over time

- Helping others (including customers)

- Voicing recommendations for change to improve things

- Adapting to and facilitating change

- Going beyond norms or expectations to make good things happen

- Taking initiative to ensure the team/unit is effective [2]

In Chapter 4, I showed the differences between satisfied and engaged employees.

Drivers of Engagement

Just as with the definition of the term, the drivers of engagement have advocates who come at it from various angles. Depending on the approach—cognitive, emotional, or behavioral—we see different emphases. Still, when all viewpoints are considered, there is remarkable consistency in at least a few top drivers.

As reported in the July 2006 *Workforce Intelligence Report*, the Great Place to Work Institute claims that trust is the single most important factor in human capital management. The Institute shows that trust is a function of credibility, respect, fairness, pride, and camaraderie.[3]

Over the past five years, a dozen independent studies have been published identifying twenty-six separate factors that have been shown to have some effect on engagement. Figure

8-3 shows the frequency of occurrence. These eight drivers appeared in several of the twelve studies.

What is remarkable to me is the parallel between these data and Fred Herzberg's theory of motivation that he published in 1959.[4] Some things, like human nature, never change.

Organizational Structures

Top management has a role to play in engagement and it comes from an angle that might not be immediately obvious. The line of sight between the individual's contribution and the organization's goals is an important engagement variable. If people cannot see the role they play in contributing to organizational success, it is unlikely that they will be motivated to perform or committed to stay.

Flattening managerial hierarchies and decision-making structures naturally leads to engagement. With a simpler structure, employees experience more freedom to act. Personal responsibility is naturally expanded. In the end, em-

Figure 8-3. Drivers of engagement.

Driver	Frequency of Mentions
Trust and Integrity	8
Nature of the Job	7
Individual/Co. Performance Sight*	6
Career Growth Opportunity	5
Pride About Company	5
Coworkers/Team	4
Employee Development	4
Relationship with Supervisor	4

*Line of sight between individual and company performance

ployees understand the impact of their contribution because their output is closer to the end results. There are fewer filters of information descending and output rising through the organization. This requires that communication be sharp and to the point and that authority to act be delegated. Structure is a significant part of a multipart employee engagement program.

Effects of Engagement

The measurement of engagement is an exercise in macro metrics. The most obvious and useful measures of engagement are financial. It would be natural to expect that an engaged workforce is more productive overall than one that is not. However, is there any data to support that assumption? In early 2006, Information Systems Research (ISR) surveyed 664,000 employees from around the world and analyzed their companies' three financial performance measures over the previous work year: operating income, net income, and earnings per share.[5]

The survey found a profound gap of 52 percent in operating income between companies with highly engaged employees and those with low engagement scores:

Engaged = 19.2 percent gain   Non-engaged = 32.7 percent decline

On net income growth, a similar pattern appeared:

Engaged = 13.2 percent gain   Non-engaged = 3.8 percent decline

On earnings per share, the trend continued:

Engaged = 27.8 percent gain   Non-engaged = 11.2 percent decline

A previous study of forty-one companies by ISR over a three-year period revealed a 5.8 percent positive difference

> Perhaps the worst outcome of low engagement is the hidden specter of workers who "quit on the job." According to various studies, it is not unusual for 15 percent to 20 percent of a workforce to drop out without leaving.

in operating margin and a 3.4 percent positive difference in net profit margin in high engagement versus low engagement companies.

Perhaps the worst outcome of low engagement is the hidden specter of workers who "quit on the job." According to various studies, it is not unusual for 15 percent to 20 percent of a workforce to drop out without leaving.

Contingent Workforce Management: The New Human Capital Challenge

The temporary workforce has grown and is growing so dramatically since the 1990s that we had to invent a name for it. That name is contingent. The dictionary defines the word *contingent* as: "Dependent for existence, occurrence, character, etc. on something not yet certain; conditional."

I'm sure that is the way a lot of contingent workers feel: not yet certain.

The rationale for the swing to a larger contingent workforce from the corporation side is flexibility. From the employee side it is a matter of work-life balance. Management can quickly increase or decrease the workforce without having to go through massive recruitment campaigns or uncomfortable layoffs. After ten years of large-scale and continual downsizing, most people were tired of the stress this put on everyone—survivors, staff, and those terminated. The argument goes that using contingent workers is a less painful way to manage the workforce and ultimately save the company money. However, not everyone agrees with that. Jeffrey Pfeffer, an outspoken Stanford professor, argues:

> If competitive success is achieved through people—if the workforce is, indeed, an increasingly important source of competitive advantage—then it is important to build a workforce that has the ability to achieve competitive success and that cannot be readily duplicated by others. Somewhat ironically, the recent trend toward using temporary help, part-timers, and contract workers, particularly when such workers are used in core activities, flies in the face of the changing basis of competitive success.[6]

Logically, he has a point. However, no matter its logic and validity, economics will rule, as it always does. So long as executives don't know how to measure the economic value of people, they will continue to treat them as an expense, not as a value-generating force, and to believe that they are saving money by using a large percentage of contingent workers. An interesting fact is that few have carried out systematic, longitudinal studies of the point of diminishing returns when using contingent workers. So again, without data, what do we think we are managing?

> Few have carried out systematic, longitudinal studies of the point of diminishing returns when using contingent workers.

Reasons for Growth

The figures on the size of the contingent workforce are muddled for several reasons. First, there is no consistent definition of what is included. The possible components are part-time on-payroll employees, temporary on- and off-payroll workers, contractors, and self-employed individuals who run their own businesses. Until there is a consensus or at least a common definition, we cannot speak reliably about the size of the contingent workforce. The figures vary from slightly over 10 percent in the middle of 1999 to claims of as much as 25 to 30 percent as early as 2003. As mentioned in Chapter 4, the best estimate at this point is that, excluding self-employed persons who run small businesses employing others, about one in five people works on a contingent basis.

The contingent segment will likely continue to grow, perhaps reaching one-third sometime early in the second decade of the twenty-first century. Barring any trauma in the economy, companies will continue to fill current needs with contingents. This growth will be driven in part by the growth of the service economy. Since the mid-1970s, services as a percentage of the total economy have doubled. Services cannot be stockpiled for later delivery, so service workers have to be available as demand waxes and wanes. Restaurants cannot produce meals for a week and then put them in the refrigerator awaiting patrons (although in some cases the food might taste like it). There is a natural flow of patrons during the day, with lulls in between. This calls for a flexible workforce.

White-collar workers now represent more than 65 percent of the workforce. Because much of white-collar administrative work is still viewed by many as more cost than value, contingents will be an attractive cost management option. Downsizing programs of the 1990s eliminated many older workers who are now coming back as contingents to work part-time. Some like making additional money to supplement their retirement incomes that were wiped out by corporate scandal. Others just want to stay busy and feel that they are still contributing members of society. Companies like these older workers because they are dependable, are already familiar with the business world, and can step into full productivity immediately.

Finally, more people are opting for less money and more time for family or avocations. They enjoy working on projects for several months and then having time off for other things in their lives. During the period they work, their average pay is sometimes more than they were making as regular employees, so in the long run they are doing well enough financially. This is especially true for people with technology skills. That includes not only systems analysts but nurses, lab technicians, pharmacists, machinists, some field service engineers, and other high-skill positions. In short, like it or not, contingent work will remain a significant segment of the workforce.

Intelligent Use of Contingents

Stanley Nollen and Helen Axel make the point that without strategy, we cannot decide on the most effective structure.[7] Absent a business and marketing plan, there is no efficient way to determine how to use contingent workers. Because short-term financial reporting drives many executives, they overreact to market swings. Downsizing is often carried out with an ax rather than a scalpel. This often leaves the corporate corpus hemorrhaging and incapacitated, requiring the companies to bring back some of the laid-off workers or employ other outsiders in core competency areas.

As illustrated many times in this book, everything must start with the enterprise's goals. Although this might sound unduly cumbersome and inhibiting, it is exactly what we find in our ongoing research study into top-performing companies. Everything rests on a commitment to a long-term vision, connected to a flexible strategy and a clear idea of long-term market position. You may choose to be the high-price, high-quality leader or the low-margin, high-volume merchant. Whatever position the company wants to occupy in the marketplace dictates every decision from vision through brand and culture. The commitment to vision and position drives the brand and a corresponding culture. The culture dictates how closely people work together, how much risk taking is condoned, and how communication takes place. The underlying ethic is the company's view of its employees. That ultimately influences how contingent staff will be used.

Advantages and Disadvantages

There are two sides to every question. For every advantage, there is often a corresponding disadvantage. So it is with the use of contingents. Figure 8-4 is a short list of the two sides. The use of contingent workers calls for more management skills than might initially be assumed.

Figure 8-4. Advantages and disadvantages of using contingent workers.

Advantages	Disadvantages
Allows for flexibility in sizing the workforce.	Limits the pool from which to draw tomorrow's managers.
Reduces fixed costs for employee pay and benefits.	Brings in people unfamiliar with company culture and policies.
Reduces hiring, laying off, and record-keeping work and expense.	May require special security precautions.
Reduces risk of violation of employment regulations.	Does not engender loyalty and motivation.
Reallocates regular staff toward value-adding functions (e.g., sales, production).	Creates a divided two-tier workforce.
Gives access to special, high-cost skills on an as-needed basis.	Requires judicious use to avoid "creeping contingents" who ultimately cost more than regular staff.

Probably one of the most difficult problems with a large contingent workforce is the split workforce. With some people enjoying a degree of job security and receiving benefits working alongside others who have neither, there are bound to be problems. Issues of inclusion in everything from corporate information to parties and picnics can drive a wedge into the work process. Professional contingents go home at five o'clock or get paid for extra work hours. Regular professionals are expected to work more than eight hours a day. Self-esteem, jealousy, fear, selfishness, and even greed affect productivity and coworker relations.

How to Measure Cost-Effectiveness

To measure cost-effectiveness, you need to gather data on pay, benefits, training, supervision, and productivity.

Pay

Regular full-time employees might have a higher hourly or monthly pay than contingent workers doing the same job, because they have been on the job longer. There are exceptions to this rule. If contingents stay for an extended period, they usually get raises. In addition, if contingent workers come from an agency, the agency marks up pay to cover its costs and a profit margin. So, in the end, an agency person can cost as much as or more than an employee.

Benefits

Regular full-time employees have benefits that part-timers might not receive, depending on the number of hours they work. Contingents may get benefits through their agencies.

Training

Regular employees usually receive some training, but each person has to be trained only once on a given task. If a new employee comes in or a contingent worker arrives, there may have to be additional training. In the case of a contingent worker, the cost of the training is lost once the person finishes his or her assignment. When the next contingent comes in, the cycle repeats itself.

Supervision

New regular employees and contingents need more supervision than do long-standing regular staffs. How much depends on the individual, but in general, the new or contingent worker will absorb more supervisor time for at least the first couple of weeks, if not longer.

Productivity

It is not possible to claim a productivity differential between the two groups. A case can be made for either type of worker. Long-term employees should be more productive because they know the job and the culture and are supposedly committed to the company. Or they may be bored or angry and deliberately perform below their capabilities, but not poorly enough to be terminated. Contingents may see the job as simply a meal ticket, or they might work hard, hoping to impress management and be offered a regular position. A large part of the difference depends on how both types of workers are treated by their supervisors.

To determine the costs of each factor, you need to track expenses and productivity levels. In cases of higher-level technicians or professionals, hard performance data might not be easy to establish. In the simplest example, the calculation looks like this:

$$\frac{\text{Pay } + \text{ Benefits } + \text{ Training } + \text{ Supervision}}{\text{Units Produced}} = \text{Cost per unit}$$

In cases of professional work, productivity measurement is more subjective. Professionals often have to work with others on a team project as well as perform their own tasks. So, the productivity or, more appropriately, the value added is a function of several behaviors. When judging a contingent professional, you can observe how much the person did in a given time and determine whether that is as good as your average regular professional staff person. Ask the following questions about contingent workers:

- Did they finish projects, and were they finished as fast as you expected?

- What was the cost from beginning to end of the project for their pay, training, and supervisory time required?

- How did the quality of their work compare with that of your regular staff?

- If they were in contact positions, were there any complaints or compliments from customers, coworkers, or staff from other departments?

The answers to these questions will help you make a judgment as to the cost-effectiveness of contingents versus regular staff.

Mergers and Acquisitions: Buy vs. Make

M&As, as they are called, are daily occurrences. Many companies have found that it is faster, cheaper, and potentially more sensible to merge with or acquire another company rather than try to build capability from scratch. However, several studies have shown that mergers and acquisitions have a very poor record of success.

In 1997, Mercer Management Consulting (MMC) looked at 215 transactions valued at $500 million-plus.[8] The data showed that 52 percent of the 1990s deals were achieving above-industry shareholder returns, compared with only 27 percent of the 1980s deals. MMC found no correlation between premiums paid and value created. Since 2000 the record has deteriorated.

- 66 percent miss original expectations.
- 83 percent don't add shareholder value.
- 50 percent are complete failures.

The reasons for this dismal performance are the same as the reasons for most business failures: neglecting preparation, ignoring warning signals, and looking at only part of the picture. Most often this is a play directed by finance or marketing, neither of which looks at the critical factor: people. Clashing cultures kill more acquisitions than anything. In the end, most ventures end up with the dominant partner dismembering the weaker one and in the course of that slaughter losing what it thought it acquired.

From 1970 through 1999, I was employed by companies on both sides of acquisitions. About half of them worked well enough, and the other half were costly failures. In the case of the failures, it was because the acquirer did not understand the dynamics of the organization it was acquiring or refused to recognize the danger signals, which were glaring.

Human Resources in M&As

Human resources has a central role to play in every stage of a merger or acquisition. Yet, in most instances, HR doesn't come into the picture until after the deal has been pretty well decided. There are a couple of reasons for this. First, most deals are finance or marketing driven. In either case, it would seem that HR does not have much to offer in the preplanning stage. This should not be true. In any deal, people and organizational culture are an important part of the purchased value. Everyone has read about deals that drove top talent out in short order, leaving a much-depreciated asset for the acquirer. This happens so often that in many mergers there is less value six months after the deal than on the day of the close. The second reason that HR is not in the front end of the deal negotiations is that HR people don't understand the dynamics of M&As.

To start with, many HR people have only a surface knowledge of their own company's business and marketing plans. They are not conversant in finance. The technology of the business is a foreign language. The strategy is not well-known. The short-term and long-term drivers are a mystery. In such a situation, why would HR be invited to the table? Mark Clemente and David Greenspan confirmed this deficiency in a survey of 370 companies that had been involved in an M&A within the past eighteen months.[9] Only 19 percent of the respondents believed that HR had the technical knowledge of an M&A to support the acquisition strategy development.

> Many HR people have only a surface knowledge of their own company's business and marketing plans.

Critical Success Factors

From preplanning to post-deal integration, Clemente and Greenspan offer ten critical success factors that are HR based.[10] Attention to these factors greatly enhances the probability that a merger or an acquisition will go off without a hitch.

1. *Address HR issues during strategy development.* By knowing industry practices regarding incentive

compensation, the acquirer can structure the offer
with equity incentives that retain key personnel.

2. *Involve HR in target company examinations.* Intelligence gathering in the market can uncover problems
   that don't show up on balance sheets but can affect
   operations and sales afterward.

3. *Include HR factors in pre-deal contracts.* Allowing HR
   access to employee records and people can help identify potential problems, as well as highlight key
   personnel to be retained after the deal.

4. *Focus HR's due diligence on cultural compatibility.*
   Beyond policies and practices, the acquirer must
   understand the culture of the firm to be merged.
   Culture clashes have highlighted some of the great
   deal failures of the past.

5. *Include HR at the table for integration planning.* HR
   often has a better feel for how to integrate people
   than does marketing or production, whose focus is
   not people-centric.

6. *Avoid hasty decisions on post-deal downsizing.* In a
   hurry to cut costs to pay for the acquisition, the dominant party often lays off large groups of people that it
   will need later to make the transition.

7. *Conduct employee sensing throughout the course of the
   integration.* It is tempting to take the employee pulse
   once and assume that everyone is comfortable with
   and knowledgeable about what is happening.

8. *Design training to support the merged objectives.* In
   some cases, people from each side will be dealing in
   operational or sales issues originating from the other
   side. Both need training in the new procedures or
   products.

9. *Pick the best people for the new positions of leadership.* Avoid the temptation of thinking that "to the victor belong the spoils" and awarding all of the top jobs to the acquirer.

10. *Maintain ongoing employee communications.* Failure to conduct ongoing communications can hamper integration efforts. People need their questions answered and need to be kept up-to-date through the entire post-deal integration.

Key Issues to Address

There are many important issues to address in the merging of two companies, including the following:

- Structural issues related to how the various functions will be combined or not

- Compensation, which is always a key concern of everyone involved

- Product lines that often have to be revamped or merged

- Reporting relationships, which are or can become sensitive matters

- Technologies to be learned or adapted

Any of these issues can be sources of lingering or explosive problems, but there are three issues from which all others seem to arise: communication, culture, and morale.

Communication has been discussed previously, because it is the most pervasive of all human activities. It is at the heart of everything we do with other people. In our research of top-performing companies, their passion for communicating with employees was evident. They stated, "You can't communicate too much."

Culture is another enveloping factor. It is everywhere and nowhere. Sometimes it is so strong that you can see it being played out over and over. At other times, it is so subtle that you kind of feel it but can't actually describe it. But make no

> Trying to buck the tide of the culture is like swimming up rapids. Ignoring culture has drowned many mergers.

mistake, it is the signature of an organization. It is what makes it different from all others. Trying to buck the tide of the culture is like swimming up rapids. Culture is a powerful force flowing in one unequivocal direction. Positive or negative, it is there. The cultures of both parties must be understood in their own terms and in terms of each other if there is to be a successful integration. Ignoring culture has drowned many mergers.

Morale is the result of how the merger was originally communicated and what really happened after the deal was done. Anyone who comes in and says that there will not be any changes is either naive or a liar. I've been involved in several M&As, and I've never seen one that didn't change many practices, structures, and people. If morale sinks, production suffers, customers are ignored, and people run over one another trying to get out the door. Morale can be managed with honest, timely communication and recognition of the effects of the merger on the acquirees' culture.

ROI: Key Success Indicators

How do you evaluate a merger or acquisition? A good way to figure that out is to ask: What human capital objectives do you hope to achieve in an M&A?

There are a number of goals common to 90 percent of M&As. Figure 8-5 is a typical list. It includes goals, programs, and measures covering retention, productivity, job

Figure 8-5. Human capital objectives, programs, measures in mergers and acquisitions.

Objective	Program	Measure
Retention of key talent Maintenance of general productivity Optimal utilization of talent Motivation of key personnel Maintenance of customer service Increased sales	Individual discussion of opportunities Employee communication program Intelligent assignment of key personnel Incentive compensation program Assimilation of the two cultures Training and cross-selling programs	Turnover rates Productivity levels Job satisfaction discussions Performance levels Customer satisfaction Sales levels

satisfaction, motivation, professional-level performance, customer satisfaction, and sales.

Retention of talent is the most common human capital issue discussed in M&As. There are many ways to keep talented people after a merger or acquisition. It starts with an honest, ongoing communication program. This includes general communication to the rank and file as well as individual sessions with key talent. Another way you retain those talented individuals is with their insightful assignment to important posts. These are the people who have the most impact and therefore deserve the most attention. That attention should start as soon as possible after you have assessed them and continue until they are firmly committed to staying. Incentives such as stock options and performance bonuses are usually necessary in the managerial and professional ranks.[11]

Alexandra Reed Lajoux makes an emphatic statement

that the acquirer's strongest defense against employee defections is a good reputation as an employer, supported by actions consistent with that reputation. Specifically, she states: "The new owner must demonstrate immediately and clearly to all of the new company's employees at all levels that their future is bright individually and collectively."[12] The operative term here is *demonstrate*. Talk is cheap. Everyone on both sides is wondering how the merger will play out. Skepticism and fear abound. Only actions are believed.

Maintenance of productivity and customer satisfaction is critical. Acquiring a company that is losing market share due to inefficiency or poor customer service is not a good deal. Sustained performance depends on a continual, effective general communication program. People need to feel that they are valued. This is especially important to the acquirees. Often the buyer comes in like a conquering army. During AOL's acquisition of Netscape in 1999, the attitude of the acquiring managers was, "They should be grateful that we saved them." The problem was that the acquirees didn't feel a need to be saved. They thought that they were doing well enough, thank you. As a result, within less than ninety days, there was a major loss of talent. To this day, the acquirers can't understand why good people left. Given the mistakes AOL has made since its merger with Time Warner, there was reason for the upset.

Motivation, and therefore productivity, depends largely on how comfortable a person feels in an environment. In a new deal, you have two main cultures and usually a number of subcultures. Assimilating people into the culture of the dominant player is a sensitive issue. It takes time, respect, communication, and often special forms of recognition. This last step is an effective way to show that the acquirer values the acquired employees. A pat on the back is often worth as much as or more than a salary increase. Everyone wants to be valued. Socialization is a higher-order need than security. Once it is clear that a person still has a job, the next step is to assure him or her that the acquirer cares. It is fundamental to self-esteem. People who feel unloved often develop negative attitudes and sometimes counter-productive behaviors.

Selling is a function of knowledge, skills, and motivation. Salespeople are inherently motivated to sell, but they expect short-term rewards. To help them sell, they need training in the new product line. This training often includes some ongoing coaching and support until they grasp how to present the unfamiliar products. In many cases, salespeople have to learn to sell a different level of product to a different group of customers. Building their confidence through training and coaching is the most effective approach.

In conclusion, a merger is successful if it retains key talent, maintains acceptable levels of productivity and customer service, keeps morale upbeat, obtains top performance out of its managers, and achieves sales targets. All of these are relatively easy to measure either quantitatively or qualitatively.

Benchmarking: A Value-Adding Approach

In preparing this section, I looked back at my book *Benchmarking Staff Performance*, published in 1993.[13] At the time, I remarked that benchmarking was still a rather new idea. Today, as we march through the early years of the new century, benchmarking is a popular but aging activity. Still, it must be addressed because of its popularity. However, I need to caution you that market volatility, industry deregulations, globalization, and other macrofactors have made benchmarking a difficult exercise. The stability that we enjoyed in the 1980s when I was one of the pioneers in benchmarking is long gone. (We launched our first report four years before Robert Camp's popular book, *Benchmarking,* came out.) Now, little is truly comparable across companies. The bottom line is that we have to spend much more effort digging into the context of the benchmarked company than we ever did before.

My approach to benchmarking—and I've done it with companies in at least a dozen countries—is to start with the goals of the enterprise and a description of the intended value of the project. Which of the following values do you have in mind?

- *Human*—helping people be more productive, less stressed, and more satisfied with their jobs

- *Production*—improving service, quality, or productivity

- *Financial*—increasing ROI, assets, or equity

- *Marketing*—gaining information on customer behaviors or market niches

Purpose and Expectation

Benchmarking is a tool with a specific purpose. It will help you find out how someone else conducts a process and perhaps allow you to transfer that discovery to your operation. It is a common practice preceding most of the programs mentioned in this chapter. But benchmarking does not provide answers, suggest priorities, or prescribe action. An effective benchmarking project develops a mass of potentially relevant and possibly useful information about functions, processes, or practices. It might guide you in uncovering problems and paths to more effective applications.

Anyone who is considering being involved in a bench-

> Looking for the holy grail of management through benchmarking is a futile exercise.

marking project should realize that it will not provide simple solutions to complex problems. Looking for the holy grail of management through benchmarking is a futile exercise. The more difficult or broad-based your problem, the more complicated the solution is likely to be. Only in rare cases will you be able to adopt the discovery directly in your operation. It is much more likely that you will have to interpret the finding and modify the practice to fit your situation.

Effective benchmarking starts by finding adaptable practices and understanding the antecedents. As I mentioned in Chapter 6, to make sense of the data we must understand the context within which it developed. What is the benchmarked company like? What is its culture, financial position, organizational structure, or brand? In what situation was this practice effective? What was the objective? Is it proving to be effective over time? How does the practice fit your situation and goals?

Common Mistakes

There are several mistakes that people make in preparing to benchmark. The following list tells you what to avoid:

- *Too Broad a Scope.* Don't take on world hunger.

- *Too Many Questions.* Keep your list short, or you will be buried in data.

- *Lack of Team Preparation.* It takes certain skills and commitment.

- *Haste.* Don't sacrifice speed for quality; do it right the first time.

- *Metrics versus Practices*. Don't ignore one for the other; get both.

- *Similar Partners*. The further afield you look, the more likely you are to find value.

- *Famous Companies*. Just because they are well-known doesn't mean they are good at everything.

In every case, the benchmarked organization is not a carbon copy of your organization. Context is everything. So, move with extreme care before adopting anything you see.

Value Benchmarking Model

Having shown the cautions, let's assume we can handle the outcome data with sensitivity. Our benchmarking approach focuses on two objectives. First, we want to find value as expressed in human or production terms. If we accomplish that, we may be rewarded with financial value. Second, we want to apply learning in a way that gives us a competitive advantage in the market. This means that the practice we adopt as a result of our learning will help us improve quality, innovation, productivity, or service (**QIPS**).

Figure 8-6 shows the value benchmarking process. It starts with an expectation of finding and adding value, not just learning something. After you know what you need to learn to add value, you can formulate questions and gather data. The fun step is evaluating what you have, learning from it, and determining what you can do to add value. Finally, you can act, monitor progress, and start over. Quite often, by the time you have fully implemented the new process, it is time to take a quantum leap and consider benchmarking world-class performance. If you're tempted to stop after improving performance by one level, you have to re-

Figure 8-6. Value benchmarking process.

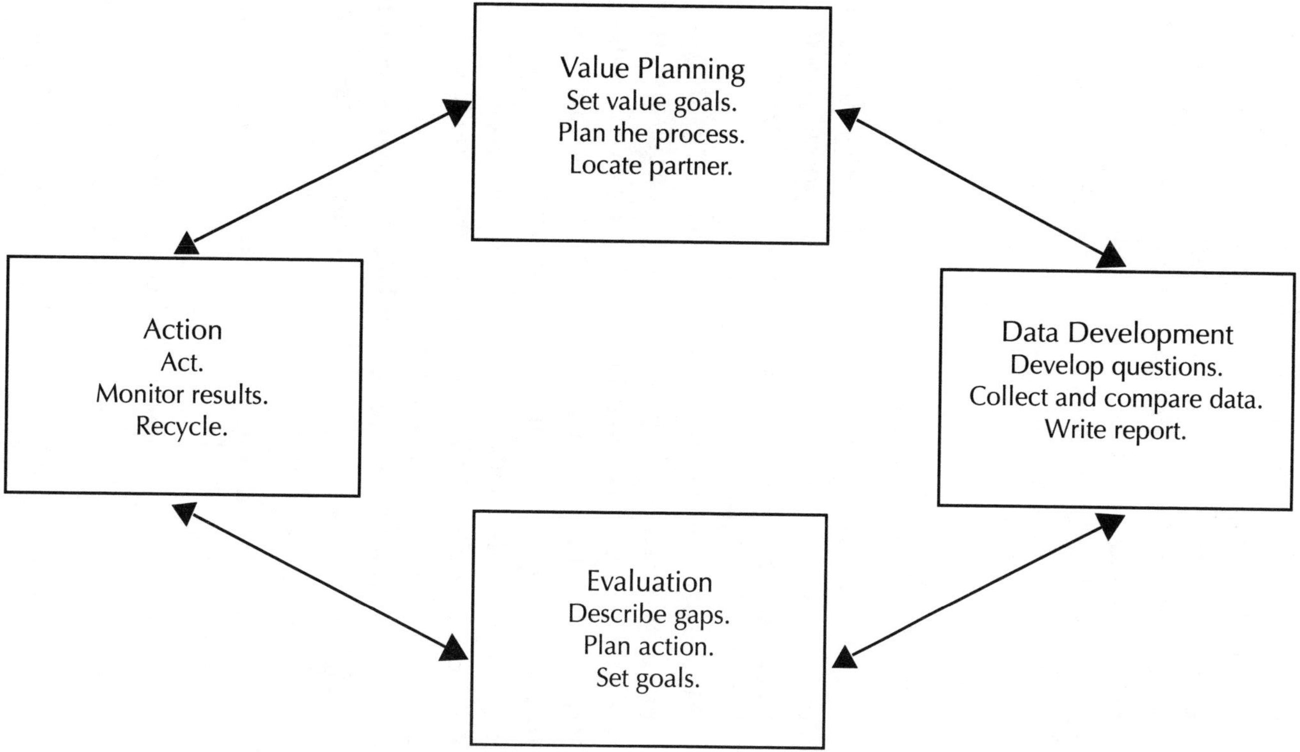

member that your competition is continuing to move to a higher level.

In practice, the benchmarking process oscillates back and forth across the four steps. If you are wise, you learn and modify or expand the process as you go. The recycling keeps you on the value path. This bouncing back and forth makes sure that you end up with more than just a lot of activity and no real applicable learning.

The ROI of Benchmarking

As in all cases in this book, we want to know how to find a return on our investment in a management process. Although benchmarking has lost much of its luster from the 1990s, it can be useful.

Figure 8-7 is a sample of some of the values that companies have obtained by benchmarking various functions in the past. You can see that benchmarking can be applied to any process. I started with human resources activities and then moved on to examples from other functions. I did not specify the potential dollar values in the value-added column because they differ across businesses and in every situation. Using your experience and imagination, you can think of how dollar values could be calculated from similar examples in your company. The thought process is always the same. The questions are:

- What is the current state of the process we want to improve?

- How is that state causing us problems?

- If we "fixed" it, what would the outcome look like?

- How is that different from the original state?

- What is the economic value of that difference?

Figure 8-7. Value added through benchmarking.

Process Improvement	Change	Impact	Value Added
Streamline requisition approvals	Hiring process shortened	Quality hires sooner	Productivity sustained
Automate applicant tracking	Number of recruiters reduced	Staffing costs cut	Operating expense reduced
Centralize transaction processing	Managers/employees empowered	Less administrative time	Output increased
Outsource payroll processing	Less supervisory time	More focus on value added	Production/service improved
Decentralize training delivery	Just in time, relevant training	Lower cost, better outcome	Efficiency/effectiveness gained
Streamline customer call center	More satisfied customers	Customer retention increased	Marketing cost cut
Upgrade building maintenance	Cleaner, safer facilities	Fewer accidents	Lower workers compensation claims
Deliver on-time, accurate reports	Timely receipt of good data	Information more useful	Sales increased
Redistribute workloads	Employee stress reduced	Less absence/turnover	Lower employee expense

- Is it worth the effort, or should we focus resources elsewhere?

Benchmarking is a tool that can help you find and generate value in almost any function—so long as you pay attention to the context.

Summary

Companies are working hard at improving their competitiveness in world markets. This is bringing about great changes within companies. Every day we read about and experience the effects of this effort. Companies are employing a variety of processes in search of more efficient and effective operations. Restructuring, outsourcing, employee engagement, employing contingent workers, merging and acquiring, and benchmarking best practices are the popular tactics. Each offers a different path from the present to the future. But at the end of the day, the most important question is, did it work? The answer can come only through an analysis of ROI.

Restructuring is, by definition, a disrupting activity. Fundamental organizational dynamics such as power, control, timing, collaboration, and risk come to the surface. As in all cases, success is most often achieved by those who have a well-developed plan. Communication is the lifeblood of a restructuring project. Since many people will be upset and some will be terminated, it is critical that honest, continual communication flow up and down the organization. During the course of a restructuring, outsourcing is always considered and often adopted. I deal with outsourcing in detail in Chapter 9.

The contingent workforce movement grew dramatically during the 1990s and has persisted through the first decade of 2000. Starting as a flexibility and cost management tool, it accounted for about 20 percent of the workforce by the end of the century. Then came the backlash. People started to ask why we used contingents in critical jobs when we claimed that people were our most important asset. The debate about contingent versus regular staff will continue so long as there is a shortage of qualified labor. I believe that it will be settled when management decides whether people are really valuable or just an expense. To know the cost-effectiveness of contingents, we have to look beyond the hourly rate comparison. We need to study issues of pay, benefits, training, supervisory time, engagement, loyalty, and productivity.

Mergers and acquisitions have generated ungodly amounts of money for investment bankers and some executives while simultaneously putting hundreds of thousands of people out of work. In the long run, the new organization occasionally provides a good return on investors' money. In the short run, many more M&As fail than succeed. From a human capital standpoint, the measurable indexes of success include maintaining productivity and customer service and meeting revenue and profit targets. These depend on the retention of key talent, because tangible assets generate no value without skilled people to apply them. The most effective tools in a merger are communication and culture management. Understanding the diversity in the merging cultures and maintaining a two-way communication system will greatly enhance the odds for a successful merger.

Benchmarking is a tool that emerged in 1990 after the publication of Robert Camp's book about Xerox's use of benchmarking to recapture market share.[14] Although people have always tried to learn from others, this technique formalized a methodology. After an overwhelming flood of benchmarking in the early years of the decade, benchmarking took a rest. Then, we came out of the dot-com crash, there was renewed interest. Benchmarking doesn't answer questions. It uncovers process methodology. When properly conducted with an eye toward context, benchmarking can reveal the rationale and conditions behind the method. The most important things to remember are to keep the project focused, plan, look at both metrics and practices, and don't benchmark a company just because it is famous.

References

1. Theodore W. Schultz, *Investing in People: The Economics of Population Quality* (Berkeley, CA: University of California, 1981) p. 21.

2. Human Capital Institute, "Differences Between Satisfaction and Engagement," 2006.

3. Great Place to Work Institute, *Workforce Intelligence Report*, 2006.

4. Fred Herzberg, B. Mausner, and B.B. Snyderman, *The Motivation to Work* (New York: John Wiley & Sons, 1959).

5. ISR, "Effects of Engagement," 2006.

6. Jeffrey Pfeffer, *Competitive Advantage Through People* (Boston: Harvard Business School Press, 1994), p. 21.

7. Stanley Nollen and Helen Axel, *Managing Contingent Workers* (New York: AMACOM, 1996).

8. Courtesy of Mercer Management Consulting, 1997.

9. Mark Clemente and David Greenspan, *Empowering Human Resources in the Merger and Acquisition Process* (Glen Rock, NJ: Clemente, Greenspan & Co., 1999), p. 109.

10. Ibid., pp. 11–18.

11. Robert Stowe England, "When Pensions Change Hands" *CFO*, August 1999, pp. 69–74.

12. Alexandra Reed Lajoux, *The Art of M&A Integration* (New York: McGraw-Hill, 1998), p. 85.

13. Jac Fitz-enz, *Benchmarking Staff Performance* (San Francisco: Jossey-Bass, 1993).

14. Robert Camp, *Benchmarking: The Search for Industry Best Practices That Lead to Superior Performance* (Milwaukee: American Society for Quality Control Press, 1989).

CHAPTER NINE

Outsourcing: A New Operating Model?

"The secret of joy in work is contained in one
word—excellence. To know how to do something
well is to enjoy it."

—PEARL BUCK

Outsourcing has been around for sixty years. In 1949, twenty-two-year-old Henry Taub started Automatic Payrolls, a manual payroll preparation service in Paterson, New Jersey. Taub's eight accounts created gross revenue of around $2,000 that year. In 1962, revenue reached $1 million for the first time. Today it is approaching $8 billion.

Outsourcing took off in the 1990s. When considering outsourcing the key question is, what are the comparable costs of processing inside versus outside? Cost is measurable in both dollars and people's reactions. Human resources and other staff functions are increasing their use of outsourcing. Beyond the traditional applications to payroll and benefits, outsourcing is claiming more of the staffing and training functions. Many employee support programs, such as employee assistance programs, are being outsourced. Outsourcing works the most cost effectively if we look at both the human and the financial aspects of it. Cutting costs while destroying morale is not a cost-effective move. We have learned from the top-performing companies that a balance of human and financial value is optimum.

In the beginning, three of the most common goals for outsourcing were cost reduction, time saving, and service-quality improvement with cost being the dominant criterion. However, there is a question that transcends those important goals and should drive any consideration of outsourcing, or any other initiative, for that matter. It is:

How do we manage human capital to optimize value and generate competitive advantage?

Outsourcing inevitably entails significant organizational change. This change affects process management, employee security, engagement, and employee service. There are a number of advantages and disadvantages to outsourcing. This chapter will look at the issues, examples, plans, and remedies.

Mixed Results

Two staff functions that have adopted outsourcing in a big way are information services and human resources. Although there was outsourcing as far back as the 1960s, it didn't become a common tactic until the 1990s. In the case of human resources, the tipping point came when Exult signed the first multimillion-dollar contract with BP in December 1999. This was followed in the next three years with similar deals with Bank of America, Prudential, and International Paper. In 2004, I coauthored a book about the trend, titled *Human Resources Business Process Outsourc-ing*, that described how these contracts were created and the attendant management issues.[1] From there other vendors emerged and the race was on. Today, there are about four thousand firms worldwide offering outsourcing services. By now, many of the early contracts have reached maturity. This has led to a reconsideration of how to use outsourcing more effectively and when it is best to keep a function in-side.

Trends in Functional Outsourcing

Having seen the rationale and success rates for the outsour-cing of various functions, the next question is, what is most often outsourced? Studies are consistent in showing which human capital management programs are increasingly being outsourced. This flies in the face of the fact that some have been unsuccessful and brought back inside. Neverthe-less, outsourcing of HR functions is not going away. People are just getting better at service contracts and their manage-ment.

I noted in the discussion of restructuring that outsourcing was one of the methods applied when redesigning or reen-gineering human resources. Benefits administration was often the first function that dealt with outsourcing. This goes back to the late 1960s. I outsourced benefits adminis-tration when I ran an HR department in the mid-1970s. As more regulations spew out of Washington, D.C., companies find it easier to contract for administration rather than try to keep up with the changes internally. Pension plans, 401(k) plans, and profit-sharing plans are most often out-sourced.

Payroll has long been an outsourcing candidate as well. A large group of payroll processing companies has developed over the past couple of decades. In a payroll processing survey, we found that the cost per paycheck varied tremendously, from as low as just over one dollar per check to as much as twelve dollars. Some companies chose to keep a costly payroll department inside because they believed that employee service was more important than cost. Others didn't even know what their cost per paycheck was. This is a classic example of managing to a gross budget rather than to a unit cost.

Staffing began to seek outsourcing help as the labor market dried up. Many large corporations have brought vendors onto the corporate campus to act as a source of temporary and, in some cases, permanent employee recruitment. In these instances, the vendor's operation looks just like the internal staffing department. This trend could well turn into a permanent change in recruitment strategy.

Training has recently become a target for outsourcing. Well over half of the training departments contacted in recent surveys report some degree of outsourcing, usually administrative services. There are two reasons for this trend. One is to reduce the fixed costs of training staff and facilities. The other is a response to a perceived lack of value added.

Some parts of the employee-relations (ER) functions are being outsourced. ER has long been the kitchen sink of human resources. Any dirty dish that did not have staffing, paying, or developing written on it was dumped into ER. Many benefits programs turn to ER to monitor or administer them. Employee-assistance programs are typically outsourced and monitored by ER. Some of the recreation and day-care benefits are outsourced under ER's direction.

One of the last functions to be outsourced is the HR information system. Although more companies are deciding to outsource their information technology functions, not as many are willing to put HR information systems in the hands of a systems company. However, that is changing. With security issues solved and the software as a service trend, new combinations of inside-outside service are arising.

Evaluating Outsourcing

A useful strategic baseline from which to start to understand and later evaluate the effects of outsourcing is a ratio of work done inside to work done outside. In effect, an outsource ratio is the ratio between the cost of employee pay and benefits—plus the cost of absence, turnover, and training—and the cost of outsourced and contingent labor. This general ratio can be modified to focus only on HR staff and programs.

You notice that I added the cost of absence, turnover, and training to the inside cost. Ignoring it is to understate the real cost of work done internally. As we will see later, another hidden expense item is the cost to supervise a governance group. It can be calculated, but seldom is, based on the claim that one also has to manage the outsource provider. One of the original premises was that supervision would be greatly reduced. This is true to a small extent. But even if the contract is well written and the vendor is effective, governance is a critical task. It can be the difference between an effective program and a disaster.

There are two sides to the outsourcing question. Books have been written about them, so I won't go into the opposing arguments. Nevertheless, I am suggesting that there is value in tracking how much of total labor cost is being spent on outsourcing and on contingent labor working in-house. Contingent labor is a form of outsourcing. Yet, I have not seen many companies take this holistic view of labor cost.

In the end, there is no *right* ratio. Still, it behooves management to know exactly where its labor investment is going and what it is yielding. Outsource ratio and depletion rates are two metrics that go beyond standard views of human-financial metrics. Together, they provide a benchmark for monitoring labor costs against a target budget.

Outsourcing Rationale Revisited

The argument for outsourcing centers on core competencies. Whether it is or isn't a core competency in a given situation, people strategy should be a core competency of the HR function. However, people administration is not a core competency according to *HR World*.[2] There is little chance for the average HR department to keep up with the changes in payroll, labor law, expatriate regulations, and the like. The best it can do is to try to hold the errors to a minimum while devoting a large amount of resources to it. This is why outsourcing has found a place.

In a 1999 study by American Management Association, only 20 percent of respondents reported satisfaction with outsourcing.[3] A 2007 survey by the Workforce Intelligence Institute, a division of Human Capital Source, asked 524 companies how satisfied they were with outsourced services.[4] Only 37 percent of companies responded positively. In addition, only 13 percent expected to outsource other functions. Conversely, this flies in the face of multimillion-dollar outsourcing contracts still being let. It also says something about survey results. You can get just about any answer you want depending on when and how you ask the question.

Changes Coming

The Everest Group predicted in 2007 that there will be a dramatic increase in demand in just a few years.[5] Applications Maintenance and Development is currently running at $7.7 billion and is expected to reach $18 billion by 2010. This will carry **HR BPO** with it. But there will be a shake-up in the vendor population. There is an oversupply that is driving down prices. Two inevitable hallmarks are margin compression and industry consolidation. For the next few years, the market will be unsettled wherein buyers pay less but have a more difficult time finding a reliable, stable, and scalable provider.

Managing for Success

Successful outsourcing depends heavily on the ability of the client to organize a governance team that understands and practices outsourcing management (OM) competencies. Vendors agree that a major cause of outsourcing problems is due to a lack of OM skills. Outsourcing is a complicated maneuver with much promise and a more than adequate amount of risk. Effective governance organizations are composed of people with various skill sets, plus a demonstrated ability for collaboration, knowledge sharing, conflict resolution, facilitation, communication, and creative problem solving. These are seldom found in the average HR function. When the staff is not prepared to function along these lines, discouragement arises as the vendor and customer butt heads over how to get the work transitioned and the service levels maintained. Figure 9-1 shows the most common opportunities and pitfalls.

> Successful outsourcing depends heavily on the ability of the client to organize a governance team that understands and practices outsourcing management (OM) competencies. Vendors agree that a major cause of outsourcing problems is due to a lack of OM skills.

Figure 9-1. Advantages and disadvantages of outsourcing.

Advantages	Disadvantages
Usually the cost of providing the service is reduced.	It is not a panacea; sometimes it does not work out due to poor planning or vendor selection.
Don't need to make large capital investments in computers and software.	Lose control and contact with employees.
Easier to hire a vendor than prepare to deliver the service in-house.	Some HR personnel will usually lose their jobs.
Cuts space and equipment needs.	A governance council needs to be organized and maintained.
Give the work to an organization that has the core competencies to handle it.	Need to hire an attorney to review the contract and possibly handle contract negotiations.
No need to hire and manage scarce, highly paid experts.	Risk fines if the vendor does not comply with government regulations.
No need to invest in training and avoids the cost of turnover.	

Outsourcing Life Cycle

According to outsourcing consultant EquaTerra, outsourcing programs have a four-phase life cycle with essential tasks associated with each phase:[6]

1. **Strategy.** The task is to analyze the potential financial benefits of outsourcing. An important part of this feasibility study is an analysis of the OM skills and experience and the costs of supporting the initiative over time.

   Checklist:

   ___ Analyze internal OM experience within the organization.

___ Analyze the local resource pool for OM-skilled professionals.

___ Interview consulting companies that specialize in OM services.

___ Develop a cost estimate for OM head count and salaries.

2. **Negotiation.** The service provider should have a plan to help the customer get organized. This will include developing the OM governance team. Typical roles include a responsible executive plus managers for finance, contract, service performance, customer relationship, and program.

Checklist:

___ Build an understanding of OM functions and the roles that support them.

___ Conduct a skills-gap analysis on potential internal personnel.

___ Identify and hire OM professionals.

___ Fill key positions and involve them in the negotiation process.

3. **Transition.** Once the agreement is signed and the transition plan approved, the responsible executive takes over. The governance team needs to be familiar with the terms of the contract as well as their roles. This is where the first major engagement of customer and provider staffs occurs.

Checklist:

___ Identify the training needs of selected governance team members.

___ Bring outside OM professionals into the governance team, if needed.

— Conduct relationship management and operations training for the team.

— Conduct joint relationship launch sessions with both governance and service delivery teams.

4. **Ongoing Management.** To ensure a smooth running operation, some companies establish an OM competency baseline. OM maturity models can be used to compare the effectiveness of your team against OM best practices. From there, an improvement plan can be drawn up to include team goals and key performance indicators (KPIs) with which to track and report progress.

Checklist:

— Set an OM competency baseline in which to measure progress.

— Develop an improvement plan for the governance team.

— Implement individual incentives to management performance.

— Provide career advancement opportunities in or out of the program.

— Participate in industry events to keep current on effective practices.

Forming a governance team with whoever is available is almost always a mistake. Outsourcing important services is a critical responsibility. It demands full attention and significant skills. We can see from this that outsourcing is a complex task requiring effective management practices at each level.

Service Initiatives and Satisfaction

If you are considering outsourcing, one place to start could be with a survey of current service satisfaction levels. Findings from a 2006 survey by Cedar Crestone highlighted relevant issues around three areas:[7]

1. *Top Ten Initiatives.* "Where are you spending at least 25 percent of your technology, time, and budget?" The top ten are listed in Figure 9-2.

In 2006, expenditures increased 5 percent or more in the war for talent and also in aligning performance over 2005. Expenditures decreased 5 percent or more in business processing, employee self-service and upgrading.

2. *Satisfaction.* "How satisfied are you with the following aspects of HR service delivery?"

Although many aspects were rated satisfactory or above, employee development and recruiting services and analytics

Figure 9-2. Top ten initiatives: how respondents spend their time and budgets worldwide.

Initiative	Time	Budget
Business process improvements and innovations	54%	42%
War for talent and talent management	47%	44%
Establishing or refining the HR application strategy	40%	27%
Aligning employee performance with organizational goals	35%	25%
Employee self-service	31%	36%
Compensation management	29%	24%
Enterprise portal allowing access to HR-related information and transactions	28%	20%
Integrating systems to do performance measurment and scorecard	28%	18%
Manage self-service	26%	22%
Upgrades	18%	19%

Source: Cedar Crestone, 2006

for decision making received the lowest scores. This indicates that the obsession with cost is no longer dominant. Higher order issues are coming into play and this is a sign of maturity.

3. *The Future.* "What do you want from the vendor of HR technologies that you are not getting today?"

Most wanted better reporting and decision tools (analytics). Another need was for more user-friendly Web services. In the analytics case, the message is that if you are going to engage in multimillion-dollar ventures, you need to be able to measure the return on your investment.

Getting It Right

Not every outsourcing program is successful. Buyers cite three main problems in failed relationships:

1. *Trust.* Provider promises were not kept or the provider did not treat ambiguous aspects of the contract in an honest and up-front manner.

2. *Money.* Buyer felt the provider nickel-and-dimed them in many instances or the buyer was not satisfied with the level of staffing from the provider.

3. *Flexibility.* Over time, the provider became unwilling to work with the client's changing needs.

The solutions are logical but not always easy to install in the heat of battle. First, don't hide a failure. The buyer should inform the new provider that it just exited an unsuccessful relationship and give some of the reasons for the failure. The buyer needs to take responsibility for its piece of the problem. Second, structure the new deal including all the various types of activities that are likely to occur. Both sides need to share a plan on how to manage situations that came up previously and may come up in the future. The deal should recognize that the customer's business may shrink or grow and take this factor into consideration. Third, an absolute necessity is a governance team. Plan for management meetings on a frequent and regular basis. This is an expensive and sensitive venture, and it needs to be treated as such. Finally, realize this is a long-term value proposition so focus on creating a mutually beneficial relationship strong enough to work through challenges that come along.

Success Factors

Throughout this book, I have been pounding away about how everything starts with the enterprise's goals, not with the process in question. Here is corroboration. In Figure 9-3, we see factors related to successful outsourcing.

The middle-range factors revolve around and depend mostly on communication—communication with the vendor, with individuals affected by the outsourcing, and with senior management. All stakeholders need to be considered and involved. It is only at the end that financial justification

Figure 9-3. Top ten factors for successful outsourcing.

1. Understanding company goals and objectives
2. A strategic vision and plan
3. Selecting the right vendor
4. Ongoing management of the relationships
5. A properly structured contract
6. Open communication with affected individuals/groups
7. Senior executive support and involvement
8. Careful attention to personnel issues
9. Near-term financial justification
10. Use of outside expertise

was noted. This is ironic because almost all outsourcing programs start with the idea of cutting expenses.

Outsourcing and Talent Development

One of the unrecognized potential values of outsourcing is the opportunity to accelerate the development of professional and managerial talent as well as increase the return on investment made in those people.

Consider the fact that as we outsource transactional work, we provide an opportunity for the remaining professional staff to shift from producing reports to analyzing them. In focusing on the human resources department, ask yourself how much time you spend in analytic work versus routine, transactional work. It is an easy trap for us to fall into and from my experience I can testify that a large majority of HR professionals and managers are caught in

> As we outsource transactional work, we provide an opportunity for the remaining professional staff to shift from producing reports to analyzing them.

that trap. When describing higher-level contributions, I am constantly confronted with the question, "How can I do that when I am swamped with daily problems?" I believe the unspoken barrier is a lack of aptitude or interest in analysis.

I understand the problem of being caught up in putting out daily fires. However, there is a solution. Once you change your focus from putting out reports on HR costs and quantities to reporting value-adding changes, management's attitude toward your function changes. I made this happen in three companies where I ran HR and you can also. Pick one important, visible problem and solve it. Report the value added to management. Then do it again, and again. As your value and credibility build, you will be given some slack by management. Executives are not stupid. They recognize value. They reward value. Believe it or not, once you have demonstrated value you will be able to hire someone to run daily operations so that you can focus on strategic issues where the highest order value resides. See Figure 9-4. The idea is to shift your time from the bottom of the pyramid toward the top.

Understand that you will never get away totally from the routine and you will never be rewarded for working hard, making budget, or handling daily problems. But I swear that you will be able to make a dramatic shift in your time allocations from routine to strategic through outsourcing, delegation, and value-added reporting.

Figure 9-4. How to add value: strategic-routine time allocation.

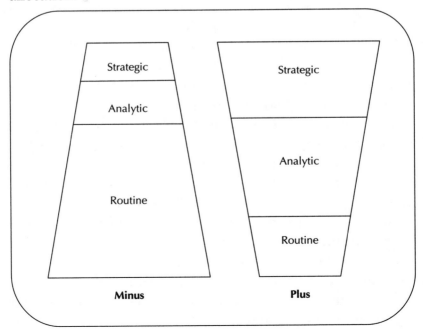

Outsourcing ROI

To know what to measure, we have to go back to the basic question: Why are we considering outsourcing? More pointedly, which major initiative of the enterprise would it support? ROI measurement starts with an assessment of the current situation. What could or should be done better? Is it a matter of deciding between upgrading our internal capability versus turning over a noncore function to an outsider? If it is, then we have to start by asking which path best leads to the enterprise's goals. The rationales and the advantages and disadvantages displayed in the preceding figures give us a set of questions we can ask as they relate to our enterprise goals and our internal capability. The following is a pathway that you might find helpful.

1. Start by listing the enterprise's key goals.

2. Next to each goal, write down how this task or process potentially affects that goal. Without calculating it, you can simply state cost, timeliness, employee morale or productivity, customer service, or whatever fits. Often there are multiple effects, so stay with the main one or two.

3. Then state the current level of performance. This can be in terms of unit cost, time to process, error rates and the number of employees committed to the process, or how happy you are with the process and result. If you don't have baseline data, how will you know what, if anything, you have accomplished?

4. List alternatives for solving the problem if the performance or cost is not satisfactory. One option is to invest in staff and equipment. What would be the cost and how long would it take to bring the capability up to speed? Another choice would be to transfer the

responsibility to another department that does similar work and perhaps gain economy of scale while avoiding additional capital expenditures. You could just stop doing it. Drop a program. It has been done. What would be the savings and the potential downside? And, of course, you could outsource it. What would that cost? How long would it take to get it up to speed? What would be the effect on employees?

5. If you choose to outsource, you already have an analysis of the cost and potential performance effects. These form the basis for your ROI or cost-benefit analysis. You know your present performance indexes. You know how much improvement is necessary to support the enterprise's goals. As the program unfolds, you can track your progress against time to implement, unit cost of the service, process times, error rates, and satisfaction of your internal customers—employees and management.

The Future: Web 2.0 and Outsourcing

Web 2.0 is not a product or a new technology; it is a new way of thinking about software.[8] It is a set of principles, business practices, social networking, community collaboration, and implementation technologies. The Internet is now a participative vehicle, so some companies are taking steps to leverage the Web 2.0 framework to enable change.

Framework's Benefits

The Web 2.0 framework builds on an approach of services rather than on products—that is, software-as-a-service and service-oriented architecture. When applied to a company's business, the framework provides the following benefits:

- Enhances data with context that conveys its meaning, thus enabling applications to use data more appropriately

- Includes an enterprise repository of information, rather than information silos

- Enables quick development of situational applications through mash-ups, where developers integrate data from various applications into a new application, thereby providing a new dimension to information

- Improves network effects as databases and applications become enhanced as people interact with them

- Provides software development cost benefits

- Allows for simpler administration than legacy platforms; facilitates the consolidation of legacy systems

Beyond Cost Cutting

Because of the growing maturity of outsourcing, companies realize its greater value lies beyond cutting costs to providing strategic solutions to business problems. The adoption of Web 2.0 facilitates collaboration and the increasing global delivery of services.

Combining Web 2.0 and outsourcing requires a different mind-set. Relationships will be more collaborative in that the parties leverage knowledge and intellectual property as a norm, not as an exception. This will require the following characteristics and functionalities:

- Shared vision and goals

- Increased transparency and trust

- Tighter integration capabilities

- Sharing of processing, storage, and communications platforms
- Use of free, open-source software

In the End

Making the shift to the Web 2.0 framework takes more than a declaration of intent. Web 2.0 is a stepchild of the dot-com experiment. Now, all aspects of operations have to adapt current and emerging best practices in areas such as strategy, organization, product development process, program management, platform, and intellectual property.

Intention is the easy part, shifting people and systems to a new model is the hard part. Operating in a Web 2.0 manner is a new way of businesses requiring changes in many commonly accepted principles and practices. Web 2.0 combined with outsourcing is a new world. Just as the introduction of the Internet in the second half of the 1990s shook up organizations and spawned the wild promises of the dot-com era, Web 2.0 requires both the customer and the vendor to fully understand the concepts, principles, technologies, level of collaboration, and change involved. Without it, a mini-dot-com bust will surely occur. The good news is that full leverage of the power of Web 2.0 and outsourcing can generate new revenues and increase value for both parties—to say nothing of improving management's ability to predict the future value of current investments.

References

1. Edward Lawler, David Ulrich, Jac Fitz-enz, and James Madden, *Human Resources Business Process Outsourcing* (San Francisco: Jossey-Bass, 2004).

2. Tom Lester, "Spare Me the Details," *HR World*, July/August 1999, pp. 32–36.

3. Mary F. Cook, *Outsourcing Human Resources Functions* (New York: AMACOM, 1999), p. 119.

4. Workforce Intelligence Report, "Human Capital Source," 2008.

5. Peter Bendor-Samuel, "How Changes in the Outsourcing World Will Affect Outsourcing in 2007," *Outsourcing Journal*, November 25, 2006.

6. D. Block, "Organizational Impacts of Outsourcing: Instituting Outsourcing Management Competency," EquaTerra, 2006.

7. Cedar Crestone, "Top Ten Initiatives," 2006.

8. Outsourcing Center, "Impact of Web 2.0 on Outsourcing," 2008.

CHAPTER TEN

How to Change the Game

"Change your thoughts and you change your world."
—NORMAN VINCENT PEALE

What do Polaroid, Xerox, Wal-Mart, Southwest Airlines, Amazon, Avon, McDonald's, and Apple Computer have in common? The answer is that these companies are examples of what Harvard professor Clay Christensen described as *disruptive technologies.*[1] In each case, these companies brought innovative ideas to market that transformed an industry. Polaroid changed photography, Xerox copying, Wal-Mart retailing, Southwest air travel, Amazon book selling, Avon cosmetic sales, McDonald's food service, and Apple personal computing. We call this *changing the game.*

From the CEO's perspective, the challenge in the twenty-first century has shifted from cost reduction through process improvement to sustaining top-line growth, leading excellence in execution, and finding top talent.[2] The magnitude of this challenge is immediately apparent when you consider what is happening in the marketplace.

Since 2006, commodities have risen 300 percent or more, housing values have crashed, the liquidity crunch is strangling business investment, and the baby boomer crisis is in full swing with 60 percent of the federal government's management cadre due to retire by 2011. These are desperate times that are seriously shocking the American dream. For the first time in over two hundred years, American children do not expect to live better than their parents.

Despite these drastic market transformations and new business challenges, very little has changed in the personnel game. In the 1960s, HR changed its name from *personnel* to *human resources* but it didn't change much else. When it comes to connecting to the business, HR people lament that they don't get invited to play with the C-level team, yet few are prepared to play effectively. Although computer technology has made the transaction work more efficient, it has not delivered strategic value because HR has not updated its management model. HR still operates in its industrial era silos, distinct from and largely disconnected from other corporate functions. Its view of the marketplace is often limited to issues around labor supply while ignoring global economic trends, competitor activities, technology advancements, and other macro forces. Internally, HR activities are not coordinated. Programs and processes are run much the same as they have always

> Very little has changed in the personnel game. A personnel generalist from the 1970s would fit right into today's HR function.

run. Planning is still viewed as gap filling. Staffing is still a fill requirement and move-on game with no analysis of sources or methods of effectiveness. Compensation has been ignoring the total rewards concept. Development thinks that blended learning fulfills the mandate for innovation. Process analysis is largely ignored and more anecdotal than scientific. Performance measurement is backward looking and out of date. At the end of the day, a personnel generalist from the 1970s would fit right into today's HR function.

HR's Disruptive Technology

HR has never been known for boldness. Perhaps this is the result of what I was told when I took my first personnel job, "This is where we put people who won't harm anyone." As demeaning as that statement was, it still applies to many of the people in human resources. But we can see that it is no longer tolerated as one HR function after another is outsourced. CEOs are increasingly calling in people from outside human resources to run the function. There is absolutely nothing to stop the C-level from outsourcing just about every HR process from planning, sourcing, and recruitment through compensation and benefits to learning and development. If HR management doesn't act boldly, it will find itself minding the kindergarten—that is, employee relations—as its primary function while the important decisions and actions are carried out by someone else, somewhere else in the organization.

Changing the Game

Fortunately, now there is a disruptive technology for HR. It is called HCM:21® (Human Capital Management for the Twenty-First Century). This breakthrough was developed over a period of eighteen months by the Predictive Initiative, a consortium of major organizations committed to transforming the HR role into a strategic function.[3] This is a major change in the personnel game shifting it to human capital management and making HR a central player in corporate management.

HCM:21, also described as *predictive management*, is both a strategic model and an operating system. It is constructed on three principles: a new type of circular rather than linear alignment, integration of service delivery, and future-facing measurement. Let me explain each aspect of the model.

1. *Alignment.* In the fifty years I have been in business, the most consistent problem I have seen and suffered through is a breakdown in linear alignment. In the beginning of the year, the C-level agrees that there are a limited number of initiatives, usually only two or three that are imperatives for the coming year. Then, each executive goes off to his or her theatre of operations and engages his or her system. Periodically, they come together to review progress and this is where alignment starts to unravel because the broad initiatives, such as improving time to market, are not delineated for each function. Specificity is lacking at the local level. Seldom is there a tight commitment to anything but the broadest goals. It is this way because functional specialization was woven into the management fabric. In the case of HCM:21, the alignment is circular in that everyone commits to move ahead together as if linked arm in arm in a giant circle along a single time line rather than several time lines. If someone fails to perform according to the agreed terms, it is immediately noticeable, disruptive, and correctable.

2. *Integration.* Within the HR function, there is likewise a lack of alignment. However, because all HR products and services are focused on the employees of the company, peak performance makes it essential that all HR functions integrate their play so that each one enhances the other. They are synchronized with each one adding value to the total

process and to each other through information sharing. The net result is that the total output is much more than the sum of the parts. For example, sourcing will let development know the level of quality that is available in the labor pool. From this, development proactively prepares the most valuable growth programs. Staffing will also tell compensation about difficulties in recruiting so that a total rewards system can be designed to give the organization a competitive advantage. The same applies to all functions, namely universal and timely communication.

3. *Measurement.* What is more important, reporting on what happened yesterday or predicting what is to come? Most data from organizations is lagging in information. Accounting, production, and sales all display what happened in some past period. Today, with the market being so uncertain, we need to know the future. Although we will always need past data about human capital activities to learn from our successes and failures, we can't simply extrapolate that into the uncertain future. We need leading indicators and measures of the intangibles that are the drivers of tomorrow. With all functions integrated and analyzing their operations and sharing data, the HR department becomes a human capital management center.

These three principles are incorporated in planning, processing, delivery, and measurement. Collectively they are a model that identifies the organizational issues and entities and then operationalizes how they interact and need to be managed. Figure 10-1 is an outline of the model. This is the core of HRP mentioned in Chapter 1.

HR typically starts its operation with workforce planning. It matches business plan staffing requirements with the labor pool and from that designs a strategy for filling gaps.

Figure 10-1. HCM:21 model.

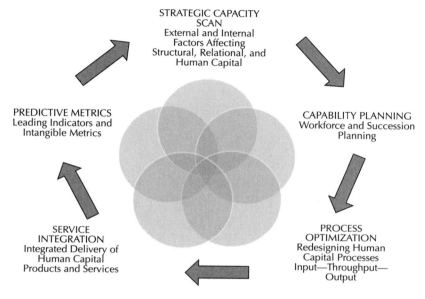

STRATEGIC CAPACITY
SCAN
External and Internal
Factors Affecting
Structural, Relational, and
Human Capital

CAPABILITY PLANNING
Workforce and Succession
Planning

PROCESS
OPTIMIZATION
Redesigning Human
Capital Processes
Input—Throughput—
Output

SERVICE
INTEGRATION
Integrated Delivery of
Human Capital
Products and Services

PREDICTIVE METRICS
Leading Indicators and
Intangible Metrics

Quite often there is no change from past practices although the marketplace has changed and is decidedly capricious. Before we can plan, we need to know what is coming. HCM:21 is launched with a strategic scan of external forces and internal factors that may affect the three fundamentals of the organization: human, structural, and relational capital. With Figure 10-2, managers determine what and how we can expect to feel effects on our organization from those forces and factors. From this corporate level scan, linked templates carry the consistent plan down throughout the organization.

In order to give the scan data a framework, we link it to the organization's three forms of capital: human, structural, and relational. Human capital is our people. Structural capital is essentially the things we own. They range from facilities and equipment to patents and codified processes,

Figure 10-2. Strategic scan template—corporate level.

Organizational Capital	Human	Structural	Relational
External Forces			
Labor Supply	Acquire and retain	Remodel facilities	Make new contacts
Economy	Incent service	Sell real property	Retain customers
Globalization	New HC sources	Reorganize	Expand suppliers
Regulations	Modify benefits	Go green	Lobby
New Technology	Train	Invest	Survey customers
Competitors	New skills	New products	Speed to market
Internal Factors			
Vision	Translate to workers	New signage	Advertise
Culture	Branding	Protocol review	Branding
Brand	Communicate	Facility design	Marketing materials
Capabilities	Facilitate	Processes	Sell competence
Leadership	Survey employees	Span of control	Personal visits
Finances	Freeze new hires	Manage cost	Less travel

including information technology software. Relational capital is our knowledge and relationships with outsiders. This includes everyone from customers and suppliers to competitors, regulators, and the communities in which we do business, here and abroad. Only after this can we begin to make plans, otherwise we are operating in a vacuum.

After the effects are noted, the department managers drill down in each cell to fully understand and communicate the details underpinning them to their staffs.

Capability Planning

Once the scan is completed as shown in the example in Figure 10-2, we can begin to lay the foundations for an advanced workforce planning process. Rather than continuing to apply an industrial model of filling holes with interchangeable bodies, we now think in terms of building capability for the Intelligence Age. The scan told us who and what we have to compete with and where our internal factors need recalibration. Now we make plans to build capabilities across mission-critical functions. The end result is a much richer appreciation for human capital and its critical leveraging capability. Being forced to think this deeply about the human element overrides biases and misconceptions that often build up over the course of management's experience.

We follow and refine the capability plan with an advanced succession planning system built around four principles:

1. Assigning an executive the primary responsibility for managing the system

2. Identifying high potential (Hi-Po) personnel as far down the organization as possible

3. Designing personal growth programs and reviewing and updating the Hi-Po list at least annually

4. Monitoring advancements and their effect on top-line
    growth

Our research reported in the 2007 "Workforce Intelligence Report" revealed that when you have at least 75 percent of your Hi-Po candidates' development programs fully
operational and replacements ready for all mission-critical
positions, you should see a rise in revenue growth per FTE.[4]
The reason is that your Hi-Pos are the key people who drive
overall performance.

Process Optimization

Now that we know what is required, we have to organize to
deliver. Periodic process analysis can greatly increase both
efficiency and effectiveness. It can be applied to the core
functions of hiring, paying, developing, and retaining as
well as initiatives such as engagement. A sample application
is staffing. In any process there are inputs, throughputs, and
outputs. In staffing, the inputs are job applicants who come
through a variety of sources such as advertising, job boards,
agencies, and employee referrals. The throughputs are the
selection and orientation methods: such as individual and
group interviews, testing, assessment, and onboarding. The
outputs are new hires who can be evaluated in terms of performance, salary progression, growth potential, and tenure.
The end goal is to find out which combination of sources
and methods yields the best hires for mission-critical jobs.
Knowing this can help cut your cost of sourcing and improve your hit rate of exceptional hires.

The typical method for improving the hiring process is an
exchange of anecdotal experience from the various sources.
The problem with this is bias, misperception, misunder-
standing, and missing the point. An effective analysis re-

quires some statistical review and applications. At the risk of scaring people, analysis can apply bivariate or multivariate approaches, in which we examine the association among specific recruitment sources, selection and orientation methods, and new hire results. For example, we can compare tenure rates among employees who are recruited from different sources, using correlations and an analysis of variance. We might apply a multivariate approach to examine the way in which multiple sources and methods are related to specific results. This helps us to answer questions like "What selection methods differentiate employees who have high-performance ratings, rapid salary increases, and high-potential ratings from those who have the opposite pattern?" A configured approach looks at the relationships among multiple variables whose particular combinations have unique effects. In short, we can identify and resolve critical issues that don't lend themselves to anecdotal descriptions. From Figure 10-3 you can see the potential interactions across several sources and methods. The question is which combination of source and method has yielded the best results in the past? More important, which is most likely to be the best combination in the future?

This process opens by gathering the records of people hired into a mission-critical job group at least two years ago. I built into Figure 10-3 a sample of what might be found. Keep in mind that in a population as small as this one, statistics are not required because we can see some of the obvious connections. If you were looking at five to ten times this many cases, the connections would not be obvious.

In this case, look at the N column in SOURCES. You see three hires: Didi, Ken, and Leo. One question is: Do applicants who come from newspaper ads stay with the company more than two years? In the T column under RESULTS, the number 1 means the person is no longer in the company

Figure 10-3. Process optimization.

NAME	SOURCES						METHODS					RESULTS			
	N	M	S	E	J	W	I	G	T	A	O	B	C	P	T
Al		M					I		T			2	2	1	1
Bea					J		I	G	T		O	2	2	2	2
Cecile				E			I	G		A	O	3	2	3	2
Didi	N						I		T		O	2	2	2	2
Earl					J		I				O	1	1	1	2
Frank					J		I		T			2	1	1	1
Gina						W	I	G		A	O	3	2	1	2
Hal		M							T		O	2	3	3	2
Isaac			S				I	G		A	O	3	3	2	2
Jon				E			I	G	T		O	2	3	2	2
Ken	N						I	G	T			1	2	2	1
Leo	N						I					2	1	1	1

N = Newspaper, M = Professional Magazine, S = Search, E = Referral, J = Job Board, W = Walk In, I = Personal Interview, G = Group Interview, T = Test, A = Assessment, O = Onboarding, B = Performance, C = Pay Increases, P = Potential Rating, T = Tenure

and 2 means the person still is. We can see that Didi is still here but the men have left. At first glance, this would indicate that newspapers might not be the best source for this job. Of the nine other hires seven are still with the company.

However, this is not the whole story. If you look at the O column under METHODS you see that four people did not go through onboarding and when you compare that to turnover, you see they all have left, regardless of their SOURCE.

You can see from this simple example that we can learn a lot about the staffing process when we analyze it in detail.

The objective is, of course, to make all our human capital management processes as cost effective as possible. This analytic exercise works for other departments as well. Wherever there is a process, be it accounting, marketing, or services, source analysis works.

Integrated Delivery

The greatest leverage opportunity can be found in how HR services are delivered. Almost all HR departments, read over 95 percent, deliver in a fragmented manner. Each function from planning and staffing through compensation and benefits to development and relations operates in its own silo.

Although there is a general HR plan, each function develops and delivers on its own time schedule without regard for what its sibling functions are doing or how its activity may conflict with or inhibit other functions. If you doubt my claim, ask yourself how often staffing, compensation, and development synchronize their offerings. In large organizations, sometimes people don't even know who is running a sister function. Development usually knows little of the quality of new hires or the introduction of new pay plans. Likewise, compensation looks only at pay and benefits neglecting to include development and employee relations investments in a total rewards system. Sourcing and recruitment are buried in their fill-the-hole game. There is no way this can be cost efficient or highly effective.

The secret to integrated delivery is leadership on the part of the CHRO supported by the CEO. Functional heads may not want to give up their autonomy. They may see it as a loss of discretion and power with little personal value in return. The CHRO must lead by showing how integrated delivery is best for the customer, our managers and employees.

The CEO must insist on it and demand reports of its effects in terms of improved ROI.

Setting aside appeals to loyalty, let's look at how integration works and the resulting values.

1. All functional heads within HR meet with the CHRO and staff to design their work plan for the year. This includes the strategic scan and capability plan that have come from the managers' meeting and working through these issues. To that is added process optimization schedules that HR managers and professionals work out.

2. From this point, operating goals and objectives are set for each function.

3. All goals and objectives are synchronized in a master plan that can be formed into a program schedule. The schedule shows when each step of each project is due and where they might affect the schedules of each other function: staffing, compensation, development, relations, or HRIS.

4. Commitment is obtained from all parties and the master plan is launched with the time line reviews.

5. Periodic reviews, usually monthly, are conducted to ensure that the plan is on schedule and any necessary changes are incorporated. More important, any change must be checked with all other functions to maintain the integrity of the plan.

The macro values are that communication is at a high level, clarity is sustained, and the superordinate goals of human capital management are attained. Operationally, the flow of information across functions not only keeps everyone informed but stimulates the sharing of ideas for innovation and program improvement. One might say that this happens in the CHRO's staff meetings anyway. My experience is that there is a good deal of slippage in meeting commitments, often a lack of confronting intergroup conflicts, and disorder to varying degrees. This is because when there is not absolute clarity and commitment to a tightly constructed master plan in the beginning, things only get worse over time. Flexibility is tolerated if there is a compelling reason.

Analysis

Given the level of detail carried out in developing the operating system, now for the first time we are able to statistically analyze connections across various human capital functions and outcomes.

In the past scanning, planning, processing, and measuring were distinct functions. Now with alignment and integration as our foundation we can find interdependencies rather easily. By applying various multivariate techniques, we see inside a function as well as between functions.

In the process optimization exercise, we were able to see connections among sources, methods, and results. We can also look for connections between the external and internal variables developed in the strategic scan. If you think about it, isn't it obvious that market factors such as a depressed economy will drive management to focus on customer service to retain customers? In the course of that, service incentives will be developed (compensation), recruiting service-oriented people will be an imperative (staffing), and training in customer service will be required (development).

When these responses are introduced, we are able to track the effects on customer retention, which leads to market share. The logic has always been there. The missing pieces have been real linear alignment across functions and effective integrated delivery within functions.

Take another look at the strategic scan. You see several natural connections that can be tested. Figure 10-4 is a graphic representation of the concept. Consider the powerful effect that HR can have on the organization when it can lead a predictive management program like this one.

Predictive Metrics

Thirty years ago, I introduced quantitative methods to the personnel function, as it was called back then. After a slow adoptive rate, we now see many HR departments doing some type of measurement. The problem is that most of them have not moved past the cost and quantity level. Typical metrics are numbers and costs related to hiring and training, occasionally time to deliver services, ratios of HR staff to employees, and HR budget benchmarks. All of these can be useful as after-the-fact data for the HR staff. How-

Figure 10-4. Connections through statistical analysis.

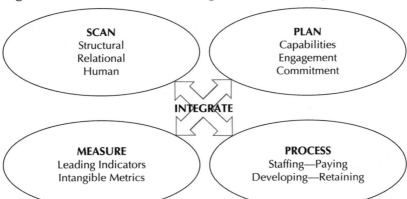

ever, they do not excite management because they focus on costly activities and say nothing of value-adding results.

Modern analytic tools and behavioral science knowledge described previously support higher levels of analysis. We can dig into turnover rates and discover what is causing them to rise or fall. We can track the return on investment of many HR services from incentive pay plans, new benefit programs, and development offerings, as well as staffing strategies and cost reductions. These address the issues that drive the current business operation. As such, they attract management's attention.

The latest and most exciting advances in measurement are leading indicators and intangible metrics. These predict what is most likely to happen in the future. In his book, *Intangibles,* Baruch Lev makes the case that intangibles are now the true indicators of organizational performance and wealth.[5] Intangibles include brands, research capabilities, processes, reputation, innovation, and certain human capital factors shown in Figure 10-5. With these data, the C-level can strategize and invest with a minimum of risk. Given the wild markets we face today and into the future, risk management is at the core of

> Given the wild markets we face today and into the future, risk management is at the core of human capital investment. High degrees of success yesterday do not guarantee similar returns tomorrow.

Figure 10-5. Leading indicators and intangibles.

Readiness	Leadership	Innovation
Market Reputation	Brand	Manager Tenure
Engagement	Culture	L&D ROI
Loyalty	Turnover	Absenteeism

human capital investment. High degrees of success yesterday do not guarantee similar returns tomorrow.

Leading Indicators

There are a number of intangible factors that can be turned into leading indicators. A short list would include engagement, leadership, culture, commitment, readiness, and knowledge management. In addition, lagging indicators such as turnover can be reverse engineered and turned into leading indicators. Issues such as manager tenure and absenteeism are signposts for the knowledgeable professional.

Note that leading indicators are often intangible. Tangibles are measures of the past or current state and therefore are lagging indicators. Intangibles can be leading or lagging. This does not mean that they cannot be measured. The value of counting past units of performance is limited. Now we have to look over the horizon by using data that has predictive potential.

The New Game

Continually working on process improvements and making additional investments in disconnected software will keep us in the pack. The only way to break out, take the lead, and drive top-line growth is to come up with an entirely new way of managing human capital.

One of the most exciting examples of a disruptive technology in sports—depending on who your favorite team is, of course—was the West Coast Offense of the San Francisco 49ers during the 1980s. They did not change the number of points for a touchdown or have more than four plays to make a first down. They worked out a new offensive strategy with which the defenses of their opponents were not prepared to cope. They changed offensive football. As a result, the 49ers were one of the most explosive scoring machines in the history of professional football and winners of five Super Bowls in a dozen years. Today, that scheme is in widespread use and it is no longer the disruptive technology. Nothing lasts forever. We have to constantly look for ways that leap the competition. In the war for talent, HCM:21 has shown its ability to do that.

Summary: Learning While Doing

This process is an excellent way to teach *management by doing* rather than playing. It has long been established that doing something teaches it better than any other process. Better than lectures, simulations, wilderness games, or even dialogues with executives, nothing is as effective as hands-on experience with the real thing. In this case, managers work with the C-level executives to realign and integrate the organization. By working through the strategic scan, building a capability plan, optimizing processes, integrating delivery, and designing a measurement system, managers learn how to organize, direct, and control an organization of any size. And HR is at the center of the action.

The first company to try this approach was a multinational engineering and construction firm of thirty thousand employees located in Asia. They had been very successful but realized they needed a quantum leap to compete with global firms operating from China to the Arabian Gulf. Forty-four executives and managers from the chairman and CEO down to all department heads and the HR director participated. As a result they revitalized their operation. More important, by working together they laid to rest the sub-rosa dissatisfactions that infect every organization. Today, they are on their way to a new level of effectiveness and profitability.

References

1. Clayton M. Christensen, *The Innovator's Dilemma* (New York: Collins Business Essentials, 2003).

2. The Conference Board, "CEO Challenge 2007."

3. Predictive Initiative Consortium: American Management Association, Accenture, Blue Shield-CA, Ceridian, Fidelity, KnowledgeAdvisors, Lehman Brothers, Monster, Oracle, Scarlett Surveys, SuccessFactors, and Target.

4. Human Capital Source, "Workforce Intelligence Report, 2007."

5. Baruch Lev, *Intangibles* (Washington, DC: Bookings Institute Press, 2001).

Eleven Principles, Seven Skills, and Five Metrics

"Every day you may make progress. Every step may be fruitful. Yet there will stretch out before you an ever-lengthening, ever-ascending, ever-improving path. You know you will never get to the end of the journey. But this, so far from discouraging, only adds to the joy and glory of the climb."

—Sir Winston Churchill

Measurement is really an exercise in evaluation. Measures are not the end in themselves. They are simply a special language to help us understand the change in value of something.

This small chapter is devoted to the fundamentals of valuation. These are the principles and skills on which value can be measured and expressed. They are the result of over thirty years of trying to understand and practice the most valid and effective ways to find value. As you review these principles, pause for a moment on each one and ask yourself what the point is behind it. Why did I decide that it would be useful to reinforce these issues?

Principle 1: People Plus Information Drive the Knowledge Economy

You've heard that this is the Information Age, and people are the most important resource. It is true—profoundly true—with implications that are still difficult to fully grasp. However, I believe it is now the Intelligence Age. We have to advance our knowledge of how to use information. We have to apply analytic tools to help us understand and to predict based on the data we generate.

As we have increasingly introduced technology into our organizations, we have changed our cultures and our structures. Communication is the bedrock of a culture and is enhanced or inhibited by structure. Bringing people and organizations along as fast as technology is growing is the primary challenge.

Principle 2: Management Demands Data; Data Helps Us Manage

We do not have a shortage of data even though we might not be collecting it. Every organization generates a plethora of data that needs to be translated into information and then upgraded to intelligence. We need relevant, valid information with which to make good decisions. Many decisions are made without adequate data. Sometimes it can't be helped. An apparent emergency springs up, and we must respond. Nevertheless, this does not provide an excuse for the lack of a human capital information database and reporting system. People who have the best information and know how to turn it into intelligence are the winners.

Principle 3: Human Capital Data Shows the How, the Why, and the Where

Since people are the only self-determining assets, it follows that they are the cause of everything that happens. If something goes well, it is due to the behaviors of the people involved. If it blows up, literally or figuratively, that is also the result of human behavior. It must follow, then, that in order to know how to improve something, we must know how people are dealing with it. Structure and policies are inert. People activate them. Cost, time, quantity, and quality data on human capital provide the base for effective action.

Principle 4: Validity Demands Consistency; Being Consistent Promotes Validity

The principal criticism of human capital measurement is that it is not as valid or accurate as financial information. When this is a fact, it is because people have started measurement programs by adopting unproven external metrics or by making up their own. When the system is not standardized, everyone who comes along is free to change it to suit his or her personal needs. Then there is no way to compare this new view with that of others, since the definitions are idiosyncratic. They build a modern Tower of Babel. However, when a standard set of metrics is established and used consistently over a long period, the metrics are as accurate as a financial system.

Principle 5: The Value Path Is Often Covered; Analysis Uncovers the Pathway

One of the major barriers to measuring qualitative, intangible human capital factors is the belief that we cannot demonstrate cause and effect. Many unknown and unknowable forces constantly in action make it impossible to prove anything in business. Nevertheless, being clear about our destination, knowing the positive and negative forces along the way, and understanding the process necessary for the journey increase the odds that we will travel by the most expeditious route and arrive ahead of the hunch players.

Principle 6: Coincidence May Look Like Correlation but Is Often Just Coincidence

It is a great temptation to claim that factors moving in a parallel path are correlated. Unfortunately, often what we observe is only a random variation. This error can be avoided if we start our observation from valid principles. Believing that two things that are basically unconnected to each other are related is the basis for most misperceptions. To produce a true correlation, we must first demonstrate the probability that A and B have something to do with each other. Starting from this base avoids false conclusions.

Principle 7: Human Capital Leverages Other Capital to Create Value

Management provides the structural capital at the best cost possible. Employees give life to that capital and create value through interaction with coworkers and outside stakeholders. Human capital is the only asset with potential. All structural capital is what it is. No amount of coercion, training, incentives, or threats is going to change it. If you view change from the people standpoint, you have a chance to generate value.

Principle 8: Success Requires Commitment; Commitment Breeds Success

The history of sustained excellence in business shows that commitments were made to a long-term core strategy. That strategy described the organization's dedication to dealing with employees, customers, suppliers, competitors, and other stakeholders, including community and government. Frequent oscillations between divergent philosophies and behaviors are a recipe for failure. Despite accounts of sensational results in isolated and short-term situations, the rule is inviolable. Building an institution of value is the only management practice that guarantees long-term excellence.

Principle 9: Volatility Demands Leading Indicators; Leading Indicators Reduce Volatility

Walking into the future with our eyes glued to the past is a very dangerous act. The wide-open, volatile, global marketplace of the twenty-first century allows everyone to compete. Cyclonic changes in technology make yesterday's processes obsolete overnight. The instantaneous access to information and the annual doubling of knowledge demand a constant view of the horizon. We absolutely must have intelligence systems that provide clues to what is coming. That includes intelligence on human, structural, and relational capital. It is as vital to a successful future as a healthy lifestyle is to extended longevity.

Principle 10: The Key Is to Supervise; the Supervisor Is the Key

All evidence points to personal relationships as the cornerstone of employee performance. The talented employee depends on the supervisor for guidance, support, and development. Throughout one's career, the supervisor is the principal crossroad for two-way communications. This person interprets what is happening and what is coming. This person describes how change will affect the employee. This person defends the employee and is the primary channel through which employee ambitions are fulfilled.

Principle 11: To Know the Future, Study the Past—but Don't Relive It

Do your homework. Study what has gone before, the good and the bad. Then take that knowledge and turn it to the future. What will be different tomorrow? How will it be different than yesterday and today? What do you need to know about tomorrow to change the game in your favor?

Seven Skills That Make It All Work

The surest way to win is to set the rules of the game.

1. *Widen the view.* There is more to human capital management than the labor supply. Consider your strategic capacity (vision-brand-culture) to deal with globalization, emerging technology, economic trends, the value of the dollar, and so on.

2. *Link people to results.* Describe in detail for all mission-critical jobs the linkage among employees, customers, and competitive advantage.

3. *Plan to win.* Tiger Woods expects to win every tournament he enters. Do you plan to be number one in human resources and human capital management? No one remembers or praises who finished second.

4. *Optimize efficiency.* Fine-tune your game. Analyze your process sources, methods, and results. Are they good enough to make you number one tomorrow?

5. *Integrate delivery.* Level the silos. All HR functions must be synchronized to serve your customers, the managers, and employees, seamlessly.

6. *Focus on the future.* Shift your attention from transactional lagging indicators to strategic leading indicators and intangibles. They are the measures of future success.

7. *Predict investment ROIs.* Manage tomorrow, today. Design and deliver everything based on its effect on future market share. Analyze the root cause and forecast the effects from the best solution before you invest.

Five Metrics of Life

Twenty years ago, I was exposed to what was called the nickel philosophy. Developed after World War II by a very wise man, it was passed on to me. My wife and I find it is very helpful in making decisions about what is important and responding reasonably when the unexpected occurs. We hope you will find it as useful.

There are five numbers that define aspects of life. Number 1 is the most important and number 5 is the least.

• **Number 1.** Your value system, your ethics, your god. This dictates everything you do, good or bad. A generous, honest, kindly value system serves you well. Your beliefs are right and good, good and evil are at the heart of your decision making. This number must always be kept intact, even in the direst circumstances. I remember Pat Brown, the governor of California in the 1960s, saying, "I always try to make my mistakes on the side of kindness and generosity."

- **Number 2.** Your health. Health is essential since we cannot function well for any long period if we are sick or injured. Of course, there are amazing stories of people with major illnesses who prevail and continue to perform at a high level. But these are exceptions. For you and me to be effective, we have to keep our bodies and minds in good condition.

- **Number 3.** Your family. This circle extends beyond your immediate kin. It encompasses that group of friends with whom you are quite fond and those who you would hate to lose. I think that people who are blessed with a good family and great friends are the happiest of all, regardless of financial circumstances.

- **Number 4.** Your job. No matter at what level you work, your labor must be fulfilling. If it is, then you are happy to go to work in the morning and don't mind putting in extra effort. If you love your job, it is not work and you are extremely fortunate.

- **Number 5.** All else. Everything else in life is of secondary importance. Small daily annoyances and major financial reversals all can be weathered if you have numbers 1 through 4 in place. Recently, there was a catastrophic fire near us and good friends lost absolutely everything. They are an eighty-year-old couple who were wiped out. Still they have 1 through 4 so they are taking it quite well. We should all be so smart.

Conclusion

If you adopt these philosophies and skills, you will not only succeed but you will have peace of mind. I don't guarantee that you will be trouble free or the most financially successful. But I do promise that the methodology that you have studied in this book and the philosophies and skills I have tried to pass on to you will give you a competitive advantage. Perhaps even more important, you will find much joy in your work and your life. Long after you have moved on, people will remember the difference you made. I promise.

Index

absenteeism, 48, 176, 179, 200
accession rate, 56
accounting, 12, 13, 133–136
acquisition
  becoming great place to work
    and, 158
  customer satisfaction and, 156
  on human capital scorecard,
    130–131, 131f
  as management activity,
    111–112
  talent availability trends and,
    205
  time to market and, 154
Adams, Scott, 94
administrative services metrics,
  99f
Alexander the Great, 76
alignment, in HCM:21®, 275
Amazon, 17, 136, 155, 272
American Management Association, 138, 257
American Productivity Center,
  211
American Society for Training
  and Development, 58
analysis, in HCM:21®, 285–286,
  286f
AOL, 240

Apple Computer, 34, 136, 272
Armstrong, Lance, 165
Ashton, Chris, 102–103
assessment, as predictive tool,
  199
assets, processes as, 70–71
AT&T, 71–72
Automatic Payrolls, 252
automobile manufacturers, 54
Avon, 272
Axel, Helen, 229

balanced scorecard, 28, 59–60
  see also human capital score-
    card
Bank of America, 253
benchmarking, 241–248
  context and, 171–172, 172f
  extrapolation and, 171
  limitations, 27, 62, 136–137
  mistakes, common, 243–244
  purpose and expectation,
    242–243
  as restructuring success
    factor, 219
  return on investment, 246,
    247f, 248
  value benchmarking model,
    244, 245f, 246
Benchmarking (Camp), 242